# SOMALIS ABROAD

INTERPRETATIONS OF CULTURE
IN THE NEW MILLENNIUM

Norman E. Whitten Jr., General Editor

*A list of books in the series appears
at the end of the book.*

# SOMALIS ABROAD

## Clan and Everyday Life in Finland

STEPHANIE R. BJORK

*with a foreword by*
*Abdulkadir Osman Farah*

UNIVERSITY OF
ILLINOIS PRESS
Urbana, Chicago, and Springfield

Library of Congress Cataloging-in-Publication Data
Names: Bjork, Stephanie R., author.
Title: Somalis abroad : clan and everyday life in Finland /
    Stephanie R. Bjork ; with a foreword by Abdulkadir Osman Farah.
Description: Urbana : University of Illinois, 2017. | Series:
    Interpretations of culture in the new millennium | Includes
    bibliographical references and index. |
Identifiers: LCCN 2016045246 (print) | LCCN 2017015280 (ebook) |
    ISBN 9780252099458 (e-book) | ISBN 9780252040931 (hardcover :
    alk. paper) | ISBN 9780252082412 (pbk. : alk. paper)
Subjects: LCSH: Somalis—Finland—Social life and customs. | Somalis—
    Social life and customs. | Somali diaspora.
Classification: LCC DL1020.S66 (ebook) | LCC DL1020.S66 B56 2017
    (print) | DDC 305.893/5404897—dc23
LC record available at https://lccn.loc.gov/2016045246

For Leif

# CONTENTS

Foreword: The Roots and Routes of Somali
Transnational Clan Formations   ix
  *Abdulkadir Osman Farah*

Acknowledgments   xv

A Note on Spelling   xvii

Prologue   1

1   Clan and Cultural Intimacy   7

2   Telling   43

3   Movement   75

4   Celebration   103

5   Crisis   131

Conclusion   157

Notes   165

Glossary   173

References   175

Index   187

# The Roots and Routes of Somali Transnational Clan Formations

Among Somalis the roots and routes of clan interactions transform and intersect, depending on time, context and agency. For example, clan orientations toward systems of power differ from clan alignments concentrating on the anthropological dimensions of diasporic lifeworld and life challenges. In a recent *New York Times* interview, the internationally celebrated Somali author Nurrudin Farah endorsed Lidwien Kapteijn's book, *Clan Cleansing in Somalia* as "a must-read for anyone wanting to unravel the complicated nature of our civil war." Under such acts of clan cleansing the agency of violent clanism constitutes the center of gravity. In contrast, in Bjork's book on "clan practicality" the emphasis rests on the roots and routes of diasporic lifeworld circumstances.

The concept of "clan practicality" suits better the circumstances in which people engage the institutions they refer to or create for themselves. For instance, historically, colonial powers used clan affiliation and eventually clanism for pursuing imperial ambitions. The aim was to "divide and rule." To counter this top-down imposition, diverse resistance grassroots movements mobilized clans to oppose colonial subjugation. Later, the military regime deployed anti-clanism rhetoric for urban-public mobilization designed for legitimacy motives. Such inconsistencies eventually precipitated de-professionalization of the army and shifted the regime balance toward neo-patrimonialism and neo-paternalism. On their part, regime opponents—within the army and beyond—employed clanism for recruitment purposes. They often eyed a power takeover through regime replacement. In retrospect, the pursuing of clanism—by the military regime and successive rebellions—failed to produce any positive collective gains. Instead, the confrontation produced disastrous factionalism and fragmentation in which corruption, nepotism and brutality became the norm. Clan factionalism expanded with internal and external alliance formations. For most urbanized Somalis, rediscovering their clans represented a survival strategy to avoid persecution and retaliation from rival clans. For some, clan affiliation provided an opportunity to regroup, to re-educate their clansmen by providing welfare to vulnerable traumatized communities. In contrast, for the warlords, clan was used to oppress, pillage and persecute often-defenseless civilians.

This legacy continues to haunt Somalis both in the homeland directly and more indirectly in host environments. As diaspora simultaneously finds itself "at home and abroad," transnational communities often operate and imagine multiple processes in coping with a tragic history and adjusting to challenges in new host environments. Although more than two decades have passed since the tragic implosion of Somalia, diaspora communities struggle to reconcile multiplicity of political and social consciousness.

Stephanie Bjork belongs to scholars in diaspora studies who critically explore the dynamics of ascribed homeland-oriented social relations (clan/ *tol*) and acquired diasporic identities often formed through transnational networks, ties, or practices. The study examines the practical transformation of social and identity constructions among people in the Somali diaspora. Similarly, to grasp and access actual lifeworld conditions among communities requires methodological sensitivity. In a more transnational perspective, Bjork illuminates how often nationalized and localized conditions can shift toward more or less institutionalized transnational trajectory. This thoughtful and reflexive approach builds on the fact that the study of Somali transnational identity formation remains largely a recent development.

The ethnographic approach offers a comprehensive opportunity to study clan dynamics in the "back stage" as people often refrain from discussing clan controversies in the "front stage." Somalis often refer to regions or other levels to avoid naming the clan in public. Therefore, active participation and observation of normal Somali social and cultural activities discovers the practicality of clan functions and thereby provides nuances. Occasionally, a non-Somali outsider researcher could be more privileged than a Somali researcher as an impartial participant. Because of their insider role, especially as the Somali war did not fully end, some respondents might worry about the Somali researcher's clan. In other circumstances, an insider researcher—due to the history of living and acting within the clan dynamics—has the assets of cultural knowledge including language fluency and thereby opportunity to filter information.

In normal circumstances, clan represents a real or imagined lineage to which people claim to belong. Among Somalis such relations remain largely patriarchal. Clans also have both exclusionary and inclusionary mechanisms to expand and restrict power relations in the community and in the society. The social and cultural rules and norms that govern such relationships depend on the context as well as the surrounding socio-political and cultural conditions. Due to the fragmentation of the Somali society since 1991, most Somalis are directly or indirectly linked to a clan for diverse motives, including the need for sociocultural and socio-political survival in sometimes harsh and complex diasporic environments.

Bjork's book, therefore, urges us not to situate identity formations and subsequent emerging social connections into particular static platforms. In essence, the book proposes a more flexible approach to the transformation of social relations among the Somalis. The aim is to transcend boundaries commonly separating classical analysis of the Somali society and the more post-structuralist conceptions of such controversial societal phenomenon. For instance, the classics of Somali studies, probably responding to colonial and post-colonial state pressures, often focused on pre-designed ideas and frames. In contrast, contemporary scholars, though incorporating their analyses with ideas and institutional mechanisms, place more emphasis on individuals and network interactions. Such scholars consider not just the socio-political manifestation of human activities, but also the actual human activities and transformations in diverse circumstances. In other words, it is not the study of the clan per se as a social phenomenon but the understanding of its application in diverse trajectories that takes us beyond the classical dichotomies of belonging versus not belonging to particular clans.

With this book, Bjork rethinks and reassesses kinship relations from a perspective, which has recently been opened by the transformation and the transnational connections of Somalis. Such a process is partially also enabled by multifaceted migration, globalization and mobilization patterns. Although clan/*tol*/*qabiil* connections remain relevant in our current era of complex mobility in the 21st century, the book critically addresses whether social relations represent a continuity reflecting historical developments (roots) or whether such connections signify discontinuity in the form of reinvention of identities and the creation of spaces for experimentation and self-realization (routes). To disclose this fact requires attentive adjustment into the current situation while simultaneously reflecting past circumstances. With regard to clanism, both proponents and opponents of the status quo either call for maintaining contextual historicity or for a total rejection of the essentializing tendencies of social affiliations. This book postulates transformational complexity in multiple levels embedded in both history and current social complexities.

Bjork suggests that in an increasingly globalized diaspora, Somalis succeed "to manipulate clan networks to manage transnational capital." Individual aspirations seeking independence and self-reliance, as well as the context of the host environment and relationship with fellow Somalis, all challenge the static clan formations. Equally important are the intersections of clan, fashion and gender among Somali women and youth. These groups creatively synthesize social spaces and redefine clan relations from an elder male dominated public sphere to the prospect of more female and youth centric sphere. The same goes to relationships formed through common refugee or neighborhood experiences that potentially alter the static clan structure. With the traditional clan conception, women belong to the clan rather than the clan belonging to the women. Among the diaspora this fact seems to reverse as women increasingly occupy spaces earlier reserved for males. Many diaspora women, more or less voluntarily, became heads of households, contribute to significant shares of remittances and organize the community's socio-political and cultural gatherings.

Somalis in the diaspora often develop, both within and outside the community, new forms of clan representation as individuals and clans have to deal with different issues abroad. Somalis might present themselves as clans to public authorities in a western country. Under such circumstances Somalis do not aim for power accumulation, retaliation or *diya* [clan compensation] paying constituency. They attempt to represent themselves as citizens of Somali origin that aim to help develop a region in Somalia where their families originate. Here clan is used as a form of a capital to develop the homeland. It is difficult to distinguish clans in the diaspora but Somalis manage to know who is who. This is particularly difficult for non-Somalis.

Both the distinction and the way in which clans relate to each other depend on the local circumstances and the prevailing political conditions. For instance, under a dictatorship, clan will circulate around the ruling regime, whereas in diaspora and in a democratic society like that in Finland, clan adjusts to the cultural and economic survival mechanisms in the community.

The clan concept also travels and goes into exile with migrants and diaspora communities. Here clanism re-emerges with blurred characteristics. In relatively peaceful host environments, people seem less preoccupied with imminent dangers and survival. Instead, many strategize to position and adjust themselves in relation to often suspicious host environments and authorities with divergent political, economic, cultural and institutional platforms. The actual strategy depends on the level of citizenship inclusion in host countries. For instance, clan might re-emerge as a symbolic cultural platform often at the backstage in a host country with expanded citizenship like Finland. In this regard, clan affiliation assumes a modified political and economic significance. Activities focus on the collection of donations, organization of cultural events such as weddings, and also the reception of high-profile Somalis from the homeland and wider diaspora. In contrast, if host countries provide restricted citizenship status like in the Arabian Gulf, clan relations presume organizational and institutional platform, including controlling the political and economic as well as the cultural aspects of the community.

Conceptually, then, clan relations can both contract and expand. Prevailing circumstances existing in particular contexts often determine whether people use it at minimum or maximum levels. The process remains hierarchical, both in the host and homeland environments. Bjork suggests that Somali women and the youth increasingly challenge exclusion mechanisms. Meanwhile, extravagant diaspora organized ceremonies such as the political including the traditional *cleema saar* (public inaugurations) remain popular among some parts of the diaspora. Such sociocultural events not only dislocate Somali clan structures from their natural environments among the Somali pastoralists, but also sustain a hierarchical order in the diaspora.

In the end, the issue is not the existing atavistic clan loyalties among competing parts of the society. It is how people legitimize the phenomenon in different social relations. Politically, if a sustainable progress has to emerge—among the diaspora and beyond—the continuing misappropriation of clan sentiments by mainly parochial political and economic elites must end. Eventually, mindful reform orientation can provide spaces for the creation of "care structures" rather than the thoughtlessness association with destructive clan structures.

Abdulkadir Osman Farah
Department of Culture and Global Studies
Aalborg University, Denmark

# ACKNOWLEDGMENTS

Above all, I express gratitude to the Somalis who participated in my research. Besides sharing their experiences and insights into clan, they offered hospitality and friendship. Although these individuals go unmentioned by name, this book is shaped by their unique experience in Finland as Somalis and our copious conversations there. Special acknowledgment goes to Hanaan, Nafiso, and Mohamed for commenting on my manuscript and thoughtful responses to my incessant questions.

Numerous scholars have also shaped me as an anthropologist and professor and influenced my understanding of the role of clan in the diaspora. Alice B. Kehoe has been a constant source of support, mentorship, and friendship since my undergraduate years studying anthropology at Marquette University. In addition to visiting me during my first stint of fieldwork in Finland, she read countless drafts. Her brilliance, academic productivity, and generosity are unequivocal. I appreciate Kathleen Bubinas's friendship, collegiality, and encouragement to complete this project, comments on several chapters, and suggestions for making the book accessible for students. Thomas Malaby, Abdi M. Kusow, Paul Brodwin, Ingrid Jordt, and Erica Bornstein were members of my dissertation committee, for which I prepared the first draft of this work.

My discussions with Abdi M. Kusow over the years about social stratification have been instrumental. Linguists Mohamed A. Eno and Georgi Kapchits graciously answered my questions about linguistic diversity and change in Somalia. Mohamed A. Eno also shared his knowledge of status claims, counter narratives, and minority groups. Georgi Kapchits contributed greatly to my understanding of language dialects and verified associations of clans with these dialects. Omar A. Eno served as a resource on Somali history and minorities. Markus Hoehne's and the late Virginia Luling's close reading of an earlier draft apprised me of slippages and oversights. Markus Hoehne challenged me to push my analysis further and kindly permitted me to reproduce his maps and offered his expertise along the way. I am grateful for Abdulkadir Osman Farah writing a strong foreword to the book about the legacy of clan from a Somali perspective. Abdulkadir also served as a resource on numerous occasions and pointed out shortcomings. It has been a pleasure working with Marika Christofides, Norm Whitten, and Daniel Nasset at the University of Illinois Press. I thank Marika and Norm for imparting advice throughout the entire process, polishing the manuscript, and carefully selecting two anonymous readers. I would like to thank both reviewers for their time and comments. In particular, I thank one reader for their meticulous review and suggestions for refining the manuscript in a myriad of ways including its usefulness as a pedagogical tool. This reviewer helped me resolve several problems I had been grappling with in the text. Geof Garvey's copyediting made the book more coherent. At Paradise Valley Community College, numerous colleagues offered their support. Special mention goes to Michele Marion for providing assistance with editing and Paula Crossman for obtaining the obscure resources I requested. Jan Downey helped make illustrations student-friendly and Mark Ordway completed image processing.

During the course of my fieldwork, I was affiliated with the Department of Sociology at the University of Helsinki as a visiting researcher. Special acknowledgment goes to Kari Pitkänen and Tapio Alkula for making me feel welcome and arranging office space when such space was a scarce resource. Friends Sanna-Kaarina Kirvesoja, Piia Jansen, Marita Heikkilä-Hertel, Emma and Timo Suni, and Olli Sallinen confirmed aspects of Finnish language and culture. The American-Scandinavian Foundation, the Wenner-Gren Foundation for Anthropological Research, and the Fulbright Foundation funded my research in Finland. The completion of this project was made possible by a 2015–2016 academic year sabbatical awarded by Maricopa Community Colleges.

I extend special thanks to my husband, Thinh, and my son, Leif, for accepting my preoccupation with this project and ubiquitous piles of books and papers. Any errors or omissions are solely mine.

# A NOTE ON SPELLING

I use Standard Somali for political figures and place names in Somalia as well as for clans (clan families, clans, and subclans). The only exception is the country's capital city, Mogadishu, since the Standard Somali spelling, Muqdisho, is less common. Although most traditional scholars in Somali studies prefer to use Standard Somali consistently throughout written work, I use a mixture of Standard Somali and Finnish transliteration to better reflect the way that the people I worked with actually write their names in Finland. For example, many of the males that I worked with were named Cali (Standard Somali) or Ali (Finnish transliteration). Thus, if I refer to Cali and Ali in the text, these names refer to two different consultants, one using Standard Somali and the other using a transliteration (in Finnish). For Standard Somali, I refer to David R. Zorc and Madina M. Osman, *Somali-English Dictionary with English Index,* 3rd ed. (Kensington, MD: Dunwood Press, 1993).

# SOMALIS ABROAD

# PROLOGUE

Since 1991 Somalia, a country of approximately ten million situated on the Horn of Africa, bordering Djibouti, Kenya, and Ethiopia, has featured prominently in international newscasts. That year, the United Somali Congress (USC)—led by a faction of the Abgaal and Habar Gidir clans who descend from the Hawiye clan family—ousted President General Maxamed Siyad Barre. Chaos ensued. This civil strife continues, albeit intermittently, to trouble the country.

This period of statelessness and unrest was preceded by the country's short-lived independence. Somalia gained its independence on July 1, 1960, after British Somaliland and the Italian Republic united to form the independent state of the Somali Democratic Republic.

In 1969 General Siyad Barre staged a coup d'état and established a military dictatorship. Barre aligned the state with the Soviet Union and instituted scientific socialism as the country's official political ideology. In an effort to curtail clan nepotism and promote nationalism, Barre led a campaign against tribalism. Clan sympathizers were arrested and detained by the regime's National Security Service.

Barre aspired to unite Somalis living outside Somalia's borders—in Djibouti, the Ogaadeen region of Ethiopia, and the Somali region of Kenya—under a greater Somalia. These three regions represented three of the five points of the star on Somalia's flag (British Somaliland and the Italian Republic served as the other two). In 1977 the Western Somali Liberation Front, led by Somalis residing in the Ogaadeen, together with Somalia's military, initiated war with Ethiopia over the disputed Ogaadeen region. Although Somalia was initially successful in driving Ethiopians out of the region, Ethiopia regained control with the Soviet Union's backing. This caused Barre to switch allegiances from the Soviet Union to the United States. Somalia's defeat resulted in the mass exodus of Ogaadeen refugees to Somalia. This loss coupled with the refugee influx strained state resources and put Somali nationalism at risk. Western aid began to flow into the country.

In 1978 a group of military officers affiliated with the Majeerteen, a Daarood clan, led an armed coup against the regime. The attempt failed. Those avoiding arrest formed the Somali Salvation Democratic Front (SSDF). The SSDF operated from across the border in Ethiopia.

During the 1980s President Barre's regime became increasingly totalitarian. Although the regime offered some stability, infrastructure development, adoption of an official Latin script for the Somali language, and literacy campaigns, it also was associated with widespread surveillance, arrests, brutality, and brain drain. The state was in economic peril and it increasingly relied upon foreign aid from the United States and Italy. Public support for the regime waned and resistance movements intensified.

The president turned to his own clan for support. Barre appointed clan affiliates from the Marreexaan, his clan, the Ogaadeen, his mother's clan, and the Dhulbahante, his son-in-law's clan, to key governmental positions. All are clans of the Daarood clan family. As nepotism became transparent, the acronym MOD was used to refer to the powerful alliance of the three affiliates, which further incited dissidence (Kapteijns 2013).

The number and strength of resistance movements soared. In the Northwest, the Isaaq clan family led the Somali National Movement (SNM). The regime persuaded the Majeerteen—a clan of the Daarood clan family and neighbor to the Isaaq—to fight the SNM. This divide and rule policy only fueled clan loyalties, which the regime had tried to repress earlier.

In 1988 the military attacked the Northwest and aerial-bombed the city of Hargeysa. A civil war ensued. Clan-based factions vied for control. The Hawiye-dominated (Habar Gidir and Abgaal clans) USC was one such faction. Barre urged Daarood affiliates to wipe out the Habar Gidir and Abgaal. In 1991 General Aideed, a Habar Gidir commander of the USC, drove Barre from Mogadishu. This led to what Lewis (2008) and Kapteijns (2013) refer to as "clan cleansing," a policy of killing and driving members of Barre's clan family from the South. The Abgaal, based in Mogadishu, set up an interim government. This action caused intraclan fighting and the USC to split along clan lines: Habar Gidir against Abgaal. The destruction and violence that plagued much of the South led to widespread famine, portrayed by international media broadcasts.

In 1991 the region previously known as British Somaliland seceded from Somalia. The clans living there, primarily the Isaaq clan family, the Gadabuursi and Ciise (clans of the Dir clan family), and the Dhulbahante and

Warsangeeli (clans of the Daarood clan family) declared the region to be the Republic of Somaliland.

Skirmishes between opposition groups continued, especially in the South. The country was divided into clan factions. Ancestral clan territories represented the spatial organization of Somalia. Groups lacking an armed militia were massacred. This was the case for minority groups such as the Somali Bantu, Madhibaan, and Benaadiri.

In 1992 the United Nations Security Council launched peacekeeping operations, and the United States assisted with famine relief efforts in the South. General Aideed attacked UN troops in Mogadishu, culminating in the infamous Battle of Mogadishu. The battle is portrayed in the Hollywood film *Black Hawk Down*. Militia ambushed U.S. Army Rangers attempting to capture Aideed. Eighteen Rangers were killed. U.S. support for assistance efforts diminished, prompting the United States to pull troops from Somalia in 1994. The UN withdrew its forces in 1995.

In 1998 a Harti clan alliance of the Daarood clan family in the northeastern territory declared itself the Puntland State of Somalia. This self-governing region aspires to a united Somalia and disputes its border with Somaliland. In 2002 the Raxanweyn Resistance Army initiated secession as Southwestern Somalia. The secession was short-lived because of an internal conflict within the resistance.

In 2000 a meeting was held in Djibouti with clan representatives and warlords to create a transitional government. The meeting resulted in the Transitional National Government (TNG) with a president and a national assembly based on clan quotas. The 275-member parliament uses a 4.5 power sharing formula among the clans: the four major clan families (Dir, Daarood, Hawiye, and Raxanweyn) are the controlling four, and the rest making up the 0.5, belongs to minority groups. The involvement of diaspora elites and former employees of Siyad Barre's regime put TNG's credibility at risk (Hoehne 2010). TNG collapsed in 2002. The Transitional Federal Government (TFG) was formed in 2004. The TFG had little influence in Somalia and controlled only Baydhabo, a city in southern Somalia.

In the 1990s various subclan-controlled Islamic courts emerged in Mogadishu to contend with crime and insecurity. The courts acted informally and "relied on recruited local clan militias to enforce their rulings. When the courts first united [around 2000] to form what would later be called the ICU [Islamic Courts Union], they also united their militias and consequently created the first significant Somali militant organization not controlled by warlords or limited to a single clan" (Stanford University 2016). In February 2006 the United States initiated talks with a coalition of warlords to form the Alliance for the Restoration of Peace and Counter-Terrorism to rid the country of foreign extremists and terrorists. The courts joined forces against the alliance. Some mark these events as the beginning of religious extremism in Somalia. By June the ICU together with clan militia took control of Mogadishu from the warlords backed by the United States. The ICU brought a degree of security and stability to southern Somalia that the TFG was unable to provide. Later that year Ethiopian troops, backed by the United States and other Western governments, drove the ICU from Mogadishu and the TFG relocated to the capital city with protection from Ethiopian and African Union forces. Al-Shabaab (Arabic for "The Youth"), a radical splinter group of the ICU—later aligning with al-Qaeda—violently resisted the TFG. In 2009 Ethiopia withdrew from Somalia and al-Shabaab took control of Baydhabo. In 2012 Kenyan, African Union, and Somali troops forced al-Shabaab out of Baydhabo.

In 2012 Somalia's first formal parliament was sworn in, marking an end to the transitional government. Parliament members elected the first president since 1967. One aim of the new government was to put an end to nepotism and clan rivalry. Al-Shabaab lost control of Kismaayo, its last hold in a major city, but continued to carry out attacks in Mogadishu and neighboring countries. As Hansen (2014) describes it, al-Shabaab "attempts to survive in an environment plagued by the fragmented forces of Somali clan politics" by taking "advantage of clans at times, while at other times clans take advantage of al-Shabaab" (10).

In 2014 officials from the United States and United Kingdom met with the new president. The UK opened an embassy at the Mogadishu International Airport. Despite the killing of the al-Shabaab leader in Somalia by a U.S. drone missile, the government faced continual threats and attacks from al-Shabaab, Hisbul Islam (another terrorist group), and various other oppositional factions. These threats spill over to neighboring countries. In 2016 Kenya announced the closing of all refugee camps because of security, economic, and environmental concerns, an action that will displace 600,000 people. The closing of Dadaab refugee camp on the Kenya–Somalia border accounts for half of those to be displaced.

Since the beginning of the civil war in 1988, Somalis have fled the country in droves. This dispersion was caused not only by war and civil unrest but also by periods of widespread drought and famine. Those living in the country's northwest region were among the first to leave in response to the government's aerial bombing against SNM attacks. Somalis sought refuge in neighboring countries in the Horn of Africa, the former colonial powers of England, Italy, and France, the Middle East, and Gulf States. They also journeyed to new destinations such as Australia, the United Arab Emirates, the United States, and Finland. Somalis can be found in nearly every part of the world. There are no accurate figures on the size of the Somali diaspora; it is estimated that two million Somalis are dispersed outside Somalia's borders. This figure does not include the one million internally displaced persons in the country and nearly another million residing in refugee camps. Some Somalis participated in voluntary repatriation programs during periods of stability in Somalia. Still, many Somalis continue to seek asylum and family reunification in the West.

Although the account of events leading up to and following Somalia's collapse seems to portray solidified clan factions vying for power, everyday life is messier than that. "Clans" are anything but stable in form, alliance, and interest. Somalis in the diaspora respond to these dynamics in complex and unpredictable ways, with many holding multiple sentiments and enjoying close relationships across clans.

# CHAPTER 1

# CLAN AND CULTURAL INTIMACY

## Moments of Scholarship

It was the first day of the Somali Studies International Association's (SSIA) Ninth International Congress of Somali Studies held in Aalborg, Denmark, in 2004.[1] Despite jet lag, I managed to make it to the hotel's breakfast buffet. As I left the hotel restaurant, another conference participant, Hussein, stopped me. Hussein introduced me to Asha, a Somali woman from Finland. I was astonished that I did not know Asha or at least recognize her. "Hello, my name is Stephanie," I said, introducing myself to Asha. "I lived in Finland for several years where I conducted research among Somalis." "Ah, Stephanie. You know Zahra?" Asha said. "Zahra who lives in Rastila? [Rastila is a neighborhood located in East Helsinki where many immigrants and refugees live in subsidized housing.] Her husband lives in Kenya and her son's name is Omar?" I asked. "Yes, she is a good friend of mine," Asha replied. "Yes, I know her well," I said. "Zahra told me I should meet you, but I was busy studying and working," Asha said. Then, Asha pointed to my name and the title of my paper printed on the conference program. She said:

> Did you see this Steven Bjork from Milwaukee who is talking about clan and practice? What is practice? How does someone from Milwaukee know about Somalis and clan in Finland? Practice? Practice is no good. My friend Ubax is studying at the university and cannot be at the conference. Ubax told me to listen to his talk and tell her about it. Ubax said that if she was here she would give him a difficult time. I received emails about the paper topic. People told me to look after this Steven.

Feeling unnerved, I pointed to the same title printed on the program that Asha held: *Clan Identities in Practice: The Somali Diaspora in Finland* (see Bjork 2007a). "I am giving that paper. I am Stephanie Bjork," I said. Taken aback, Asha asked, "No, really?" "Yes, I realize that clan is a sensitive topic, but I think that clan is important to discuss," I said. Then I added, "I have tried to approach clan in a neutral manner. I will not refer to clans by name." Noticing that Asha looked distraught, I said, "Now I am apprehensive about reading my paper." "No, don't worry," Asha said. Then, I asked Asha to critique my paper before I presented it at the congress. In that way, I could include Asha's comments in my presentation. Asha agreed, and we planned to meet that evening at the hotel.

That afternoon, I attended a panel where a distinguished scholar's mere mention of a clan, *qabiil* in Somali, was met with opposition. When this scholar referred to the implication of clan in asylum decisions in Europe, a Somali man in the audience stood up and objected to the clan reference. He said, "Why do you always divide Somalis?" This public outburst stunned the panelists and the audience.

Later that evening, I met Asha in her hotel room, and I read my paper to her. "I agree with what you said. That sounds like Somalis," Asha said. Then, she added, "I have never heard clan talked like this way before." It is conceivable that Asha might have rejected my paper if I had referred to clans by name. Instead of naming names, that is, the actual names of clans, I used clan family A, clan B, subclan A, and so forth.

It was the first paper I gave about clan at a professional conference and my first experience presenting at an SSIA congress. Because kinship was no longer in vogue, and increasingly marginalized, in Somali studies, Asha's query about "Steven Bjork" was especially unnerving. It was also my first experience presenting for a largely Somali audience. In fact, a few of my consultants living in Finland attended my talk. I had understood that clan was a sensitive cultural issue to discuss. Looking back at this and other experiences at SSIA congresses, I feel fortunate to have opportunities to engage in open dialogue and disseminate my work to Somalis, for this still is not the norm for many anthropologists. I anticipated seeing a number of my consultants at the Twelfth SSIA Congress held in 2015 in Helsinki, but that was not the case. The participation of local Somalis at the congress was significantly lower than at the previous congresses held in Aalborg, Denmark, and Columbus, Ohio. Early anthropologists rarely experienced the kind of feedback Asha gave me in Denmark. I no longer refer to clans as clan family A, clan B, subclan A, and so forth as I did as a doctoral student. I have learned how to discuss clan more sensitively by highlighting the multivocality of consultants' own discourse.

Globalization continues to alter the relationship between anthropologists and the people they work with. Since leaving the field, I maintain contact with consultants via email, social media, FaceTime, and Skype. Our ongoing communication not only keeps me in touch with dear friends dispersed around the world, but also facilitates discussion and my own reflexivity. I have routinely found myself asking consultants questions about Somali history, their interpretations of what I saw or heard during fieldwork, and reflecting upon my own position in the field. Following the suggestion of an anonymous reviewer, I asked a few consultants to comment on this manuscript before publication, collaborating more formally. Fortunately, I had planned a trip to Finland to present at the Twelfth SSIA Congress in Helsinki. I met with three consultants, Hanaan, Nafiso, and Mohamed, during this trip to look at and discuss the manuscript. I incorporate their comments throughout this book and offer their updates on changes since the fieldwork period. I endeavor also to write in a way that is accessible to many of the people I have worked with, students of anthropology, and others interested in the topic.

## Things That Make Unprogress

I was not surprised that Asha and her friend Ubax were suspicious about my paper. Nor was I surprised when Asha admitted that other Somalis told her "to look after this Steven." I anticipated opposition to my paper. I concealed clan names in an effort to avoid clan politics and to minimize dissonance.

In most cases, clan is a taboo topic for public discourse. The Somali man's open criticism of the scholar who uttered a clan reference is a testament to that. Surely, the outburst was not only projected toward that scholar but also toward the numerous other scholars who have studied clan. Studies of Somali kinship figure prominently in the ethnographic literature on Somalia (see Cerulli 1957–1964; Colucci 1924; Helander 1996, 2003; Lewis 1961, 1962, 1994; Luling 1971, 2002; Marlowe 1963). It has been through the lens of clan that Somalis have been primarily viewed and represented. When Somalis working for refugee resettlement agencies visit my anthropology classes to provide an overview of Somali culture, they usually mention that Somalis have clans. Rarely do they add further details. A few have said that clans remain important for those living in Somalia's countryside or referred to clans' role in the civil war. There is no mention of what clan means to Somalis abroad or its role in daily life. One reason they might touch on clan during these talks is because they know that outsiders (and particularly anthropology students) already have a notion of Somali clans from scholarship and media representations.

In addition to blaming scholars for dividing Somalis by clan, Somalis tend to blame cultural outsiders, including international media, refugee organizations, and host governments for dividing Somalis by clan. Somalis extend this blame to cultural insiders who appear to be concerned with clan or to be clannish. Such constant blaming underscores the disconcerting relationship that Somalis have with clan. When I visited Finland in 2015, I met with Mohamed, a man in his forties. After we read the section on this disconcerting relationship, Mohamed said, "Somalis use clan issues themselves, but, for some authorities, they force you to tell your clan, otherwise no [refugee] status. You have to have a clan name."

As Somalis migrate to the West, they do not readily acknowledge to outsiders that clan is ever-present in their daily lives, even though Somalis understand that to be the case. The notion of clan embarrasses Somalis who live abroad. This perplexing relationship with clan developed long before the civil war. Mohamed (2007) argues that colonial governments focused solely on genealogical kinship and disregarded Somalis' flexible traditional governing principles, particularly *xeer*, the social contract, that binds kin and unrelated groups together (Mohamed 2007:226). "Since the colonial administration insisted on ruling the Somalis as clans and factions of clans, the latter began to compete with each other through and for the state" (Kapteijns 2013:76). Under colonial rule, clan became a political force. Somalis' long-established oral history is evidence of Somali notions of kinship and belonging that predate European colonialism. European colonialism made kinship more concrete and ordered, replacing what were likely more fluid forms.

Somalia's postcolonial elite regarded tribalism as backward and kinship a threat to national solidarity but still used clan ties for their own political endeavors (see Lewis 2002; Hoehne 2006; Mohamed 2007). In 1970, President General Maxamed Siyad Barre led a national campaign against tribalism in the name of progress. Barre's military regime aligned with the Soviet Union and instituted scientific socialism as Somalia's official political ideology in an effort to unify a nation divided by kinship loyalties (see Lewis 2002; Samatar 1988). "One of Barre's first actions was to 'bury tribalism' by burning the tribe in the form of an effigy at pre-organized gatherings in every city and town in Somalia" (Kusow 2014:94). By 1971 the recitation of clan genealogy was illegal. Somalis were instructed to "replace this kin term [*ina'adeer*] in general salutations by the word *jaalle*, 'comrade' or 'mate'" (Lewis 1994:87). In addition to the literal meaning of the kinship term *ina'adeer*, child of father's brother, the term also is used as a form of address among patrilineal kin of the same generation (Lewis 1994:87). The regime's National Security Service (NSS), modeled after the Soviet Union's and East Germany's, worked to repress Somalis' public recognition of clan. It is unlikely that private expressions of clan were suppressed.

After Somalia's defeat in the war with Ethiopia to reclaim the Ogaa-deeniya (Ogaden region in southeast Ethiopia largely inhabited by the Ogaadeen clan), refugees from the region flooded into the country. Barre's alliance with the Soviet Union had dissolved as a result of the Soviet's military support for Ethiopia in the Ogaden War. Unparalleled amounts of international aid began to flow into Somalia. Simons (1995) refers to this influx of economic capital as "the aid avalanche" (52) of which the United States was a key contributor. Growing dissension, especially in the North, was met with harsh military rule and surveillance. By the 1980s, the particular clan alliance Barre was believed to rely on was referred to by the acronym MOD (Marreexaan, Ogaadeen, Dhulbahante; Kapteijns 2013:78). Marreexaan is Barre's clan, Ogaadeen his mother's clan, and Dhulbahante his son-in-law's clan. All are clans of the Daarood clan family. Simons (1995) notes, "In hindsight, it now seems that it was *this* avalanche of aid—and the influx of aid workers and Western diplomats accompanying it—that bent the system" (52–53). Besteman (2016) echoes this sentiment: "the wealth flowing into Somalia from foreign aid enabled the growth of an elite, urban class of politicians and businessmen with close government connections. Inequalities between clans had arrived in Somalia, joining hierarchies of race and ancestry created previously through the slave trade and migration" (43).

Western media coverage of the Somali conflict, coupled with the celebrity of *Black Hawk Down*, a 2001 Hollywood film, led the international community to associate Somalis with warlords, clans, and violence.[2] And Somalis themselves blame tribalism as the cause of the war and ongoing civil unrest in poststate collapse Somalia.[3] Clans seem antiquated in the lives of diasporic Somalis, as the following quote from an in-depth interview reveals:

AUTHOR: If I ask Somalis about tribe[4] [consultants used clan and tribe interchangeably], they tell me that they are against it; but when I am with them, they talk about it all the time and question the tribal affiliation of others. Why?

FARAH: Tribe was a primitive system used by people in the countryside. Tribes fought for land and water. Tribe was not used by educated people living in cities. People from different tribes were friends, lived together in neighborhoods, and had business together. Tribe is one of those *things that make unprogress* [emphasis added]. You have to know other people and who they are. Are they a good person? Tribe is only to recognize each other. But in this world now, if you say I just want to be with my tribe, you cannot go far. You must be with everyone, even whites and other Africans—wider than a small group.

The concept of *cultural intimacy* provides an apt foundation to understand the cultural intricacies that shape Somalis' contestation of clan. As defined by Herzfeld, cultural intimacy is "the recognition of those aspects of a cultural identity that are considered a source of external embarrassment but that nevertheless provide insiders with their assurance of common sociability" (Herzfeld 1997:3). Perhaps because clan is associated with the barbarity of the warlords and seems antithetical to modernity, Somalis abroad deny significance of their clan affiliations even as they point out their own clans and those of their associates.

Cultural intimacy shapes Somalis' contestation of clan in the diaspora. Several moments at the Ninth SSIA Congress in Denmark illustrated this. During a session break, I sat with a group of Somali men who attended my talk. Most of them were conference observers. A few resided in Finland and the rest lived in other European countries. Although none of them objected to my paper, each pointed to the cultural intimacy of clan. The men contested the notion that clan influenced their daily lives, yet they were quick to point out other Somalis who were clannish.

The following day, Hassan, with whom I sat at the conference, approached me with a business proposition. Hassan asked me to write a book about his clan, explaining that other Somalis disagreed about the origins of his clan. He assured me that he could provide the appropriate references for such a book. I thanked Hassan, but I declined his offer. Sometime later, Ahmed, another man with whom I sat took me aside. Ahmed told me that Mukhtar, still another man from the group who attended my talk, was preoccupied with clan and clan politics.

None of these culturally intimate moments surprised me. The people I worked with constructed clan and contested clan and persons who were clannish in the same way. It struck me that, apart from my paper, talks on clan were conspicuously absent from the conference proceedings. The previous SSIA conferences held in 1998 and in 2001 revealed a similar pattern (see Ford, Adam, and Ismail 2003; Lilius 2001).[5] This omission is remarkable when the prominence of kinship in the scholarship of Somalia is considered.

In 2015 Hanaan commented on the cultural intimacy of clan. She said, "In my opinion, most of Somalis when they speak about clan or tribe to an outsider, not a Somali person, they try to cover in a diplomatic way that shows Somali society is no longer clan- or tribe-oriented, which is not one hundred percent honest." After Nafiso and I read this section together, she said, "A woman supports me and I support her, but she said she supports me more than a woman from her same clan. I didn't like it." I asked Nafiso to clarify what caused her displeasure. She explained that the woman brought up the clan issue by pointing out they belong to different clans.

## Studies of Somali Kinship

Historically, kinship is central to the discipline of anthropology. The field emerged during Western expansion and an increase in contact between cultures. During European colonialism, British social anthropology's theoretical school of structural functionalism was at the forefront of kinship studies.[6] That theoretical tradition views society as a holistic integrated system without considering how historical or political factors such as colonial imposition may influence kin relations. Much of the work dealt with creating and applying kinship typologies and terminologies and describing the structure and function of kinship in terms of descent groups, politics, alliances, residence rules, marriage rules, inheritance, and obligations. From that perspective, colonial ethnographers studied and compared what they termed African acephalous societies (societies that function without formally named officials). They viewed kinship as the basis for political structure and order in stateless societies. Colonial administrators used this information to inform indirect rule in British colonies. Studies of Somali kinship are part of this tradition.

British anthropologist Ioan M. Lewis, a student of E. E. Evans-Pritchard, was among the first scholars to study Somali kinship. Lewis applied Evans-Pritchard's (1940) classic kinship model, the segmentary lineage system, to Somalis (Lewis 1998a). The model was first used to explain how unilineal descent groups function as political groups among the Nuer in what was then Sudan (now South Sudan).[7] Unilineal descent, descent traced through either the mother or the father, is the most common type of descent across cultures. The Nuer and Somalis practice patrilineal descent (tracing descent through males in their father's line and remaining members of their father's patrilineal clan throughout their lives). In theory, the father's patriline constitutes the most significant kin relationship. Lewis fit Somalis into this academic model before he began fieldwork in the British Somaliland Protectorate.[8]

According to Lewis's (1998a) model, Somali society is organized into segmenting units based on patrilineal reckoning of descent. The six clan families are segmented into clans whose members believe they descend from the same apical ancestor (the first common ancestor). Clans tend to associate with particular territories, but with undefined boundaries. Clans segment into primary lineages (subclans) that further segment into *diya*-paying groups (blood compensation-paying groups). In this complementary opposition, clans have equal status, and conflict is managed through shifting clan alliances. In theory, when two subclans fight, the two clans from which they descend also will fight.

In Lewis's (1957) terms, this *total genealogy* links Somalis to Hiil, who descends from the Qurayshitic lineage of the Prophet Muhammad. From Hiil's two sons, Sab and Samaale, a key subdivision among Somali clan families occurred. The two agropastoral clan families (Digil-Mirifle or Digil and Raxanweyn) descend from Sab and the four pastoral-nomadic clan families (Daarood, Dir, Hawiye, and Isaaq) descend from Samaale. This total genealogy legitimates the Arab origins of Somalis, their ties to Islam, and the Sab–Samaale distinction.

Lewis's work among northerners indicates that the Sab–Samaale distinction is a basis for status claims. The Samaale despise the Sab for their sedentary agricultural lifestyle, ambiguous origins, and mixed genealogies (Lewis 1957, 1961, 1998a). Persons descending from the two agropastoral clan families likely employed their own counternarratives during the time of Lewis's research. Despite the Sab–Samaale cleavage, Lewis considers Somali society to be egalitarian and homogeneous. Groups that fall outside the total genealogy fall outside the boundary of Somaliness.

Lewis's (1961) ethnographic work among pastoral-nomadic clans in British Somaliland reveals that both *tol* (agnatic descent) and *xeer* (contract) order alliances.[9] And the *diya*-paying group tends to be the most vital political unit among these clans. At times, *diya*-paying groups form *xeer* in response to their changing interests and conditions and supersede genealogy (see Lewis 1961, 1994, 2002). This makes Lewis's model more fluid than the model that Evans-Pritchard, his predecessor, used to explain Nuer kinship. Still, genealogy tends to be the primary organizing principle among pastoral nomads.

Research in southern Somalia among the Digil and Raxanweyn (Digil-Mirifle) indicates that affiliated clans tend to form alliances based on residence rather than on genealogy. It is important to note here that Lewis also understood that to be the case (see Lewis 1969). Virginia Luling (1971, 2002) reveals that the Geledi clan—inhabiting the town of Afgooye along the lower Shabeelle River—is a confederation of lineages comparable to southern coastal city-states.[10] Bernhard Helander (1996, 2003) demonstrates that the Hubeer, an inland, agropastoral clan, adopts unaffiliated

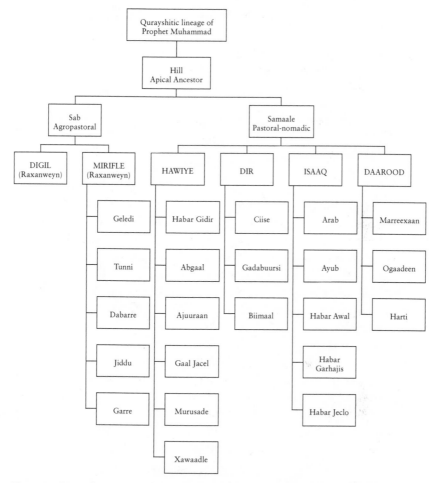

Figure 1. General overview of Somali kinship. Clan families are indicated in uppercase. The Digil and Mirifle clan family is often combined as Raxanweyn. Following Hoehne (2006), Isaaq is depicted as a clan family rather than a clan of Dir because of its size and political standing. The clans descending from each clan family further segment into subclans and lineages, and Somali minorities have their own clans.

individuals and groups who may have relocated for fertile soil. Adopted individuals become members of a new clan, but they continue to claim the genealogy of their paternal clan. This fictitious descent does not diminish the ideological importance for Somalis of the segmentary lineage model (Helander 2003). Helander's work also reveals the importance of other ties of solidarity including those with neighbors and mother's paternal clan.

In the 1970s and 1980s, kinship studies in anthropology declined. This was in part due to a rejection of colonial ethnography and its deterministic theories and the advent of newer theoretical perspectives, particularly practice theory and postmodernist theory. Many anthropologists considered traditional kinship theory to be rigid, algebraic, and constrained by structural functionalism. This led to reexamination of early kinship studies in which the segmentary lineage system was challenged widely (see Gough 1971; Hutchinson 1996; Southall 1970, 1986; Verdon 1982). Revisions reveal the messier realities of kinship. For example, Gough's research among the Nuer of Sudan, conducted nearly forty years later than Evans-Pritchard's work, found that the group practices bilateral filiation (tracing kinship connections through both parents without reference to a unilineal construct). Gough suggests that Evan-Pritchard's findings that strictly favor patrilineal descent groups were influenced by colonial officials' practice. Studies on power, hegemony, gender, personhood, and ethnicity replaced kinship as a central analytical category (Carsten 2004; Holy 1996).

A new generation of social scientists conducting research in Somalia followed this trend. These researchers, mostly anthropologists—grounded in postmodernist theory, feminist theory, and Marxist theory—sought to illuminate Somalis' heterogeneity and challenge the notion of Somalia as one nation with a shared culture and language. Instead of focusing on kinship, these researchers focused on class, gender, race, and Somalia's dissolution (see Besteman 1991, 1999; Bhoola 1989; Declich 1992; Menkhaus 1989; Simons 1995). Menkhaus (2010) reflects upon how the academic climate of the 1980s affected his doctoral research in international studies in Somalia, and it is worth including here:

> My own doctoral field research, in pre-war Somalia's Lower Jubba Valley, was not initially informed by considerations of ethno-politics of any sort, though I had read Lewis' works closely. Like most of my peers in the 1980s, I was a product of an academic environment dominated by political economy approaches, and so was trained to approach the question of land, production, and the state through that prism. As a consequence of that socialisation process, I uncritically accepted the dismissal of the earlier scholarship of cultural anthropologists and their fellow travellers in political science who reified ethnic identity and whose writing incautiously echoed the discredited tone of colonial administrators. As a result, in preparing for my fieldwork, I intentionally downplayed matters of clan and ethnic identity, and kept a quiet distance from the ideas and analyses of scholars like Professor Lewis. (Menkhaus 2010:90–91)

Simons's *Networks of Dissolution: Somalia Undone* offers a taste of clan at the local level. Simons's intention to focus her research on livestock domestication among camel nomads in central Somalia was thwarted by the country's instability. Simons situated her fieldwork in Mogadishu, the country's capital city, from 1988 to 1989 as an affiliate of the World Bank's Central Rangelands Development Project (CRDP). Although the field project in central Somalia was put on hold, Simons and her coworkers—Somalis and expatriates—met daily at the CRDP office. The NSS's increased policing of government dissidents and clan sympathizers did not stop Simons's Somali coworkers from telling their clan and talking about clan. They told clan through dialect and used euphemisms to elude eavesdroppers who might have worked for the NSS (Simons 1995:7). Simons argues that when the state became undone and its institutions failed, Somali kinship endured.

The collapse of Somalia's government and mass exodus triggered other movements within Somali studies. The number of Somali-born scholars contributing to the literature rose considerably. *The Invention of Somalia* (A. Ahmed 1995), marks a pivotal departure from earlier studies on Somalia.[11] The contributors to this volume, more than half Somali-born, contest the epistemology of the Somali canon by deconstructing colonial scholarship and the proclivity of scholars to embrace the Somali "one nation, one language, and one religion" myth. The volume offers new perspectives on gender, southern Somalis, minorities, and kinship. This book set forth a new agenda for Somali studies, which is by and large a Somali perspective. Works on clan reexamine colonial representations by scrutinizing clan origin myths and segmentary lineage theory and examine its role in the collapse of Somalia (A. Abdullahi 2001; Besteman 1995; Eno 1997, 2004; Kusow 1995, 2004; Laitin and Samatar 1987; Mansur 1995, 1997; Mohamed 1997; Mukhtar 1995, 1997; Samatar 2001).

Research on the Somali diaspora continues to overlook clan. Most of this work looks at the following: transnational families (Al-Sharmani 2004; Decimo 2007; Horst 2007a, b); migration patterns and asylum policies (Abdi 2015; Hautaniemi 2007; Luling 2007); refugee experience (Abdi 2015; Huisman et al. 2011); diasporic identity (Abdi 2015; Al-Sharmani 2007; Fangen 2007; Kusow 1998); integration (Alitolppa-Niitamo 2000, 2004; Farah and Stenum 2014; Jinnah 2010); mental health and female circumcision (Johansen 2006; Warfa et al. 2012); religious changes (Berns McGown 1999, 2004; Tiilikainen 2003, 2007); remittances (Horst 2006, 2007a, b; Lindley 2010); and transnational civic and associational mobilization (Farah 2013, 2015, 2016). These works deal little with clan aside from the few that offer a brief overview of Somali kinship or mention that Somalis belong to different clans. Two notable exceptions are Horst (2006) and Lindley (2010). Horst examines the role of clan, among other social networks, as a means to cope with daily insecurity in Dadaab refugee camp in Kenya and Lindley implicates the role of clan in remittances in Hargeysa, Nairobi, and London. I return to these two works later in the present book.

Somali scholar Cawo M. Abdi's (2015) lack of emphasis on clan in her recent book is intentional and it is worth including the reasons here:

> Unlike most books written by non-Somalis, and in some cases by Somalis, there is no section that outlines the Somali clan structure in this book. This is intentional and based on the nonrelevance of clan as a topic of discussion in my own interactions with Somalis in all the settings covered in this book. I grew up in an era when asking others their clan was frowned on. This remains so for many in my age group and especially for many in the Somali communities in the diaspora. But the place of clan and what it means in society has become a major political topic since the collapse of the Somali nation in 1991. Nevertheless, the only Somalis who ever inquired about my clan affiliation were men and women in their sixties and seventies. In no interaction in Somalia, Kenya, South Africa, UAE, or the United States did a research participant make an issue of what my clan membership was. This is not to say that interviewees did not inquire about what clan I belonged to with others, but it was never a point of discussion of contention with me. (24)

Has scholarship been inhibited by the cultural intimacy of clan? Many Somalis claim that clan is no longer relevant and overtly deny significance of clan ties. An increasing number of scholars also claim that clan is no longer relevant as a focus of analysis. Some scholars consider clan to be a quasi-taboo topic for scholarship, in part because of colonial anthropology's preoccupation with kinship and clan. And some blame Lewis's clan-based view of Somali society for the rise of tribalism and challenge the notion of the segmentary lineage system's centrality in Somali society.

The collapse of the Somali state triggered a flood of academic publications and NGO and media reports explaining why the country failed. Lewis's stance that Somali kinship was the primary cause of collapse and continuation of the conflict is clear when one considers the title of his 1994 book on the subject: *Blood and Bone: The Call of Kinship in Somali Society*. Most media and political outlets shared Lewis's estimation (Besteman 1996a). Besteman (1996a, see also 1996b) argues that the segmentary lineage system and "ancient hatreds and [clan] rivalries" (120–21) offer a simplistic explanation of Somalia's collapse and ensuing violence and contributes to "othering" Somalia. The impassioned exchange that followed between Lewis (1998b) and Besteman (1998) highlights the tension in what Barnes (2006) characterizes as "the generational and paradigmatic battle lines of Somali studies, as well as the regional divide between north and south Somalia" (488).[12]

Besteman (1998) argues that Lewis's "primordial blinders" (109) prevent him from seeing how the changing global political economy, increasing urbanization, militarization, foreign aid, and class divisions caused the state to fail and how patterns of violence played out along class, race, and regional lines in southern Somalia. As many scholars do, Besteman contends that Lewis relegates Somalis to an unchanging "tradition of aggression and the tradition of lineage segmentation" (111). Lewis (1998) argues that Besteman was "doing violence to ethnography" (100) by giving credence to the role of class, race, and regional differences in Somalia's collapse in preference to that of kinship and by discounting his forty years of scholarship on segmentary lineage. Lewis's all-or-nothing approach to kinship continues to marginalize studies of clan. Both scholars, however, agree that Somalis turned to clan networks to cope with the uncertainty and insecurity of the state's collapse.

Although kinship studies remain marginalized in scholarship on Somalia and its diaspora, Lidwien Kapteijns and Markus Hoehne are scholars who have recently added to the literature on Somali kinship and have moved beyond Lewis's all-or-nothing approach. Kapteijns (2013) exposes the clan-cleansing campaign in Mogadishu and southern Somalia after the country's collapse by analyzing Somali poetry and survivor accounts. Hoehne's work (2006, 2009, 2010, forthcoming) highlights shifting regional and clan identities in northern Somalia.

## Practicing Clan in the Somali Diaspora

This book is an ethnography of everyday life in the Somali diaspora depicted through the lives of Somalis in Finland. The primary data for this book stem from ethnographic fieldwork conducted in the Helsinki metropolitan area between January 2003 and April 2004 (see Bjork 2007c). The Helsinki metropolitan region, inhabited by 1.2 million persons, consists of four municipalities: Helsinki, the capital of Finland, and the surrounding cities of Espoo, Vantaa, and Kauniainen. Earlier fieldwork conducted in Finland from 2000 to 2001 and summer 2002 also informs this work. Since 2004, I have maintained contact with several key consultants whom I consider close friends by email and, more recently, by social networking sites such as Facebook and Instagram. This communication has been vital for maintaining friendships and keeping up to date on changes since the fieldwork. As mentioned earlier, the comments and updates from the three consultants that I met with in 2015 add another important dimension to this book.

At first, I intended to focus my research on how Somalis use social networks, including clan networks, networks with Finns, and other means, to access work in the Somali informal sector and in the Finnish formal sector. In the field, I became fascinated with consultants' contestation of clan and their efforts to tell clan. This led me to examine everyday practices that build and exchange capital among clan relatives. Despite the attitudes of Somalis that clan recognitions are to be glossed over, the anthropologist observer sees clan to be an ever-present feature of life abroad. Somalis are aware that Westerners do not recognize clan in their own cultures and do not want to emphasize this difference between them and their host society. Although some Finns, particularly service providers, may have a notion that Somalis belong to clans, they do not understand the nuances or insider dynamics.

We ethnographers are in a unique position to not only see what is tacit but to recognize the importance of clan, which may or may not be apparent to cultural insiders and to understand the everyday lives of the people we work with. Anthropological methods uncover insights about cultural phenomena that quantitative studies cannot reveal. Through intensive fieldwork, we participate in our consultants' daily life to see the world from their varied perspectives and in their own terms. The observations we make are objective and nonjudgmental. Ethnography is a collaborative process. We establish rapport and build trust, and often, friendships, with consultants. Through interviews, informal conversations, and surveys, we gain insight into beliefs, values, behaviors, discourse, and practices. We also learn how culture is constructed, negotiated, and contested. This is the way, and the reason, that I approach the study of clan in this book.

Traditional structural functionalist approaches to Somali kinship or clan-based societies in general cannot capture the cultural intricacies of clan under current conditions of global movements of people, objects, and ideas. I want to understand this classic anthropological concept in a novel way. A practice theory approach highlights clan on a practical and discursive basis rather than on a formal kinship model. Practice theory has reconciled the dilemma of structure and individual agency and accounts for change. What looks like hard structure is achieved through practices on the ground.

By focusing on everyday life, we see Somalis' seemingly habitual efforts to construct clan and cultivate clan networks. Cultivation involves a number of practices that integrate kin and hone, in Pierre Bourdieu's (1998) terms, a *family feeling* among clan relatives (or group feeling, *tolnimo* in Somali; see Mohamed 2007). In the same way, a *clan feeling* is vital for creating a sense of clan identity and trust among clan members. Cultivation involves a number of practices that use clan networks. Somalis use local and global clan networks in the moments of movement, celebration, and crisis. Using clan is what makes these everyday practices become a durable pattern that structures relationships over time and as the result of constant effort.

Because of clan's role in social networks, Bourdieu's (1986) formulation of social capital provides an apt foundation for understanding how clan is experienced and employed. Somalis must maintain clan networks in order for those networks to be potentially useful in the future. Through clan networks, Somalis accumulate capital and exchange capital globally. Bourdieu's economy of practices is a framework that sees all forms of capital in concert: economic, cultural, social, and symbolic.

Although I disagree with Lewis's traditional approach to clan, I agree with his contention that Somalis can use clan in modern ways. Lewis argues that Somalis "embrace it [modernity], adopting and adapting what interests them for their own purposes" (Lewis 1998b:105). Daily life exposes networks as flexible and reveals innovative configurations and uses. Consultants may use clan networks in certain contexts, but they may draw from other networks that crosscut clans.

Daily life also elucidates the messiness of clan as opposed to the orderliness of clan. In the diaspora, creating a *clan feeling* and obligation among clan relatives is cumbersome. Somalis in Finland came from various places: Somalia and other countries in the Horn of Africa, the Middle East, and Europe. Individuals possess various degrees of clan competency, that is, knowledge of clan genealogies and clan relationships. Individual investment in this cultural capital requires individual effort.

In the diaspora, Somalis encounter different ideologies that compete with a hierarchical clan ideology. In Finland, Somalis see their rights and obligations toward family, clan, and—in Al-Sharmani's (2004) terms—interdependent transnational families alongside ideas of autonomy and gender equality. In Finland and elsewhere, clan networks both limit individuality and offer a chance to build capital among kin. The diaspora broadens Somalis' opportunities to use clan in modern ways.

It would be a grave error to give readers the impression that clan interests drive all social networks. This is untrue and a gross oversimplification and one reason why many Somalis refute some earlier work on kinship and are not keen on contemporary studies on clan. The daily lives of Somalis in the diaspora, and in Somalia, are more complicated than that. On numerous occasions, I observed consultants engage with nonrelatives in many of the same everyday practices that hone a clan feeling among clan relatives. Throughout this book, I provide examples of them. Some consultants feel more kinship with nonrelatives than with clan relatives. Some Somalis feel more affinity toward individuals affiliated with their mother's paternal clan than with their own paternal clan, or with others who share similar migration experiences, prior residence, time of arrival, religious practices, Somali dialect or other spoken languages, and interests. Affinal relationships, ties through marriage, also play significant roles in daily life. At times, it is an individual's or group's interest to form horizontal links across clans. I provide examples of these efforts to build and exchange capital across clans. And a few of the people I worked with had little interest in cultivating relationships with other Somalis.

Throughout this book, I illustrate how Somalis socially construct associations of clans with status claims. Status claims are prevalent in daily life: in stereotypes, language use, marriage practices, efforts at distinction, and so forth. Symbolic effects of capital are messy because clan identities and clan status claims are constantly shifting because of cultural, social, economic and political processes on local and global scales. And status claims can be tied to various times and spaces. The size of a local community or network abroad, a historical event or famous ancestor, the development of ancestral clan territory, participation in homeland politics, and holding political positions in Finland can all be a basis for status claims.

Two well-known models of clan hierarchy are the lineage-based narrative and the territorial-based narrative. The lineage-based narrative is perhaps the most widely known of the two because of Lewis's extensive work among northern clans. From this viewpoint, northern clans claim higher status than southern clans because they claim that they are more closely related to the Arab and Muslim founding ancestor and geographically closer to the ancestor's original entry point (Kusow 2004:6; see also Cassanelli 2010). During Siyad Barre's regime, this notion of clan hierarchy found support at the national level through state-sponsored media, language, literature, and education.

Kusow (2004) argues that the territorial-based narrative reverses the lineage-based narrative's version of clan hierarchy. Territorial priorities exclude northern clans from any ancestral claim to the South's fertile, productive land. Here southern Somalis claim higher status than northern clans because they view themselves as "true owners of the land versus newcomers [northern clans] who have taken the land by force" (Kusow 2004:10). This narrative links southern clans with peaceful, collective values and northern clans with anarchistic and urban nomadic values (Kusow 2004:8). Barnes (2006) argues that 'u dhashay "born to (a family/clan)" and ku dhashay "born in a place/region)" (487) has a historical basis and informs current debates of political legitimacy in contemporary Somalia and its diaspora. Although the lineage-based narrative and territorial-based narratives are widely known narratives, there are unlimited ways to construct and contest status claims. Minority groups produce and circulate their own counternarratives to the status claims of the so-called majority Somalis, adding other layers to the messiness of status claims. In the conclusion, I touch on some of these counternarratives from my work with Somali Bantu refugees in the United States.

## An Unlikely Place

Finland (*Suomi* in Finnish) does seem like an unlikely place for a U.S. anthropologist to situate her fieldwork on the Somali diaspora. I easily could have conducted this study in the United States, Canada, or England. These countries host the largest Somali communities outside the Horn of Africa. Somalis are well represented in cities like Minneapolis, Minnesota; Columbus, Ohio; Toronto, Canada; and London, England. Also, I do not claim Finnish heritage and English is my native language. For many anthropologists, previous experiences or ties to a particular place and its people influence selection of field sites.

Unpredictably, my high school exchange in Finland (1990–91) aroused my interest in Somali refugees. I spent my exchange year in Uusikaupunki (Finnish for New Town), a small town of about fifteen thousand inhabitants on the country's southwest coast. This charming town by the Baltic Sea is known for its well preserved wooden houses dating from the eighteenth and early nineteenth centuries, cobblestone marketplace, and sailing culture. I immersed myself in Finnish culture, acquired some Finnish language skills, and formed lifetime friendships. I learned to appreciate Finns' fondness for solitude and efficient conversation style and their stoic qualities. I reveled in the independent lives my peers and I led. During the summertime, I went sailing and visited *kesämökkit* (Finnish for summer cottages) dotting the coastline or on one of the thousands of small islands in the archipelago. I spent many sunlit summer nights with friends hanging out at the marketplace and swimming in the sea. My favorite tradition was partaking in the sauna ritual with my three host families and friends and feeling comfortable doing so *au naturel*. During the winter, I learned to deal with the darkness by lighting candles, staying active outdoors, attending house parties, and waiting for a blanket of snow to lighten the landscape.

Some months into my exchange, I heard international newscasts about widespread devastation in the Horn of Africa and the breakdown of Somalia. Most Finns at that time were at least trilingual, speaking Finnish, Swedish (the other national language), and German, French, or English. Both my second host parents spoke English fluently, which was not the case for my other host parents, who learned German or French at school. So listening to English newscasts was not unusual. At the time, Finnish television was limited to a few channels and this was before the internet era. English was replacing German and French in popularity at school and was increasingly spoken among my peers. I clearly recall watching BBC broadcasts of the famine and strife caused by the civil war with my second host family. The poignant images weighed heavily on us.

About two months later, we visited Turku, a nearby city with a large Swedish-speaking population. We frequented Turku for shopping, art, and entertainment. As we walked through the city's cobblestone streets, I noticed graffiti on a few buildings. The writing and its racial content puzzled me. Until that moment, I had not seen graffiti in Finland. I asked Päivi, my second host mother, about the graffiti, and she explained that some Finns did not want Somalis to live in Finland.

As it happened, my year as an exchange student coincided with the influx of the first Somalis seeking asylum in Finland. My host family and I never talked about Somalis again, and I do not recall hearing any Finns discuss the Somalis finding refuge in Finland. There were no Somalis living in Uusikaupunki. If I had lived in Turku or Helsinki, the Somali situation or "Somali Shock" as it was widely called, would have likely been an everyday topic of conversation. Finland is a relatively homogeneous country and this was the country's first experience settling a large refugee population.

Nearly ten years passed before I was able to return to Finland. At the time, I was a first-year graduate student in anthropology. In addition to visiting with friends and host families, I was interested in finding a suitable topic for my master's thesis. When I arrived in Helsinki, I was immediately struck by the city's changing cultural landscape, especially the sizable Somali population living there. A decade earlier, there were few foreigners living in Finland. After I returned to the States, I started tutoring Somali refugee women in English at a vocational school. In turn, they provided me with instruction in the Somali language. Soon we became friends and I spent my weekends at their homes, met more members of the community, and started to learn about their culture.

In 2000 I returned to Finland on a Fulbright fellowship to conduct ethnographic field research among the Somali community (August 2000–August 2001). This research culminated in my master's thesis, which focused on the production and circulation of wedding videos. I had no interest in focusing on clan for many of the same reasons other scholars suggest. In addition to being my first fieldwork project, it also was my first direct contact with a refugee population in Finland.

I became accustomed to Finns' routine questions: "Why do you want to study Somali culture?" "Why study Somalis in Finland?" I became accustomed to friends' warnings: "Be careful." "Don't go to their [Somalis'] homes." It is likely that Finnish researchers experience these moments more frequently. Still, some Finns were curious about my work and about Somali culture. Several friends asked to read my finished work.

At first, Finland was not a destination for Somalis. Most consultants arriving in Finland in the 1990s characterized their move as being accidental. They had planned to resettle elsewhere, in Sweden, Western Europe, or North America.[13] Abdi, a male consultant, said, "I planned to go to the U.S. but the flight refused to take Somalis." Once these Somalis arrived in Finland, their journey ended or was at least interrupted. At that time, Somalia's civil war was in full force, making it unfeasible for Somalis to return home or travel beyond Finland. Somali passports were no longer valid, and some persons lacked documentation.

Cold War alliances between Siyad Barre's regime and the former Soviet Union served as a catalyst for the initial migration of Somalis to Finland (Alitolppa-Niitamo 2000).[14] Consultants studying in Moscow on scholarships financed by the failed nations—Somalia and the Soviet Union—lost their support. By chance, some students made their way to neighboring Finland.

Another vestige of these Cold War ties was the weekly direct flight via Aeroflot (the Soviet Union's national airline) that connected Moscow and Mogadishu. Cali, a man whom I worked with, caught the final flight out of Mogadishu in 1991 before the civil war deterred air travel. He said, "One flight from Mogadishu remained after November thirty-first [1991] on Aeroflot and flew once a week to Moscow." Farah, who had taken another flight, said, "Most people who came to Finland came from Mogadishu by accident by Aeroflot." Together with students, individuals securing tickets on Aeroflot were among the first Somali asylum seekers in Finland. The majority of them were men.

This influx of Somalis coincided with changes in Finnish society: deep recession, high unemployment, and the influx of Russian and Estonian immigrants

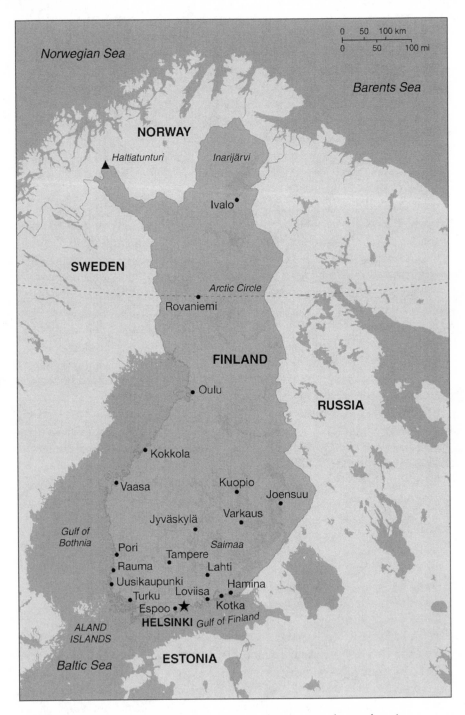

Map 1. Finland and neighboring countries. Consultants reported more than sixty different migration routes to Finland. The most common route was Mogadishu to Finland via Moscow. The second most common route was via Ethiopia or Kenya. Courtesy of University of Texas Libraries.

after the collapse of the Soviet Union. During that time, Finns' negative attitudes were largely directed toward Russians, Arabs, and Somalis because these newcomers were unemployed and accused of living off social security (Jaakkola 2000:139). Such views are compounded in a welfare state where high taxes support public services, and welfare benefits are distributed equally among Finns and permanent foreign residents.

The accidental arrivals prompted other Somalis to enter Finland, in particular spouses and immediate kin. Finland's family reunification program significantly increased Somalis' presence. Finnish law permits refugees and residence permit holders to have their family reunited with them in the country. Just over half of consultants reported that they entered Finland through the family reunification program.[15] The Finnish state defines family in terms of a nuclear family rather than the more extensive Somali family (see Hautaniemi 2007). In Somalia, polygyny, a marriage between one man and two or more women, is a fairly common practice. Islam permits men to marry up to four wives concurrently. In Somalia, polygyny is most common among older men with status or wealth (Lewis 1994:29). This form of marriage is not legally recognized in Finland.

As a further screening of Somali families, the Finnish government instituted DNA testing for cases of family reunification that appeared to be ambiguous.[16] In 2000 a new Finnish law made DNA testing more accessible (Hautaniemi 2007). Hautaniemi notes, "Somalis were the main target of the law for they often lacked valid documentation to prove 'real' family ties" (Hautaniemi 2007:124). This practice is highly controversial not only because of how Somalis define family but also in instances of rape and extramarital relationships (Tapaninen and Halme-Tuomisaari 2015). Finland's strategy of imposing its state-sponsored definition of family upon Somalis does not inhibit Somali migration to Finland. They assume they will be able to continue to live as interdependent transnational families with collective family interests.

Despite high unemployment and widespread discrimination, Somalis continue to arrive in Finland as quota refugees, as asylum seekers, and through the country's family reunification program.[17] In 2004 Somalis were the fourth-largest minority population and the largest African population living in Finland: Russians, Estonians, and Swedes constituted the largest minority populations. By the end of 2004, 8,096 native Somali speakers resided in Finland, and the ratio of men to women was almost 1:1 (Official Statistics of Finland 2004). When I returned in 2015, the Somali population had risen to about 16,000. They constitute the third-largest minority group in Finland and the country's largest refugee, African, and Muslim group (see Official Statistics Finland 2013).

It is fitting to highlight a few impressions of racism and xenophobia from my fieldwork and return trip in 2015. During the fieldwork period, physical separation between Somalis and Finns was observable in everyday life. As I will explain later in this chapter, there also were instances when this was not the case. Racism was one reason for this dissociation. Many of the people I worked with complained to me about racism.

Perhaps the best-known violent attacks against Somalis took place in Joensuu, a city in eastern Finland, in 1995, and in Hakunila, a suburb of Vantaa, in 2000. The former case involved the attacks of Finnish skinhead youth on Somali refugee youth. Joensuu is notorious for ethnic tensions partially due to the skinhead groups living there (Kulsoom 2002).

In the latter case in 2000, a series of violent clashes occurred between Somali and Finnish youth in Hakunila. In response to the violence, Somali parents kept their children home from school for several days. Soon after the Somali children returned to school, further violence occurred. This clash occurred during my initial fieldwork in Finland. At that time, reports of the clash dominated Finnish media. President Tarja Halonen, the country's first female president and a strong opponent of Finnish racism, showed her support for Somalis when she personally met with Somali students in Hakunila.

Surely, racism and xenophobia contributed to social exclusion of Somalis in Finnish society. My research suggests that some consultants segregated themselves from Finnish society. The majority of my consultants did not accept the notion of permanent residence in Finland. And some consultants had little interest in interacting with Finns.

On occasion, I accompanied Somali women to intercultural meeting places for women. Although an aim of these gatherings was to increase interethnic communication, I observed almost no interaction between the Somali and Finnish women. The Somali women tended to congregate in one room and the Finnish women congregated in another room. Often the Somali women gathered around the facility's sewing machines, where they mended or altered clothing (usually veils or dresses). I recall one instance in which a Finnish woman working at the meeting place told the Somali women to speak Finnish. This suggestion offended the group. The Finnish woman later explained that even if the Somali women could speak Finnish, they still spoke Somali. The Finnish women suspected that the Somali women talked about them when they socialized in Somali. I observed a wide range of opportunities for Somali–Finnish interaction for women, organized and facilitated by Finnish women, but such occasions were few for Somali men.

Some of the people I worked with deemed Finnish culture immoral. This led some Somali parents to limit their children's interaction with Finnish peers. Mukhtar, a father, said, "It is no [not] good that Finns go to sauna naked with their families. It is shameful to see your parents naked. And [Finnish] kids drink, smoke, and everything else [have sex] at a young age. In Somali culture, youth respect their parents."

The sauna is a national symbol of Finnish culture. Nearly every Finnish home and summer cottage has a sauna. The sauna is a wood-lined room with wooden steps and benches that is commonly heated up to 80–90° Celsius (176–194° Fahrenheit) with wood or electricity. Most Finns use the sauna at least once a week with family or friends for deep cleansing and relaxation. One friend of mine uses it daily. Sauna bathers take off their clothes and jewelry and shower before entering, place a small towel on a bench to sit upon, and throw water on the heated rocks to increase the heat and humidity. Since Finns first partake in the sauna ritual as children with their family, they are not embarrassed by nudity and consider the sauna a nonsexual place. Other differences in morality regarding drinking alcohol, premarital sex, and cohabiting may affect levels of integration and belonging. I return to these topics later in this book. D'Alisera's (2004) work indicates a similar pattern among Sierra Leoneans in the United States. Parents have "the notion of an 'authentic' Sierra Leonean Muslim culture" and they "often lament the 'Americanization' of children and work" (125).

When Somalis arrived in Finland they represented a culturally distinct population in Finland and had striking differences in language, religion, dating, family, and gender roles. Somalis in Finland mainly speak Somali and they are predominately Sunni Muslim whereas Finns mainly speak Finnish and they are predominately Lutheran but society is secular. Somalis tend to date without the knowledge of their parents before they are briefly engaged, marry, and have children. Finns tend to date a number of people and begin in their early teens without much interference from parents. It is not unusual for Finns to cohabit and have children before (or if) they marry. Somalis typically have large families (five to eight children), whereas Finns have small families (one or two children). In contrast to Finnish households, which typically comprise two or three persons, Somali households tend to be larger and more fluid. In addition to Somalis having more children, their household may comprise extended relatives, visiting relatives, and friends. Somali fathers tend to hold the authoritative role within families, whereas Finnish mothers and fathers tend to share this role. Gender roles are more clearly defined among Somalis: men should not cook or clean. Finnish men and women tend to share such responsibilities (at least more than Somalis do). Although these generalities highlight differences between Somalis and Finns, there are always exceptions. Migration opens up the possibility, and

often the necessity, for people to modify gender roles and family size as well
as other cultural forms.

Even during the fieldwork period, not all consultants fit neatly into the
generalizations above. In 2015 it was apparent that such contrasts were less
defined. Morality is shaped by culture but varies by individual. Individuals
adapt to a new culture and pick and choose what appeals to them. What
one considers as moral can change in the same way that cultural practices
change. In 2015 Hanaan commented on changes in gender roles since the
fieldwork period. She said, "It's ideal that women do household and take
care of kids, but [this is] not [the] reality nowadays. Both work. Share. [To]
Show to next generation that life is not the same." Both Hanaan and Nafiso
commented on the increase of divorce. Hanaan said, "More single mothers.
Older generation women tend to be more independent than in Somalia with
the help of the government of Finland supporting them and help integrating
them to find jobs. A lot of older women are working, about forty percent
[of them]. [Finnish] language skills [are] hard for them." She mentioned that
these women tend to work as nursing assistants or at daycares. After they
learn about the rights they have in Finland, there is more divorce among
them. Nafiso commented that in addition to more single mothers, there are
also more single fathers. When I met with Hanaan, she said, "I can dress
nicely but I don't dress showing out, like body, because I need to protect my
image, my name, and my parent's name in the Somali society. We do have
some people who give up."

Some consultants well integrated into Finnish society claimed that other
Somalis used racism as an excuse for their own lack of success in Finnish
society. Cali, a man in his twenties, described his first job in Finland as a
teacher's aide as taxing because he worked as a liaison between Finnish
teachers and Somali students and parents. Cali said that Somali parents
refused to believe that their children misbehaved or missed school. "The
parents told me that [the] Finnish teacher was racist," Cali said. Still, Mohamed and Faadumo, other consultants I worked with, believed that social
networks with Finns were necessary for gaining employment. Faadumo, a
female consultant in her early thirties, said, "I have been working since 1998.
If you have Finnish friends, they will help you get a job. I am still friends
with [a] Finn from [my] first job." Faadumo landed her first job after living
eight years in the country.

Consultants who immigrated to Finland from the Middle East tended to
characterize Finland as not overtly racist:

ABDI: Is there racism in Finland?
AUTHOR: Yes.

ABDI: I don't think so. I came from Arabian countries [Egypt and Syria] and there, [there is] is racism. They [the locals] yell to [at] you [Somalis]. In Finland, it is peaceful.

HUSSEIN: He just came here [Finland]. It [racism] was worse before.

Racial violence was less common in Finland during the fieldwork period than it was in the early to mid-1990s. Al-Sharmani (2004, 2007) and Kroner (2007) note the various forms of overt discrimination Somalis face daily in Cairo (from the government, police, and Egyptians). Al-Sharmani argues that Somalis in Egypt tend to promote a nationalistic identity known as *Soomaalinimo* (Somaliness or being a Somali), which Al-Sharmani describes as a moral, diasporic identity as opposed to a self-interested or clan identity. In this way, *Soomaalinimo* helps counteract "their harsh living conditions and limited legal rights" (Al-Sharmani 2007:72). *Soomaalinimo* existed prior to the mass exodus of Somalis. As noted earlier, precolonial elites and various institutions during Siyad Barre's regime cultivated this identity. It is hard for me to imagine that Somalis in Cairo do not use clans as channels for transnational capital as they do in Finland. In some contexts, the people I worked with displayed *Soomaalinimo*. I observed consultants across clans celebrating Somalia's independence day, dancing and singing together at community parties, and reminiscing about the past and sharing their hopes for Somalia's future. More recently, I have noticed friends displaying Soomaalinimo on Facebook by celebrating Mo Farah's recent Olympic gold medal for the United Kingdom in Rio and for "liking" *All Things Somali*.

In 2015 anti-immigrant and anti-Islam sentiment had become more pervasive. This was evident in the rise of the True Finn Party (*Perussuomalaiset* in Finnish), now called Finns Party. Hanaan commented on the polarizing political climate. She said, "In my opinion, because of the member of Parliament [Olli Immonen] speaking out about the racism it gives everyone the right to say whatever they want to whom they want.[18] As long as the member of Parliament [Olli Immonen] continues True Finns' racism things like that will continue. They are the third-largest party in Finland. The True Finns have good things such as they want the integration to go better. They want we have studies and work. But, saying in the election days, that all Somalians need to leave from the country, does not give a good image of Somalis. It brings more problems. It's a very negative image." There also was controversy about the possibility of building a great mosque in Helsinki. Hanaan commented on the examples of racism in the text. She said, "Sad part it happens in 2015. The same things that happened twenty years ago. We have not progressed in terms of integration."

## Navigating Somalis in the Field

The more I immersed myself into the field, the less contact I had with Finns. Somalis did not tend to frequent the places my longtime Finnish friends did: *Esplanadin Puisto* (Esplanade Park); Stockmann Department Store, a high-end store in Helsinki's city center that features a specialty grocery store on its ground flour; fitness centers; pubs; nightclubs; Seurasaari and Suomenlinna Islands; Fazer Café, a café renowned for its architecture, ambiance, and epic Fazer chocolate; Finnish households; and *mökki* or *kesämökki*, cottage or summer cottage built with a sauna located near the sea or a lake. My Finnish friends did not tend to patronize the places my consultants did: Itäkeskus (*Itis*) Shopping Center, a mall located in eastern Helsinki that attracts diverse shoppers; mosques; Global Shop, a Somali-owned business; R&B (rhythm and blues) nights at Tiger, a Helsinki night club; *aroosyo* (Somali wedding celebrations); concerts featuring famous diaspora singers; the McDonald's at Helsinki's central railway station; the Cable Book Library, a small library in Helsinki's city center that offers free computer use and internet access; and Somali households.

In many ways, this everyday separation of Finns from Somalis resulted in my everyday separation from Finns. The more I became involved in the lives of consultants, the more I became socially distant from Finnish society. From time to time, when I did meet with longtime Finnish friends, I felt this detachment more strongly. For example, at times I tagged along to R&B nights at Tiger with groups of single Somalis between the ages of eighteen and mid-twenties. When I mentioned this to a group of Finnish friends, one woman told me that "*Siellä on liian tummaa* [It is too dark there]." By this statement she meant that the patrons who frequent this club on those nights have dark skin and it is therefore a place that she avoids. Indeed, these nights attracted a diverse crowd of Somalis and other refugees and immigrants, primarily from Arab countries or other African nations. It is possible that the dissociation I felt and experienced was in some ways biased by my personal relationships with longtime Finnish friends their age (thirties) and social class. Although some had relocated to the Helsinki area, they did not have the opportunity to build friendships with Somalis at school. In other ways, I came to know a variety of Finns through my interactions with Somalis: teachers, volunteers at refugee reception centers, school friends, coworkers, and spouses.

Such cultural distance and social distance from the host society was auspicious for my research among Somalis. Over coffee, I chatted with four young female consultants and their friend Asha. Dega, one of my consultants, asked Asha to participate in my research: "Do you want to be interviewed by a university student?"

ASHA: Maya. En mä jaksa. [No. I don't want.]
DEGA: Maya? [No?] You don't want?
ASHA: Oh, I didn't know it was you. Yes, I want [to participate in the research].

Initially, Asha was unwilling to be interviewed because she thought the interviewer was a Finnish university student. This episode was not exceptional.

It is worth mentioning here that consultants like Asha who arrived in Finland as children commonly switched languages when they spoke. In this example, Asha spoke Somali and Finnish. *Maya* is a Somali term. The phrase *en mä jaksä* is Finnish. It is a slang phrase that roughly translates as: I don't want. In this context, Asha's use of the phrase also implies that she is uninterested and tired. In spite of Asha's refusal to take part in a Finn's research, her use of *en mä jaksä* points to her familiarity with colloquial Finnish. In fact, Asha and other Somalis from her age group tended to interact more frequently and intimately with Finns than other Somalis did. Often these Somalis met Finnish friends and, in some cases, romantic interests, at school, work, or discos.

Although some consultants reported a belief that Finnish researchers worked for the Finnish government, I was not exempt from such suspicion. For example, on two separate occasions, a young man and an elderly man refused to participate in my research because they suspected that I worked for the United States Central Intelligence Agency. In light of the United States-led War on Terror, such moments were surprisingly few.

Still, this political climate affected my research. Some consultants were bothered by this survey question: "Which mosque do you attend?" I asked the question as one technique to map social networks. After one of the aforementioned men noticed this question on my survey, he told me that I was looking for terrorists. So, after having a series of hesitant responses to this question, I omitted it. In an effort to minimize such concern, I refused consultants' invitations to mosques. On one occasion, though, I joined female friends at a *Ciid* (a religious holiday or holy day) celebration for women and children held at a mosque.

Osman, a *sheekh* (learned man of Islam), told me that "We tell in the mosque not to be part of research unless you trust the person." I did not want to access Somalis through Finns. I intended to navigate the Somali community through consultants' own social networks. In this way, I mapped social networks and I established relationships with consultants through persons they trusted.

This methodology was vital for documenting how consultants' everyday social interactions and relationships played out on the ground in comparison with the way consultants purported them to be. Participant observation and social network mapping revealed that clan shaped social networks. I accessed most consultants through their clan relatives. Still, a number of the people I worked with introduced me to their friends and coworkers from other clan backgrounds. Because I was not affiliated with any clan, I could move relatively freely among different groups. A native researcher might have had difficulty in accessing consultants this way and in gaining trust with consultants from different clans. It is possible that nonrelatives would be less likely to discuss clan with a native researcher. The people I worked with considered persons uncouth who appeared to be occupied with clan or to be clannish. Likewise, the cultural intimacy of clan inhibits native researchers from discussing clan with consultants (see Kusow 2003).

Because of my previous research in Finland, I had a wide range of consultants affiliated with each clan family as well as with various clans and subclans and with the Benaadiri minority group. I was confident that I could attain my projected population sample of 300. Consultants agreed. For example, Dega said, "It will be easy for you to get three hundred people if you already know people. Then they trust you." Nevertheless, I encountered challenges.

Some consultants were hesitant to introduce me to other Somalis. This was especially true among consultants who embraced a Finnish lifestyle and who were active in Finnish society (those educated in Finland or employed in formal Finnish employment). These individuals tended to limit their interaction with other Somalis. At the same time, these consultants were more likely to introduce me to nonrelatives. When I asked Mohamed, a key male consultant, to help me access Somali men, he said, "If I help you, others will suspect that you pay me. Then, they will ask me to do something for them." Other Somalis regularly asked Mohamed for help: fixing computers; assisting with weddings; and filling out papers in Finnish.[19]

After some persuasion, Mohamed agreed to help me. Mohamed took out his mobile phone, and we looked through his phonebook. Entry by entry, Mohamed told me which of his contacts I could call. A considerable number of Mohamed's contacts had migrated elsewhere: to Sweden, to England, and to Belgium. Mohamed warned me that some of the phone numbers had likely changed, a situation with which I was certainly familiar.

Not only is Finland home to Nokia, the world's largest producer of mobile phones prior to the advent of Apple's iPhone, Finland also has the largest number of mobile phones per capita in the world. These phones are an everyday necessity in Finland, and it is hard to imagine maintaining contact with Somalis or Finns without my Nokia. Mobile phones were vital for fieldwork. Since I conducted most interviews in Somali households, I traveled to unfamiliar places each week. A telephone call helped me find my way. Upon arrival at my destination, I often called consultants again because the main entrance to the apartment building was locked. At times, I used my mobile to schedule or confirm meetings. Mobile phone use was considerably more widespread in Finland before it was in North America.

This technology also presented challenges to the fieldwork process. Just as is common among Finns, Somalis canceled meetings by sending a text message. Helsinki residents were often on the move traveling to and fro by public transport. When people travel, they may meet friends or relatives. Consultants may get caught up in conversation or decide to forgo a meeting and go elsewhere. At times, when I called consultants who did not show up at meetings, they did not answer my phone call, or their phones were conveniently "*kiinni*" (Finnish term for closed, also meaning turned off). More frequently, a phone number changed because a consultant found a better deal with another mobile phone company, or a bill went unpaid, closing that account.

Helsinki's urban setting presented few challenges as a research site. Since I was familiar with Helsinki, and the city had affordable and efficient public transportation, it was easy to navigate. Connections tended to be fewer in areas peripheral to the city center where most Somalis lived. Perhaps the greatest hardship was waiting for the last night commuter train at the Koivukylä train station in the dead of winter. The station is located in the city of Vantaa and is about twelve and a half miles (twenty kilometers) from Helsinki's central railway station. One of those winter nights was especially wearing: I mistakenly hopped on the wrong (and last scheduled) train for the evening. This was one of the few times that I paid cab fare. I never felt unsafe when I traveled home late at night.

The Somali community in Finland was of ample size for research yet manageable for an ethnographer to navigate. It was the frequent movement of a number of people I worked with that hindered my research. Some consultants traveled to other diaspora communities and to the Horn of Africa. And a few individuals spent almost half the year outside Finland. Numerous consultants emigrated from Finland before the research period ended. This fluid, transnational movement of people, objects, and ideas characterizes the Somali diaspora.

In addition to the frequent movement of Somalis and their suspicion of researchers, my gender influenced access. I spent most of my time with women because it was socially appropriate to do so. I dressed modestly in pants and long-sleeved tops. When I conducted surveys or interviews, I also spent more time with women than I did with men. I met most male consultants at cafés or at workplaces. These meetings tended to be efficient and one-on-one. On the few occasions when I did work with men in households, their wives or female relatives were present. Conversely, many female consultants wanted to spend time with me rather than to answer my questions. I might spend several days at the home of a female consultant visiting, cooking and eating, playing with children, and watching wedding videos before I conducted a survey or an interview. On occasion, I went home without a completed survey.

Despite my efforts to follow gender norms, I was still a target for gossip. For example, a young woman whom I worked with told me that when she asked an older woman whether I could interview her she responded, "Oh, that teenager? I heard that she is looking for a Somali husband." My consultant responded to this comment by explaining that I had just turned thirty years old and was too busy to get married. It is likely that the older woman referred to me as a girl because the term also refers to an unmarried female.

Although I did not reach my target population of 300 Somalis, I might have realized my goal with another year of fieldwork. The population sample for this study consisted of 186 Somalis: 77 men and 109 women eighteen years old and older. Informed consent forms were written in Somali, Finnish, and English. Nearly all consultants read the form on their own. In the few cases where consultants were illiterate, a native Somali speaker read the form to them. I conducted surveys with all research participants in the language of their choice: Somali, Finnish, or English. A native Somali speaker who worked as a translator and interpreter in Finland prepared the informed consent forms and surveys in Somali. A native Finnish speaker prepared the Finnish informed consent forms and looked over my survey. I read aloud each survey question (sometimes with consultants' assistance) and manually recorded each respondent's answers.[20] Sometimes I conducted surveys in groups where consultants had various degrees of abilities in these languages. Often, during surveys, consultants and I switched from one language to another. In many cases, consultants' Finnish language skills surpassed mine, which was always true for the Somali language. Interviews were conducted in English.

Surveys served several purposes: to amass sociodemographic information, to gather information on consultant's social networks inside and outside the Somali community, and to collect information on everyday practices. In-depth interviews with male and female consultants consisted of open-ended questions. Participant observation situated me in places where Somalis interacted. I evaluated observations against survey data and interview data.

Like many other refugee groups, Somalis tend to be wary of researchers. To facilitate my research, I did not tape-record surveys or interviews, and I limited notetaking for them. Often, I feverishly wrote up my field notes as I traveled home on various modes of public transport. I thought about carrying a small voice recorder for dictating notes when I traveled home, but that was too risky. It was not unusual for children to go through the contents of my purse during household visits. A chance discovery could cause consultants to suspect me of recording them without their permission. When consultants revealed supplementary information, I noted such data directly on surveys. During in-depth interviews, key consultants permitted me to take notes.

In accordance with the ethics of anthropological research, I use pseudonyms rather than real names and removed or altered identifying information to ensure confidentiality for consultants. At times, I removed the names of consultants' clans (especially for consultants who affiliate with clans that are small in numbers residing in Finland). The Somali community in Finland is relatively small, and the identity of the people I worked with would be easy to discern otherwise. I took photographs at culturally appropriate moments: when consultants took pictures at an *aroos* (wedding) and at other parties. No consultant's identity is revealed in the photographs in this book.

Multisited ethnography can be instructive for understanding populations in the diaspora (see Falzon 2004; Hannerz 2003; Marcus 1995). Hage (2005) notes pitfalls of multisited research from his own work among Lebanese migrants in various international settings. Besides jet lag and strained relationships, Hage argues this trend in migration and diaspora studies inhibits the anthropologist's immersion, which is at odds with the goal of ethnography. Hage (2005) argues, "in the study of migrants sharing a unifying culture across a number of global locations, multi-sitedness is less helpful than a notion of a single geographically discontinuous site" (463). Irrespective of field location, Somalis consider clan to be culturally intimate and tell clan in similar ways. Moments from the Ninth SSIA Congress in Denmark are a testament to this.

The cultural intimacy of clan is another challenge to multisited ethnography. I did not explicitly delve into clan issues until after I conducted my first stint of year-long fieldwork. During research for my master's thesis, I steered clear of clan. Although I desisted from asking Somalis about clan, I observed how consultants told clan and talked about clan. These observations, together with my relationships with consultants, allowed me to approach clan with cultural sensitivity. Even if I accessed Somalis in other locations through my consultants' own social networks, rapid fieldwork would not produce the type of understanding I strive for.

In 2015 I noticed more young Somalis hanging around in the city center with friends than I did in 2000–2004. After my first meeting with Hanaan at a hip coffee shop in downtown Helsinki, she suggested that we check out the countless pop-up restaurants at *Esplanadin Puisto* (Esplanadi Park) in celebration of Restaurant Day, a multicultural food extravaganza. We spotted two stands where Somali women were selling traditional food, ran into a few Somalis we knew, and spotted only a few more in the crowd of people. When we met again a few days later to look over the manuscript, she again selected the place. We met for lunch at the trendy *Teatteri* (Finnish for theater) restaurant and nightclub in the city center. It was and still is a popular place among my longtime Finnish friends. Hanaan commented on how she and her international group of friends spend time together. She said, "We have dinners together at home or restaurants, go to music festivals, coffee, summer cottages (not so often), and travel together." Although she mentioned that *Itis* was still popular among Somalis, she said, "I haven't been to Itäkeskus, not for four, five, or six months. I avoid that place and other places where most Somalians live [East Helsinki and Vantaa]. [It's] Well divided in those environments. Here in the centrum [Swedish for city center] is mixed: foreigners and tourists. In the suburbs, you see the real division. What people are complaining about. Most True Finns [now Finns Party] supporters live in those areas. My area is where many SDP [Social Democratic Party of Finland] and Green Party supporters live."

Nafiso and Mohamed treated me to dinner at Stockmann's restaurant. We met another day to talk about the manuscript. This time, I treated them to dinner and they selected an Italian restaurant in the city center. We grabbed an ice cream from a kiosk before finding a quiet place to talk. As we walked to our destination, Mohamed pointed out a number of Finnish landmarks as if I was a new visitor to his hometown of the last twenty-five years: the Parliament Building, Kiasma, the contemporary museum of art, and Finlandia Hall. D'Alisera (2004) notes a similar experience she had with Sierra Leoneans in Washington, D.C. Unfortunately, we both failed to ask consultants what these places meant to them.

Nafiso commented on the example of social distance I noted during the fieldwork period. She said, "No [not] summer cottages so much. Young people who have grown up here go to those places with their friends." She further commented on integration of young Somalis. She said, "The young generation speak Somali but do not know [the] language well. When they speak Somali, they mix Somali and Finnish language and at home with their siblings. Nowadays, they have a lot of friends from different backgrounds." Nafiso explained when her child travels to Somalia, he is relieved to return home to Finland where "it is calm and everything is working."

Some readers may question my use of Finns and Somalis over Somali-Finn, Finnish-Somali, or Finn of Somali origin. Many Somalis are Finnish citizens, a large number are Finnish-born, and many speak Finnish fluently. At eighteen years of age, Somali boys join other Finnish nationals in military conscription. I saw a young Somali man catch a commuter train wearing his army uniform. Some Somalis have found success in Finnish politics. After twenty-five years, consultants still verbalize and internalize this difference, albeit in various and complicated ways. The three consultants that I met with in 2015 are all well integrated into Finnish society but they still make a distinction between Somalis and Finns in their comments throughout the book. Hanaan commented on the notion of belonging and identity for Somalis in Finland. She said, "There is no Somali person I have met for the last thirty years that says they are something else or from some other nation." I asked her how she felt when she traveled abroad. She said, "Somali-Finnish when I go abroad. I live in Finland but originally from Somalia. To Finns, I am Somalian." Then, she said, "More Finn than Somali but at the end I am Somali. My mentality is Finnish: open-minded. I don't eat the same food [she follows the Islamic prohibition on pork] with them or drink the same drinks [alcohol] as them and not as open-minded as them. I have this back of my mind." At the same time, a Somali cannot admit openly being Finnish because the larger Finnish society does not accept that identity for them (see also Tiilikainen et al. 2013).

As I complete this book in 2016, I am not sure whether I would have had the same experience in accessing consultants now. I question how my outsider status (not Somali and not Finnish), U.S. citizenship, and the current political climate could affect my access. I wonder whether my age, now forty-two, would hinder my social engagement with twenty-somethings. At the 2015 SSIA congress in Helsinki, a Finnish professor and doctoral student shared their difficulties in finding even a small number of research participants. I spoke with Mohamed, Nafiso, and Hanaan about this issue during our meetings. There seemed to be some consensus that there were too many research projects with little benefit to the Somali community.

## Diasporic Moments

Diasporic moments are the core of this book. Diasporic moments reveal Somalis in everyday situations where they manipulate clan networks to manage transnational capital. In the worldwide dispersal of Somalis, clan networks prove an efficient way to access resources. Caldwell (2004) notes that Muscovites deal with daily uncertainty by employing tactics embedded "with perceptions and processes of sociability" (29) to access capital. Practices that integrate kin and transform capital among kin are embedded in Somali culture. With frequent travel and real-time communication by means of several media, practices are flexible and mobile. Because clan relatives invest in capital on a global scale, the diasporic moments that I present transcend locality. In each chapter, I delve into various moments when Somalis contest clan and employ everyday tactics to maneuver within clan networks.

In chapter 2, "Telling," I elucidate how Somalis tell and read clan in daily life. The everyday social practice of telling helps legitimize clan affiliation and social boundaries of Somaliness and denotes a personal investment in clan competence. Telling opens up the potential for individuals to access clan networks. That is, once an individual legitimizes her or his clan through telling and is successful at having fellow clan members recognize the claim, the individual is in a position to build clan-based social capital. The chapter also discusses social conventions of telling clan, how telling forms links across clans, tactics to make clan status claims, and counternarratives to such claims.

In chapter 3, "Movement," I focus on movement in various forms: young Somalis away from family households, during online interactions, and to Finland as a strategic way to position themselves in a Nordic welfare state. Yet when Somalis move, continuing the construction of clan is at risk because Somalis consider their own obligations toward family and clan alongside differing ideologies such as autonomy and equality. That is especially the case for young, single Somalis in their late teens and early to mid-twenties who live independently from parents or guardian(s) in apartments with other youth. They rebel against their family by "becoming too Finnish" and challenging moral ideals by dating, cohabiting, and drinking alcohol. In this liminal space, these young Somalis form connections with each other irrespective of clan affiliation. They may live together, work together, and party together. For these Somalis who embrace a Finnish lifestyle, clan networks seem to be more of a constraint than an opportunity. Clan relatives may pressure them to follow family and gender norms and live at home until they marry. When they move, they may gain financial independence and keep their wage earnings for their own consumption rather than add-

ing to a family's pooled resources. (Portions of these resources are remitted
to dispersed family in the Horn of Africa, a practice that cultivates clan
networks.) Nevertheless, research indicates independent young people tend
to cultivate clan networks in ways similar to those of other Somalis. They
do not, however, exert as much effort to cultivate clan networks as other
Somalis do.

In chapter 4, "Celebration," I reveal that Somali women perform clan in
gender-specific ways. I illustrate how *aroosyo* (weddings), communitywide
events for Somalis, are key sites for legitimizing clan claims and integrating
kin through exchange of capital. During these rites of integration, women
perform and honor their clans publicly by displaying their clan competence.
Some women may unveil new forms of distinction such as a Djibouti-style
*diric* women's dress worn at the interclan celebration. Because Somalis consider clan to be a sensitive if not taboo topic for public discourse, tensions
among clans may arise in response to efforts to establish clan hegemony.
Sites of integration also become sites of resistance. Some women may use
the public event to initiate horizontal links between clans. At the same time,
*aroos* hones a shared sense of being Somali.

In chapter 5, "Crisis," I explore how Somalis may use or avoid networks
with local clan relatives when they face an everyday crisis. In particular, Somalis successful in the Finnish formal sector who embrace a Finnish lifestyle
tend to desist from asking relatives and nonrelatives for help because they
believe doing so will escalate into a series of endless obligations. Some such
consultants forged relationships in refugee camps in Finland in the 1990s
based on neighborhood or hometown rather than on clan, relationships
that have endured. Other Somalis, particularly those who have little interaction with Finns and may be unemployed, consider these individuals to be
exceptionally useful because they tend to have access to economic capital,
Finnish cultural capital, and Finnish social capital. Although successful individuals evade other Somalis' frequent requests for help, they tend to meet
the requests of close clan relatives. Prosperous Somalis use clan networks
to avoid crisis: a crisis of clan legitimacy and a security crisis in Somalia.
Clanship can be set aside when Somalis face discrimination and racism.

Finally, in the Conclusion, I summarize the key points of the book and
elucidate how my case study furthers our understanding of kinship, identity,
and diaspora. I consider how and why telling will likely change with the
return of Somalis to ancestral clan territories, south to north migration,
linguistic changes, shifting political engagements, and identity constructions.
I highlight the targeted resettlement of Somali Bantu refugees in the United
States by contrasting my more recent work among this group in the United
States with Somalis in Finland.

# CHAPTER 2

# Telling

## Chance Encounters

Ayaan and I stood near the lounge area of the adult education school, just outside the classroom where the Finnish language class for foreigners met. We were waiting for two of Ayaan's female relatives whom I had met with Ayaan the previous day. We would have waited sitting on the sofa or chairs, but four Somali men already occupied the seats. I asked Ayaan whether she knew any of the men. They were unfamiliar to her. After a few minutes, one of the men asked Ayaan whether she was Ethiopian. She slyly smiled at his assertion. "No, you are Somali," another man interjected. The third man asked, "Where are you from?" "Mogadishu," Ayaan replied. The man probed further, "I don't believe you. Where there?" "Wardhiigleey," Ayaan replied. The man noted that he, too, was from Wardhiigleey and inquired about her clan, "Abgaal?" "No," Ayaan answered before voluntarily adding, "Buur Hindi." "Aah, you are [name of subclan]. You are from Gaalkacyo," the man declared. Then, Ayaan asked the men where they were from. One by one, the four men revealed their clan affiliations to Ayaan: Habar Gidir-Cayr, Majeerteen, Sheekhaal (also Sheikhal), and Isaaq.

This elaborate exchange between Ayaan and a group of strangers is riddled with telling signs intended for knowing observers. The use of each place name (Mogadishu, Wardhiigleey, Buur Hindi, and Gaalkacyo) is deliberate. As the interaction unfolds, each stated place serves as a cue to further delimit Ayaan's clan. The meanings that Somalis attach to these places are not static. It is the routine use of such place names in specific ways and contexts that make such constructions appear to be fixed. Although each place denotes historical and contemporary meaning, linking to particular clans, these associations are constructed, negotiated, and contested. If conditions change, meanings can change.

Weeks after the encounter at the adult education school, I met with Ayaan and her husband, Hassan, for an in-depth interview at their remarkably Scandinavian apartment in eastern Helsinki. Their home was calm, featuring minimalist trends: Ikea-like furniture with clean lines and understated décor. This was in stark contrast to most of the other Somali family households that I visited. These spaces bustle with children's play, conversations with visitors or family and friends by phone or computer, and sounds of wedding videos blaring on television. Incense permeates these ornately decorated spaces. Arabian-styled carpets cover floors and silk curtains in rich bold colors conceal windows, and, in some cases, neutral walls. Islamic wall art and a flag of Somalia, Somaliland, or Puntland are on display. In 1991 the Republic of Somaliland, located in Somalia's northwest region, declared its independence and seceded. In 1998, Puntland was founded as an autonomous state in Somalia's northeast region. Puntland aspires to unify Somalia. Particular clans or confederations of clans founded these states and continue to exercise political authority.

During the interview, I asked Ayaan whether she remembered the last time someone in Finland asked where she was from, meaning, "What is your clan?" She did not recall any such interaction. "No one asks this now," she proclaimed. I reminded her of our chance meeting with the group of men at the adult education school. "These men asked your clan," I said. "Yes, I remember," Ayaan replied. We all laughed. Recalling the incident, Ayaan told us that one of the men assumed she was Ethiopian because of her appearance. Ayaan further explained that if she had worn a *xijaab* like most Somali women in Finland her age (in their thirties), the man would have assumed she was Somali.[1] *Xijaab* is the Somali form of the Arabic term *hijab*, which translates as barrier. In this context, *xijaab* refers to a veil or headscarf that some Muslim women wear in public to display religious affiliation and modesty by concealing their hair and neck. Since many Somali girls and women in Finland don *xijaab*, it can serve as a visual marker for Somalis. This was still the case in 2015. Hanaan commented, "I am the only girl in my family including my sister's daughters that does not use *xijaab* but yet I still can respect their choices and they can respect mine. Who knows? One day I may also use it."

Ayaan recounted the strategies she used to tell her clan to the group of strangers. "First, I told the man that I was from Mogadishu. Second, I told Wardhiigleey." Hassan, Ayaan's husband, interjected as if to justify his wife's actions, "If you ask tribe [clan], they must tell back. It's our culture." Continuing her story, Ayaan said, "The man then thought I was Abgaal because most of the people living there [in Wardhiigleey] are Abgaal. Then, I told Buur Hindi. Everyone knows who I am when I say Buur Hindi."

Ayaan could have ignored the stranger's inquiry or cut the conversation short by simply stating her affiliation. Instead Ayaan replied as if she had answered the same way before or at least observed others using similar tactics. Ayaan's first response left her clan ambiguous seeing as individuals affiliated with all clans resided in Mogadishu, the country's capital city. Wardhiigleey is one of Mogadishu's sixteen administrative districts. According to linguist Georgi Kapchits, "At the time of the civil war, the district was dominated by the representatives of the Habar Gidir clan [a clan of the Hawiye clan family] speaking in one of the Daarood dialects" (email to author, March 11, 2015). Buur Hindi is a neighborhood in the Wardhiigleey district.

Nafiso, born and raised in Mogadishu, offered further comments on identifying clans by place. In 2015 she said, "You can recognize the clans that live in these areas but all other areas were mixed. Wardhiigleey and maybe two or three other areas in Mogadishu—some clans populated more than others." Nafiso did not name the other areas telling of particular clans. Mohamed commented on the various ways Somalis ask a person's clan. He said, "I know how people try to get your clan details if you're not willing to tell them. They ask you where [were] you born? (Halkee ku dhalatay? or Intee ku dhalatay?) or 'Where are you from?' (Halkee ka timi? or Intee ka timi?) Then, if you mention a big city like Mogadishu, then it is not clear for which clan you belong to, so they start to ask where your father [was] born? After that, if it is not clear for them, they will ask you a direct question which is "Which clan you are from?" (Tolmaa tahay?) or "Which clan do you belong to?" (Qabiilkee u dhalatay?)" Hanaan commented, "Normally when a South person is from a big city they need to identify who he is by saying which clan he is from. But when a person is [has] grown up and [was] raised in a village or smaller city, they don't need to identify who they are by saying the clan because mostly everybody knows each other: same clan only lives in that village."

When Ayaan specified Buur Hindi, one of the men considered this place in association with the other cues and sorted out her affiliation. He determined her subclan and linked the group with Gaalkacyo. Gaalkacyo is the capital city of the Mudug region in central Somalia. The Mudug region is one of the country's eighteen administrative regions. The Habar Gidir claims this region as their ancestral clan territory. After Ayaan's clan family, clan, and subclan (Hawiye-Habar Gidir [name of subclan]) were made known, the men self-identified in purposeful ways in light of this new information.

The first man to recognize Ayaan's clan identified as Habar Gidir-Cayr. He and Ayaan both affiliate with Habar Gidir, a clan of the Hawiye clan family. Cayr is a subclan of the Habar Gidir. The second man identified as Majeerteen, a clan of the Daarood clan family. The third man identified as Sheekhaal, a clan of the Hawiye clan family.[2] The fourth man identified by his clan family, the Isaaq. It is remarkable that the men self-identified at different levels of segmentation: clan family, clan, and subclan. I did not have the opportunity to ask the men why they answered in different ways. Perhaps the men's answers are telling of local relationships or divisions among groups in Finland or political alliances at home. The manner of self-identification may also reflect situational positioning in terms of status claims. I asked Mohamed A. Eno about his take on the matter:

> They respond at different levels due to a person's choice of how they would mention their identity at a specific time. It also reflects their loyalty to the specific branch they come from. At a certain level, although these are supposed to be equal, some believe that they are even better than their cousin of the same subclan due to influence in wealth, number of prominent persons in government, size, bellicosity, first-born status, and so on and so forth. These are not more than personal beliefs though, since they are all the same as descendants of the same forefather. It is simply a personal choice of how someone feels good to present their identity at a particular time; of course with some hidden pride in at the background. (email to author, March 13, 2015)

In 2015 Nafiso commented on why a person responds in a particular way. She said, "It depends on the situation. Where they are and who is asking." Although she did not offer further details, her answer added the information that social conventions for public and private settings and mixed clan settings can vary. Where a person is in Finland or Somalia will influence the way they answer. The age and dialect of the person asking may elicit a certain response. Is the person a cultural insider or cultural outsider? What is the motivation behind the inquiry? An answer can be ambiguous by stating Mogadishu, Somalia, or a birthplace outside Somalia, such as Saudi Arabia or Finland, or be more direct by using a place associated with their clan, such as a neighborhood, birthplace, or parent's birthplace. And, certainly, individuals can refuse to entertain the question for any number of reasons.

I cannot comment on how the stranger's inquiry of Ayaan's clan and the subsequent interaction may have cultivated a sense of familiarity or affinity among the group. Nor can I state whether this was anyone's intention. As mentioned in the previous chapter, Cawo M. Abdi experienced only a few instances where someone directly asked her clan during her multisited research on the Somali diaspora (Abdi 2015:24). "But even the elders who asked this question often found a way to connect with me around shared kinship linkages. Thus, when I told one elder what my clan was, he automatically went on to discuss how his daughter is married to this clan, thus identifying a kinship affinity with me, even if it is through a level other than direct clan relations" (25). Ayaan did not offer this reading of her encounter nor did I consider it during our discussions. The man who stated "Habar Gidir," the clan he shared with Ayaan, may have done this to create a kinship affinity. He could have simply answered at the subclan level (Cayr). This subtlety might be more apparent to a native anthropologist or a fluent Somali speaker.

In *The Politics of Legitimacy*, Frank Burton introduces the concept of telling to elucidate the practice of sectarian differentiation among Catholics and Protestants in Northern Ireland. According to Burton, "Telling is based on the social significance attached to name, face and dress, area of residence, school attended, linguistic and possibly phonetic use, colour and symbolism. It is not based on undisputed fact but as an ideological representation is a mixture of 'myth and reality'" (Burton 1978:37). Even individuals politically opposed to this sectarian ideology tend to use telling cues in their everyday interactions (Burton 1978).

Throughout my visits with Ayaan and Hassan, they adamantly contested the notion that clan in any way influenced their daily lives. As in Burton's (1978) findings in Northern Ireland, even consultants such as Ayaan and Hassan who oppose the ubiquity of clan in the diaspora utilize telling signs in their everyday interactions. During an interview with another married couple, they proudly told me that they did not teach their children about clan. To prove this, the man asked his oldest son, who was less than ten years of age, where he was from. His son replied, "Wardhiigleey." This is notable because the boy was Finnish-born and had never visited Somalia. Wardhiigleey was where his father grew up (this man and Ayaan self-identify as the same clan).

## Telling as Strategy

If the people I worked with claimed that clan does not influence their daily lives or make sense within the cosmopolitan milieu of Somalis abroad, why is it important for them to tell clan? Telling is an everyday practice that is imperative for the continuous construction of clan for Somalis abroad. Somalis use this social practice to politely legitimize personal claims to clan membership. Telling simultaneously includes and excludes individuals and groups from the boundary of Somaliness: those who descend from the common apical ancestor and affiliate with majority clans versus those who exist outside Somali clanship. This perpetuates racial and ethnic divisions as well as marriage taboos. Telling constructs clan boundaries and associated status claims, thereby maintaining clan distinctions.

Once an individual legitimizes his or her clan through telling and obtaining recognition of that claim by fellow clan members, the individual is in a position to build local and transnational clan networks. Because of the role of clan in social networks, Bourdieu's (1986) concept of social capital provides an apt foundation to sort out why clan is ubiquitous in daily life. Bourdieu defines *social capital* as "the aggregate of the actual or potential resources which are linked to possession of a durable network of more or less institutionalized relationships of mutual acquaintance and recognition—or in other words, to membership in a group—which provides each of its members with the backing of the collectively-owned capital, a 'credential' which entitles them to credit, in the various senses of the word" (248–49).

Some scholars posit that social capital decreases with mobility (Alitolppa-Niitamo 2004; Faist 2000; McMichael and Manderson 2004). My research findings suggest that a vital aspect of maintaining Somaliness in diaspora amounts to maintaining mobile social capital through globalized social networks shaped by clan relationships. Clan, a form of social capital, is not a latent and accruing value, but rather it is capital actively maintained. Membership in a clan or any other group does not ensure access to social networks. Somalis must work to maintain clan networks in order for these networks to be useful. Success in garnering clan-based social capital results from an individual's constant effort at engaging social capital (accessing networks and cultivating networks through reciprocal relationships).

Bourdieu (1998) argues that kinship and family structures must be continuously maintained in order for them to be useful: "The structures of kinship and family as *bodies* can be perpetuated only through a continuous creation of family feeling, a cognitive principle of vision and division that is at the same time an effective principle of *cohesion*, that is, the adhesion that is vital to the existence of a family group and its interests" (68). As with nurturing a *family feeling* among family members (see Bourdieu 1998), a number of everyday practices build a *clan feeling* among clan members: telling, household visiting, telephone calls, emails, instant messaging, text messaging, using regional dialect and clan dialect, lending money, sending remittances, collective gift giving, viewing and sharing photographs and wedding videos, sharing distinctive food, selling and consuming goods and services in the informal economy, and participating in rites of institution such as birth, marriage, and death. These continuous practices integrate clan relatives and build social capital among kin. It is worth reiterating here that I observed consultants engaging with nonrelatives in many of the same everyday practices that hone a clan feeling. I provide examples of these in this chapter and those to follow.

In order to elucidate the connection between class and capital, Bourdieu (1986) expands the notion of capital to include noneconomic forms. In this formulation, the structure and distribution of capital or resources in its various forms (economic, capital, social, and symbolic) represents the structure of the social world. This work stems from the French sociology of conflict and the structuralist tradition, deeply embedded in Bourdieu's theory of practice (see Bourdieu 1977). In this view, the connection between class and capital is understood from the perspective of individual actors who strategize in pursuit of their interests within the limits of their experiences or imaginable possibilities. Accordingly, clan provides connections through social networks as well as economic, cultural, and symbolic forms.

The strategy of converting social capital into economic and cultural capital or cultural goods is evident in the following example: clan networks, formed and maintained in the diaspora, are channels through which many goods sold in the Somali informal economy originate and are later consumed by clan relatives in Finland. Some of the goods could be fabric for women's dresses and coordinating scarves, handicrafts for display at home, and *uunsi* (incense) for making homes fragrant and inviting, especially after cooking. In Bourdieu's (1984) formulation of cultural capital, culture becomes a power resource that is cultivated through socialization. Clan distinction is cultivated in the habitus (dispositions and competence) and realized and reaffirmed through practices that transform and exchange various forms of capital. This exchange is necessary for the development of capital. Perpetuation of clan or regional dialect in Somali households during rites of institution and online discussions reinforces clan distinction and associated status claims. Language and dialect are a form of cultural capital, a specific cultural competence. For Bourdieu, symbolic capital is the legitimization of power relations through symbolic forms (status or recognition). In social networks, symbolic effects of clan boundaries and associated status claims are often made visible on the ground. Social networks visually include and exclude individuals from the boundaries of clan and Somaliness. Obvious groupings of individuals, especially during rites of institutions such as *aroosyo* (weddings), link affiliated groups of individuals with symbolic capital when they refer to prestigious clan names, well-known ancestors, or pride-provoking historical and contemporary events.

The three consultants that I met with in 2015 mentioned that graduations have become important occasions to cultivate kin networks. In 2015 Hanaan stated, "Nowadays when kids graduate from high school or university, parents make parties for the kids. The strange part is in those parties you can feel the environment where the kid is from or which clan he belongs to. Kids invite their friends regardless from which clan they are. Most adults who attend the party are from the same clan as the graduate. Then clan relatives give gifts like books, perfume, money, [and] *diric* (Somali women's dress)." Mohamed explained that these practices are similar to the way Finns typically celebrate graduations. He said, "It is also a Finnish tradition to invite relatives. Finns first invite close relatives and later in the evening they invite friends."

During my earlier fieldwork in Finland from 2000 to 2001, I attended two graduations: a girl's *lukio* (high school) graduation and a woman's vocational school graduation. The girl was the first Somali to graduate from that particular *lukio*. The number of Somalis completing upper-secondary education (high school and vocational)[3] and higher education (polytechnic and university) has increased significantly since my research. Still, only about a third of Somali students continue to general upper-secondary schools (Tiilikainen et al. 2013:53).

## Initial Encounters

In the early to mid-1990s, initial encounters among strangers in Finland were more direct and less sociable than Ayaan's chance 2004 encounter reported in the previous section. Many such interactions took place in Finnish refugee reception centers around the country, where the first large groups of Somali asylum seekers were housed. Consultants commonly referred to the reception centers as camps or refugee camps. In these spaces, many Somalis found themselves living alongside strangers. The following excerpts from in-depth interviews reveal how the early arrivals interacted with one another and came to know newcomers:

ABUKAR: We were on the same flight from Mogadishu, then they put us in a camp six hundred kilometers away from here [Helsinki]. It was Joensuu [Joensuu is a city of 75,000 inhabitants located in eastern Finland]. Most of them know each other already. They were in Russia long time and they lived by tribes [clans]. I asked people right away if there were any Samaroon[4] [Samaroon is a subclan of the Gadabuursi, a clan of the Dir clan family] there. They said no, but there was a guy who is Samaroon. He lied and told he was Isaaq. He was afraid.

SHUKRI: When I first came to Finland there was [were] one hundred sixty-three person[s]. We came together because we was [were] trying to find a place to live. Most of the people were friendly. We were in the refugee camp near Helsinki and it started. People lived by clan.

HODAN: In the camp, everyone who was there was looking for their own tribe [clan]—asking everyone because there was this war still going on. They were asking everything, details. There was no trust. 'Who are you and what is your tribe?' And you had to know all the names. If you make a mistake, they do not trust you. Grandfather, blah blah blah.

MOHAMED: At the camp, one man was asking me almost every day, every month. He was from the countryside in the North. And also he was living in Saudi Arabia—it tells a lot about his behavior. He told everyone, 'He is Midgaan' [Midgaan is a Somali ethnic minority group]. Somalis asked my clan for three years but I would not tell. It took almost three months to know my clan. I told everyone that I did not know [my clan]. People were calling me Midgaan and a person who hides their clan. This continued until a guy I went to high school with in Somalia told other people I was Majeerteen [Majeerteen is a clan of the Daarood clan family].

It is not surprising that clan was the focal point of these early encounters at refugee reception centers. This was during the height of Somalia's civil war when groups vying for power used kinship as a political tool. Residents urgently sought out clan relatives for camaraderie, support, and protection. Knowing where someone was from was vital for those who arrived during this time as many sought to align themselves with persons they could trust: clan relatives. In some cases, each floor of refugee reception centers became one clan's domain. Consultants reported fighting that mirrored a clan conflict in Somalia that erupted between two clans at a reception center in Helsinki.

Residents directed newcomers to self-identify by clan, reckoning ancestors through their father's line (*abtirsiino* in Somali). Each claim tested an individual's ability to exhibit cultural competence. By cultural competence, I mean "knowledge of genealogical relationships and of real connections and skill at using them" (Bourdieu 1986:250). This specific cultural competence, a form of cultural capital, in its embodied state, is transmitted through socialization (Bourdieu 1986:245). Some residents at the camps were skilled at reciting the names of clan ancestors and the relationship of their clan to other clans and others lacked this competence, as the following excerpts from in-depth interviews illustrate:

> NUURA: I didn't know much about clan when I arrived in Finland at the age of fourteen. I was asked my clan and I could name my father and grandfather's name but no more. People said that I was a person who hides their clan. When my mother came to Finland, I asked her to teach me about my clan. Now I can name many in my lineage.
>
> NUR: When I come to Finland, I went to a Finnish course. It was October 1994. 'Who am I'? 'Who is my tribe'? They [other Somalis] told me what tribe I belong. I did not know. I had to call my father to ask. It was very stupid.

The civil war intensified the lack of trust felt among strangers. Persons affiliated with rival clans were met with suspicion. These conditions made it vital for newcomers to know where they were from. This prompted consultants like Nuura and Nur to contact parents or other relatives to teach them clan genealogy as a way to legitimize their clan ties. But there was still another reason for this investment in cultural competence. Beyond the suspicion of clan rivals, there was a prevailing fear that people could easily hide their affiliation in diaspora.

Nuura was suspected of being "a person who hides their clan" because she lacked extensive knowledge of her clan genealogy. According to historian Omar A. Eno who self-identifies as Somali Bantu, a minority group, Somalis do not have a specific word for persons who hide their clan. Eno notes that "People normally create a word spontaneously. For example: *qabiil-diid* (someone who rejects tribalism), *sheegato* (a newcomer who identifies himself with the natives), and *tol-laabe* (someone who does not belong to a clan); probably he is hiding it" (email to author, July 7, 2005). Luling translates *sheegad* (sheegato) as "adopted, client group" (Luling 2002:278).[5]

Often persons suspected of hiding their clan in Finland, like Nur, were assumed to be Midgaan. Midgaan is a derogatory term. The preferred term is Madhibaan. The Madhibaan are an endogamous occupational caste group traditionally working as hunters, leatherworkers, and barbers. They held a servile status with Somalis from the so-called dominant clans who acted as their patrons (Lewis 1994:127). This relationship changed somewhat when they migrated to cities, but other Somalis regarded the neighborhoods where they lived as the least desirable areas (Lewis 1994:127). Majority Somalis view them as existing outside Somali kinship genealogy, unmarriageable, and socially polluting (see Kusow and Eno 2015). Although the Madhibaan are physically and linguistically indistinguishable from majority clans, occupation, living quarters, and social networks are telling of their ascribed status. These aspects make the Madhibaan similar to the untouchables in India, who refer to themselves as Dalits. Even though Mohamed claimed to stand firm amid repeated inquiries about his clan at the camp, he was aware that a fellow resident, a former high school classmate, could verify his affiliation. Through my many conversations with Mohamed through the years, it was clear they did not care what others believed.

Less commonly, consultants suspected others of being Somali Bantu. This group also falls outside Somali kinship genealogy and marriageability and is marked as racially and linguistically distinguishable from majority clans (see Besteman 1999; Eno 1997). Majority Somalis believe they have *jileec* (soft-textured hair), which is Arab-like, as opposed to *jareer* (hard-textured hair), which is African-like (Besteman 1999). This group's disparity is evident in its disparate origin narratives, languages, cultural traditions, and clans. Some are indigenous to Somalia and others are descendants of slaves who were brought to the country in the nineteenth century (Eno and Eno 2007; Eno 2008). *Af-Maay* (also called *Maay Maay*) is the dominant language of most Somali Bantus and in Somalia "from the central regions to the south" (Mukhtar 2010:282). Many Raxanweyn (Digil Mirifle) speak *Af-Maay*, as do others living in the region. Some Somali Bantus speak *Af-Maxaa*, Standard Somali, and fewer speak their ancestral languages such as *Ki-Zegua* (Menkhaus 2010:93). In addition to working as agriculturalists, they worked as carpenters, house builders, weavers, potters, and butchers (Luling 2002). A few of the people I worked with who resided in Mogadishu reported that their families employed Somali Bantu girls and women as live-in domestic help. "Some have tribal identities outside the Somali lineage, while others are fully assimilated in a Somali clan" (Menkhaus 2010:94). Some such Somali clans are the Biimaal, a clan of the Dir clan family, and the Jiddu and the Geledi, clans of the Digil-Mirifle clan family (see Luling 1984).

Consultants commonly reported that individuals who entered into marriages with a Somali Bantu or Madhibaan risked losing family support. In the past, such marriages were punishable by death (Mohamed 1997:149). In theory, any children resulting from such marriages belong to their father's clan. However, even if the father is affiliated with a majority clan, the children will experience stigma in association with their mother's minority group. Marriage taboos, however ubiquitous in diaspora, do not go unchallenged. I heard about three couples that defied marriage restrictions.

Others claimed the couples married before they arrived in Finland. When I conducted an in-depth interview with an unmarried man in his mid-thirties from a northern pastoral clan, he expressed discontent with marriage taboos against minorities. He said, "Sometimes you wonder why when you see someone from their clan [Madhibaan]. The women are very beautiful, and they [other Somalis] say, 'You can't marry them.' They [Madhibaan] are Somalis. What's the point?"

These ideas and practices persist. In 2015 Hanaan commented, "Midgaan is difficult to identify by the look because they might have normal Somalian features, but *jareer* it's easier to identify because they have West African features." In relation to marriage taboos, she said, "It is still going on. There are several situations at this time going on." Hanaan spoke of a few cases where young people of marriageable age are unable to find a Somali spouse because others believe they are Somali Bantu. Hanaan explained, "It affects your children's future if you get married with *jareer* or Midgaan. The other Somalian clans somehow feel that they are superior so they don't want to mix with lower class clan. So nobody wants to give their children to a *jareer* or Midgaan even though the other parent might be a superior clan. It's who your father is, is who you are. As long as your father is a Midgaan or *jareer*."

Hanaan expressed confusion over the term Somali Bantu. This is likely because few Somali Bantus and minorities live in Finland. Remarkably, after I presented a paper on the Somali Bantus in the United States at the SSIA congress held in Helsinki in 2015, my fellow panelists, mostly European scholars working with Somalis in Europe, voiced their unfamiliarity with the term and minority group. The term Somali Bantu was coined in 1991 by international aid organizations and media outlets (Menkhaus 2010:92). Older literature on Somalia refers to this group as *Gosha* people (people of the forest), *WaGosha*, and *jareer*. I return to Somali Bantus in the final chapter.

Some consultants who reportedly formed initial alliances across clans in camps based on prior place of residence claimed that others influenced them to organize by clan. According to Abukar, Somalis who lived in Russia and Arab countries such as Saudi Arabia and Iraq told him and others at the camp, "He is from that tribe and you should come with us." Hassan explained that persons "from Arab [countries] already know organization of clans . . . lived by clan. [They] Must find a relative for job, paper to work, need apartment to live. There they learn what a tribe is. In Mogadishu it was different. Neighbors could be anyone."

Hassan's argument is convincing. Somalis residing in these foreign environments tended to occupy vulnerable positions (minority, international student, or migrant worker). Kinship was one way to organize and create association. Less convincing is Abukar and Hassan's insistence that others, particularly those who had already lived abroad or from the North, are to blame for tribalism at the camps. Abukar stated that upon arrival at the camp he immediately asked whether there was anyone from his clan. Hassan claims that he and others from Mogadishu were different from the rest. They were used to living in mixed-clan neighborhoods. Yet Ayaan, the woman in the previous section, made her clan and subclan explicit by stating her neighborhood and specific quarter in the capital city.

During the 1990s, Somalis formed more than forty associations in Finland. Clan affiliation served as the basis for most of these groups (Alitolppa-Niitamo 2000). Finns assumed the newly arrived Somalis to embody little more than the label of refugee: "an almost generic, ideal-typical figure" (Malkki 1995:8). Finnish authorities anticipated uniformity among Somali asylum seekers and refugees and were perplexed by the group's inability to unite to represent their community.

Abdul, a male consultant, offered an explanation for the prevalence of Somali associations in Finland. Abdul said, "There are many Somali associations in Finland. Finland lets anyone start a club instead of only allowing one club in Finland. Every clan has an organization so we don't have to work together. We want to work together." Abdul blamed the Finnish government for the high incidence of clan-based Somali associations instead of the Somalis that founded and supported these groups. This moment of blaming others for inciting tribalism, together with the examples of Abukar, Hassan, and Ayaan, underscore the cultural intimacy of clan.

During surveys, I asked consultants about their memberships in associations. I intentionally omitted the words Somali and clan from my question so as not to influence answers. A little more than one-third of consultants reported membership in some kind of association. The most common response was membership in a Somali association. Besides Somali associations, consultants reported other affiliations, listed in descending order of frequency: professional occupation, multicultural, recreational, political parties, human rights, and Muslim associations. Thirteen individuals did not respond to the question.

The number of active Somali associations declined by the time I entered the field. Men continued to manage and were the primary supporters of the few clan-based associations. Just less than one-quarter of consultants reporting membership in a Somali association were women. McMichael and Manderson (2004) report that Somali men in Australia play a similar role in these associations. A reduction in clan-based associations may not support consultants' claims that clan was less important then than it was in the 1990s. Following Herzfeld (1997), the decline or concealment of clan-based associations because of the cultural intimacy of clan for Somalis abroad may point to the opposite. When I asked the consultants without association affiliations why they did not support any, it was clear that many took my question to be about clan-based associations. Many cited tribalism and misuse of funds as reasons for avoiding them.[6] Others stated they were not interested or too busy, it was a waste of time, and membership was only for men.

Three consultants working as public servants expressed the importance of maintaining a neutral position within the Somali community. By neutral, I mean maintaining an unaligned position, in terms of clan, within the Somali community. These consultants equated membership in clan-based Somali associations, a seemingly overt sign of clan affiliation in Finland, as sufficient evidence for other Somalis to conclude that they favored one group over another. Abdirahman, who worked with youth at risk, said, "Somali associations take money for themselves, and I need to be neutral in my work."

I refused invitations to two Somali associations because I, not unlike the public servants, did not want to appear as favoring one clan over another. Despite my cautions, several consultants told me that they heard a rumor that I had visited one association that—although controversial among many consultants who deemed it corrupt and clannish—the Finnish government considered an umbrella for Somali groups. The fact was that during the fieldwork period, the association was unable to attract a diverse clan membership base. The organization's governing board contacted me in hopes of helping them broaden their membership base beyond the three clans represented.

Pirkkalainen (2009) conducted a study that indicated a considerable increase in the number of Somali associations from the time of my fieldwork: more than a hundred, of which about fifty are fully operational (78). Men continue to control these organizations (85). Findings from interviews with representatives of sixteen associations suggest that regional and clan affiliations of chairpersons and members inform development locations. Interviewees noted trust with local relatives and security as reasons for this and reported that they assist everyone living in the area regardless of affiliation (79–80). Two associations operating in areas unaffiliated with its membership used a needs assessment to determine its location for development projects (79).

Suomen-Somalia Verkosto (Finnish-Somalia Network), founded in 2004 and registered in 2009, replaced the older Somali umbrella association, assuming the role of an independent umbrella organization for Somali associations. A Somali woman acts as chair and members include native Finns and

Somalis. The organization promotes capacity building and facilitates cooperation for Somali associations seeking to conduct development in Somalia.
In 2009, eighteen associations were part of the network: sixteen Somali
associations and two native Finnish associations (Pirkkalainen 2009:80).
Pirkkalainen questions whether Suomen-Somalia Verkosto can be considered as a representative umbrella organization because the participation of
Somali associations is low (Pirkkalainen 2009:80). I was unaware of the
current participation of Somali associations in the umbrella organization.
None of the consultants I met with in 2015 provided further details.

I cannot help but wonder how the cultural intimacy of clan may have
affected this research. Does this account for the low participation of representatives from Somali associations in the study? Certainly, as participants
reported, associations would have a hard time gaining access, trust, and
security in areas without clan networks. Besides those reasons given to the
researcher, do men feel obligated to develop their ancestral clan territory,
region, or hometown if other men in Finland and in other diaspora locations
do the same? In what ways do these practices cultivate a clan, regional, or
hometown feeling? How do these practices cultivate reciprocal relationships
with local and dispersed clan relatives and persons across clans? Do some
men engage in development initiatives as a means of facilitating their own
plans for return, business ventures, marriage arrangements, and perhaps
better position their clan in ongoing power struggles?

In 2015 Hanaan commented on the status of Somali associations in Finland. She said, "There are several Somali associations. None have clans in
name or description but they do in membership. Associations help with
integration and develop [development] of clan territory in Somalia." It is
remarkable that clan names no longer appear in associations' names or
descriptions as during the fieldwork period. This shift points to the cultural
intimacy of clan. It is likely that the use of clan names has fallen out of favor
in the same way that telling has changed: from the reckoning of ancestors to
the more discreet forms that I describe in the following section. Moreover,
such an adjustment could reflect a strategy to access resources from money
granting institutions and partnering organizations by appearing more inclusive. During my meeting with Hanaan, she voiced disapproval of Somali
associations that only support development in clan territories.

## Everyday Encounters

During my two stints of fieldwork (2000–2001 and 2003–4), Somalis ami-
cably greeted each other in public spaces, particularly while traveling on
public transport; shopping; taking children to school; hanging out at cafés,

nightclubs, multicultural centers, and women's groups; attending Finnish language courses; celebrating at weddings and performances of diaspora singers and DJs; and visiting with neighbors at apartment complexes. The people I worked with reported a few other local places where these everyday interactions occurred: mosques, schools, workplaces, libraries, bureaucratic offices, youth centers, pubs, and football games (soccer games).

Apart from the chance meeting detailed at the onset of this chapter, I rarely observed occasions where Somalis asked "Where are you from?" The Somali community was more settled during my fieldwork than it was in the early to mid-1990s. And, as Ayaan stated, "No one asks this now." Because the first large numbers of asylum seekers established each other's descent in the camps, it is likely the affiliations of later arrivals became known in similar ways. Those who arrived through family reunification may have been the exception. Beginning in 2000, the Finnish government instituted the use of DNA testing to establish family ties for family members of asylum seekers and refugees when documentation was inconclusive.

All these circumstances defined the local clan landscape. Many consultants claimed to recognize each other's clan. A woman I worked with stated, "No, no one asked 'Tolmaa tahay' [Which clan are you from?] because everyone knew each other." It was not always possible to know everyone. The community was too sizable and Somalis continued to arrive from abroad. Still, consultants expressed their belief that certain persons hid their clan and that the behavior was especially threatening in diaspora. This together with the possibility of encountering anyone—especially in public spaces—made it necessary to know where others were from. During the time of my research, consultants considered the direct questioning and recitation of clan genealogies as old-fashioned, unsophisticated, and rude. This sentiment prevailed in Somalia before the country's collapse. As mentioned in the introductory chapter, Siyad Barre's regime made public references to clan and other tribalism illegal.

Because Somalis abroad consider clan to be culturally intimate and a sensitive, if not taboo, topic for public discourse, they use an array of tactics within conventional social practice to tell clan. According to fieldwork data gathered in the Helsinki metropolitan area, Somalis distinguish clan and minority group affiliation through the following telling signs: language and dialect, gestures, names (given names, family names, and nicknames), places (birthplace, prior residence, areas associated with particular clans, and local hangouts), tastes (clothing, cuisine, and dancing styles), social networks, memberships in Somali associations, and physical appearance (facial features and hair texture).

This social construction of difference is in Bourdieu's (1977) terms a *structuring structure*: deeply rooted in the habitus and "partially realized and re-affirmed" through the everyday practice of telling (Burton 1978:4). Somalis construct these signs from their own life experiences: personal upbringing, interactions with other Somalis, knowledge of genealogical relationships, Somalia's history and current events, and stereotypes. The signs consultants use to tell clan are often performed tactically, in exaggeration, as in Bourdieu's (1984) terms, to mark distinction. The cues Somalis use to tell are selected and open to dispute, often leaving the practice of telling ambiguous and open to negotiation. In some cases, Somalis conceal these signs to mask clan ascription.

When Abdi, a male consultant in his mid-thirties, encounters an unfamiliar Somali, he reveals his clan by the strategic use of a telling name rather than by brazenly identifying his clan by name. Somalis have three names. The first name is a given name. The second name is the given name of their father, and the third name is the given name of their paternal grandfather. It is customary for married women to retain their names after marriage. In this way, a married woman's second and third names are the same as her siblings' names: second is father's given name and third is paternal grandfather's given name. A few women who married outside the Somali community assumed their husband's surnames. Hanaan commented on this break from tradition. She said, "It is disrespectful to change your last name because it disrespects your father. You don't respect your heritage or background."

Abdi said, "I like to tell my clan. I tell my second name. They know it's Abgaal. If I meet someone on the train, I introduce myself using my second name. Then they will know who I am. Then we are free to speak. My clan and his clan are put aside, and we are free to talk about other clans." Abdi introduces himself with his second name, Xaayoow, rather than with his given name, Abdi, a common man's name that lacks any recognizable clan significance. To other Somalis, with the necessary cultural competence, Xaayoow is recognizably Abgaal. "Xaayoow is a typical Abgaal name. At times, this name is used derogatorily to identify an Abgaal male" (Mohamed A. Eno, email to author, February 17, 2015). Abgaal is a clan of the Hawiye clan family.

Abdi's dialect also may help others decipher his clan. Linguistic differences distinguish clans and minority groups (see Eno 2008; Eno, Dammak, and Eno 2016; Kapchits 2010; Lamberti 1986). Somali is an Eastern Cushitic language belonging to the Afro-Asiatic language family. Linguists disagree on the number of dialects in Somali, citing from three to five major dialects, each with multiple variants. Lamberti (1986) notes fifty-two dialect variants.

Table 1. Primary dialects and dialect variants of Somali and related kin groups.

| Primary Dialect | Northern Somali | Daarood Group | Benaadir Group | Maay Dialects* | Digil Group |
|---|---|---|---|---|---|
| Variant Kin group | Af-Ciise<br>Dir clan | Af-Warsangeeli<br>Daarood clan | Af-Abgaal<br>Hawiye clan | | Af-Tunni<br>Raxanweyn clan |
| Variant Kin group | Af-Gadabuursi<br>Dir clan | Af-Dhulbahante<br>Daarood clan | Af-Ajuuraan<br>Hawiye clan | | Af-Dabarre<br>Raxanweyn clan |
| Variant Kin group | Af-Isaaq<br>Clan family | Af-Ogaadeen<br>Daarood clan | Af-Gaal Jacel<br>Hawiye clan | | Af-Garre<br>Raxanweyn clan |
| Variant Kin group | Af-Warsangeeli<br>Daarood clan | Af-Degodiya<br>Hawiye clan | Af-Xamari<br>Reer Xamar<br>or Benaadiri,<br>a minority group | | Af-Jiddu<br>Raxanweyn clan |
| Variant Kin group | Af-Dhulbahante<br>Daarood clan | Af-Wardaay<br>Dir clan | Af-Biimaal<br>Dir clan | | |
| Variant Kin group | | Af-Marreexaan<br>Daarood clan | | | |

This table is based on Lamberti's (1984, 1986) work.
* The variants of Maay dialects are unspecified in Lamberti's work.

For the purposes of this book, I draw from Lamberti's (1984, 1986) linguistic research in Somalia that identifies five primary Somali dialects linking to particular kinship groups and geographical regions (see table 1, map 2, and table 2).[7] Abdi's clan, the Abgaal, typically speak *Af-Abgaal*, a dialect variant of the primary dialect group *Af-Benaadir* (see tables 1 and 2). *Af* directly translates as language. When *af* is used in conjunction with a clan name, it means dialect (Georgi Kapchits, email to author, March 11, 2015).

The Maay Dialect and Digil Group Dialect distinguish the Digil and Mirifle clan families (Digil and Raxanweyn) from the other clan families. This distinction follows the Sab–Saamaale split in Somali clanship illustrated in the previous chapter (see figure 1).[8] Some scholars argue that *Af-Maay* is a distinct language with its own dialects and variations and note that it includes distinct sounds not found in Standard Somali (Eno 2008; Eno et al. forthcoming; Mohamed A. Eno, email to author, February 17, 2015). In the Maay dialect, the correct pronunciation is *Reewiin* and not "Raxanweyn" (Kusow 1995; Luling 2002; Mukhtar 1995). The Raxanweyn take great pride in their dialect (Helander 1996:197). As noted earlier, most Somali Bantus speak *Af-Maay*. In addition to consultants who self-identify as Raxanweyn, four other people I worked with who affiliate with the Daarood, Dir, and Hawiye clan families speak *Af-Maay*. Two of these consultants

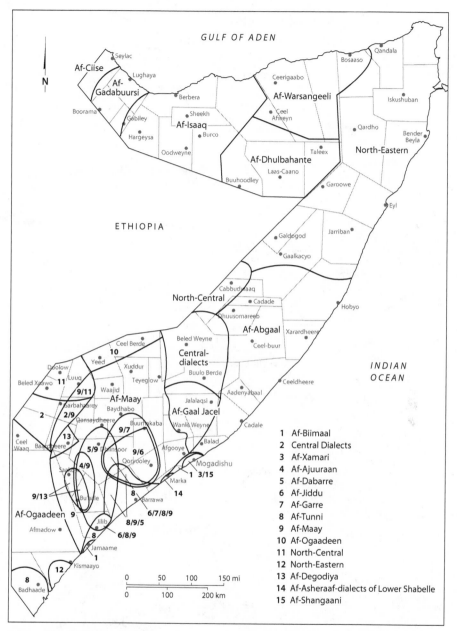

Map 2. Somali dialects in the Somali Democratic Republic. With kind permission of Helmut Buske Verlag, Hamburg, Germany. First published in 1986 in Marcello Lamberti as "Map of Somali Dialects."

Table 2. Influence of language and dialect on everyday phrases

| Af-Maay/Maay language | Abgaal/Hawiye (southern dialect) | Woqooyi (northern dialect) | English |
|---|---|---|---|
| Maay fathaase? | Xaad rabtaa? | Maxaad dooneysaa? | What do you want? |
| Surungkuungaa ka neebsathooyne. | Mahaanaan isaga bajeeynaa. | Halkan baan isaga nasaneynaa. | We're just resting here. |
| Meela iska roog. (Meelaa surunaaw) | Rabtaan iska joog. (Mahaaga iska rorog) | Halkan iska joog. (Halkaaga taagnoow). | Just stay here. (Be where you are) |
| Igaarti kooyteey? | Igaarti ma timid? | Wiilashi ma yimaadeen? | Have the boys come? |
| Ikorooy. | Iikaadi. | Isug. | Wait for me. |

Reproduced by permission from Mohamed A. Eno, *The Bantu-Jareer Somalis: Unearthing Apartheid in the Horn of Africa* (London: Adonis & Abbey, 2008).

lived in Baydhabo, a city in south central Somalia, where *Af-Maay* is widely spoken. Linguists and Somalis commonly use *Maay tiri* and *Maxaa tiri* as opposed to *Af-Maay* and *Af-Maxaa*. "*Maay tiri* and *Maxaa tiri* translate as 'What did you say?' in the respective dialects or languages" (Georgi Kapchits, email to author, March 13, 2015).

The politics of Somali language learning in Finnish schools set off rifts between parents and Somali language teachers. The Finnish government supports municipalities to provide two hours of native language instruction per week for immigrant children. At least three students with the same mother tongue must attend the school to receive this support. Several language teachers claimed that parents complained if their children were taught a dialect different from their own. Certainly this is not a clear-cut issue for children with parents speaking different dialects. During my fieldwork period, teaching materials featured *Af-Maxaa*, Standard Somali. It is unlikely that children who speak *Af-Maay* at home will learn their dialect at school because they comprise a small proportion of the Somali population in Finland.

Finland's own language history accounts for its legal protection of immigrant languages in schools. The Finnish language (*Suomen kieli* in Finnish) endured despite Swedish and Russian rule and played a critical role in Finland's nationalist and independence movements. Finnish is a non–Indo European language belonging to the Finno-Ugrian language family. This distinguishes Finnish from Swedish and other Scandinavian languages and Russian. Finnish shares linguistic roots with Estonian; Sámi, the language spoken by the indigenous Sámi population; and Hungarian. In 1902 Finnish was adopted as an official language along with Swedish. Only five million people speak Finnish as native speakers.

*Aroos* (wedding), a communitywide event for Somalis, is perhaps the most important occasion for maintaining clan networks. After attending a wedding celebration in Vantaa, Mariam, a female consultant, told me that she was surprised to discover the rightful clan affiliation of another woman, Fatima. Like Mariam, Fatima arrived as an asylum seeker in the early 1990s. For years, Mariam had falsely assumed Fatima's clan affiliation to be Abgaal. Mariam based this assumption on a series of telling signs such as Fatima's Somali dialect, birthplace, and social networks.

During the wedding celebration, however, Mariam deciphered Fatima's rightful clan affiliation from Fatima's close association with women from her paternal clan family. After the wedding, Mariam explained why Fatima's clan affiliation was difficult to decipher. Mariam said, "Fatima is [name of clan family], but raised Abgaal." Fatima did not grow up in the northern territory traditionally associated with her paternal clan family. Nor did she speak the northern Somali dialect typical of her paternal kin (see table 1). Since she was born and raised in the south, among her mother's clan, she spoke a Benaadir Group dialect (see table 1).

Misreading Fatima's clan from her dialect and social networks exposed the key role of her mother's clan, not her paternal clan, in Fatima's everyday life. Survey and interview data indicates that Fatima maintains networks with women from both her father's clan and mother's clan. She does this through household visiting, attending wedding celebrations, and as an entrepreneur selling goods such as *diric* (Somali women's dress worn at weddings and other special occasions) in the informal economy. The term *diric* is typically used in the North, whereas *dirac* is preferred in the South. Fatima maintained dispersed clan networks outside Finland through her social networks in Finland by sharing news and via telephone, travel, and the circulation of videos. Fatima called upon her networks in Europe, the Middle East, and East Africa established during her travels, where she purchased goods for resale and rental in Finland. The misidentification of Fatima's clan affiliation is just one of many examples in which an individual's clan affiliation is open to obfuscation. These situations indicate the difficulties in determining clan based solely on observational strategies.

Men tend to meet at restaurants, cafés (some for men only), and the Helsinki railway station to discuss current events. In Helsinki, some public places are known by consultants to be meeting places for men of particular clans even though other Somalis may frequent the same establishments. A male consultant reported, "Now people go to the internet to check what is going on, and when they meet together, they defend their own tribe, but they do talk to each other."

Abdi, a man in his thirties, told me that if he met a group of Habar Gidir men from his clan and brought another man with him, his clansmen would assume that his companion also was Habar Gidir. Habar Gidir is a clan of the Hawiye clan family. Explaining the social convention for this type of mixed-clan setting, Abdi said, "I must say before the conversation begins that the man is, for example, Daarood, to set it up. So nothing bad is said about Daarood. It's polite." Daarood is a clan family.

In more intimate settings, such as family households, mixed-clan interactions might be less common or even exceptional, as it was in the following case. One evening I accompanied two female consultants to the household of one of the women's relatives. After we entered the family apartment, our hostess and mutual friend, Kadijah, introduced Lul to her husband as Lul-Habar Gidir-Cayr (Cayr is a subclan of the Habar Gidir clan). Kadijah's husband greeted Lul: "*Salaan* (greetings) Cayr Queen." Directly, yet politely, Kadijah informed her husband that Lul was not a clan relative. Kadijah's assertiveness was socially savvy. This strategic move cued her husband to be cautious of his words in Lul's presence. Kadijah, as Abdi noted earlier, knew all too well that without identifying a newcomer's clan, an unpleasant situation might arise because something ill-mannered might be mentioned about the stranger's clan or clan relative.

Although most consultants claimed to decipher the clan affiliation of others through telling signs, some people, like Fadumo, were always held suspect. Fadumo was aware that other Somalis suspected her of masking her clan affiliation. As Fadumo and I chatted at her sister's home, she pulled a few pieces of hair loose from her ponytail and said, "People [other Somalis] say I am *jareer* [hard-textured hair, suggesting Bantu origins] because of my hair." Fadumo rarely styled her hair or had it chemically relaxed as some women did.

Women's performative acts such as chemical hair straightening and skin bleaching blur the notion of ascribed physical features. I recall one occasion when I was preparing for an *aroos* with a group of women. When Ruqiyo brushed my hair before fixing it into an elaborate updo, she said, "Stephanie, your hair is like mine." Ruqiyo meant that we both have *jileec* (soft-textured hair) hair. It is remarkable that she and the other women believed that their hair was *jileec* when they exerted great effort that day to make their hair appear "soft" for *aroos*. In the event that consultants acknowledged African-like hair or facial features among relatives or others who were backed by a clan collective, these exceptions were dismissed in terms of "They are not beautiful." Luling (2002) notes "such anomalous characteristics in individuals are noticed and admitted to, often with laughter, but they do not disturb the stereotype" (94).

Individuals or families with few relatives in Finland are likely to be considered suspect if a collective does not support their claim to clan membership. Persons affiliated with smaller clans (either in terms of numbers residing in Finland or Somalia) are especially subject to suspicion. As I traveled with a female consultant by metro to Helsinki's city center, she explained why other Somalis did not accept the clan affiliation of Saed, whom she suspected was Madhibaan:

> Saed says his mother is Hawiye and his father is Asheraaf, but nobody [in Finland] will say he is Hawiye. He says [name of subclan], but they are so small. The [name of subclan] who live here [in Finland] say he is not [name of subclan], and Asheraaf nobody knows. No one will marry him and have children with him.

In addition to claiming descent from small clans, Saed's paternal clan, the Asheraaf Sarman (also Ashraf Sarman), a southern inland minority group associated with the Raxanweyn, was not well known among other local Somalis. Because Saed could not garner support from clan relatives in Finland, he was likely excluded from clan-based social networks.

Hiding and avoiding other Somalis are strategies available to minority Somalis, but these strategies are also telling of ascribed status. A man that I worked with told me how two men—whom he believed to be Madhibaan—used these two tactics. He said, "I have one friend who is Midgaan. When anyone talks about clan, he leaves. Another man [who is Madhibaan] drinks [alcohol] and stays away from other Somalis. When we [Somalis] came to Finland, we [Somalis] were all the same or at least the Finns think so. Some are like Arabs, others like Africans—it's in the face."

Although I never came across a consultant who claimed to be Madhibaan or Somali Bantu, several of the people I worked with claimed that I had interviewed individuals affiliated with these groups. It is possible to imagine that persons with few ties and obligations to local Somalis are perhaps more likely to build networks with Finns and other immigrants and seek individual success in Finnish society.

Consultants excused the naming clan names for polite purposes as noted earlier and for practical reasons. In everyday speech, the people I worked with used clan names as a practical way to set apart individuals and groups. After conducting a survey with Ahmed, a civil servant, he asked me whether I had interviewed his colleague Hassan. "Who, Hassan?" our friend, Hawa, inquired. Ahmed responded, "Hassan, Dir." Ahmed explained, "There are too many Hassan. Then, we know which Hassan." Since Hassan is a common Somali name and the individual in question did not have a well-known nickname, Ahmed utilized Hassan's clan family, Dir, as a reference marker. Few persons were affiliated with this clan family in Finland.

Somalis with common names such as Maxamed and Ayaan typically have nicknames to help others distinguish them. Nicknames may denote physical characteristics such as body shape, hair color and texture, skin color, eye color and shape, nose shape, personality traits, or family names. Some nicknames are telling of clan affiliation by means of clan dialect. In other cases, a name like Hassan was followed by a place name. The place name can refer to a previous place of residence or current residence if uncommon for local Somalis. For example, if Hassan previously lived in Qatar, his nickname could be Hassan Qatar. Since few Somalis lived in a West Helsinki neighborhood like Espoo, a nickname like Hassan Espoo can point to a particular individual. I developed my own nicknaming strategy in the field to distinguish individuals. On my mobile phone, I listed individual names followed by their place of residence, and in some cases, clan names. I used nicknames like "Abdi Havukoski" for a consultant named Abdi, a common man's name, who resided in Havukoski, an area in the city of Vantaa.

In 2015 Hanaan commented on how greeting practices have changed. She said, "Nowadays people don't say hi to each other, they just smile because the society is much bigger than it used to be—fifteen thousand. We say hi to each other if we know or have seen each other in some parties or weddings. If you stay and talk you say, '*Is ka warran*? (How are you?)'" She used the term *Titanic* to refer to recent arrivals. *Titanic* is derogatory, much like the phrase *fresh off the boat*, commonly referred by the acronym FOB, to denote recent immigrants in the United States. The term connotes a lack of integration in terms of demeanor, dress, language skills, and so forth. In 2016 Mohamed explained the term on Facebook Messenger. He wrote, "I've heard *Titanic* is referred to someone who has traveled from North Africa by boat through [the] Mediterranean Sea to Greece or Italy and took a high risk by taking the sea route to Europe. [The] word Titanic is familiar to almost every Somali living in Finland, and it roughly means bold, newcomers, shameless, and sometimes very aggressive and intrusive." In 2016 Idil offered a few examples of how the term is used in everyday speech via Facebook Messenger. She wrote, "Guys, here the Titanic are coming. Check the Titanic. She is Titanic." Nafiso added that they tend to stand out from other Somalis with their loud and aggressive behavior. Nafiso noted another reason for changing sociability. She said, "Some don't say hi. Before people came from same camp, but now the people don't know each other."

Although people still keep abreast of happenings at home through the internet and social networks, satellite television and travel are increasingly widespread. In 2015 men no longer congregated at the central railway station. They favor meeting at cafés for men located near the mosque at Itis or at gas stations. Gas stations are popular meeting places because they are open late, usually until midnight, they serve coffee, and the staff does not mind if patrons linger. Few men visit the Cable Library to use its free internet connections because most own smartphones. Free wi-fi is readily accessible: the city of Helsinki and public transport offer free wi-fi.

## Telling Cultivates Links across Clans

Telling can link individuals to particular clans at various levels of segmentation, but another use of telling is to form horizontal links across clans. As I have already shown, Somalis from various clan backgrounds may speak the same dialect. Lamberti's (1984, 1986) work clearly demonstrates this (see table 1 and map 2). The example of a woman speaking a dialect telling of her mother's paternal clan rather than her own paternal clan points to messy realities on the ground. Many of the signs Somalis use to decipher clan also reflect regional cultural forms. Just as using and sharing a distinctive dialect creates a sense of familiarity and shared identity, the same can be said for regionally distinctive foods. Most consultants were multilingual and spoke two or three languages in addition to Somali. The use of these languages—particularly Swahili, Oromo, *Af-Maay*, Amharic, Arabic, English, Italian, French, Russian, Swedish, and Finnish—also cultivates a group feeling among Somalis and with other speakers. In the same way, using telling place names can integrate persons from the same city or region and provide an opportunity to build social capital across clans.

Consultants routinely used the English terms *North* (*Waqooyi* in Somali) and *South* (*Koonfur* in Somali) to point to groupings of clans. These categories connote a wide array of perceived differences based on geographical location of ancestral clan territory, colonial history, current political association, language, dialect, livelihood, social manner, taste, and habit. Like the telling signs Somalis use to reveal clan, *North* and *South* are ambiguous and open to negotiation. The performance of North and South varies. In some contexts, it is exaggerated, and in other contexts it is downplayed. What is important here is that these broader categories present yet another possibility for lining up, cultivating networks, and exchanging capital.

The most common construction of North and South is based on political configurations: British Somaliland and Somaliland Republic as North and Italian Somaliland and Puntland and the rest of the country as South (see map 3 and map 5 in chapter 5). The people I worked with employed other constructions. At times, they used *North* exclusively for the Isaaq clan family. At other times, they included Somaliland and Puntland into constructions of North. One constant was exclusion of ethnic minority groups in these constructions. Local conditions, including individual relationships and those

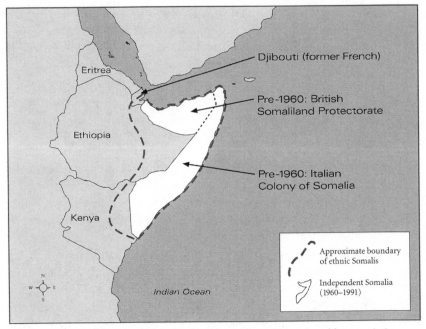

Map 3. Distribution of Somalis and colonial partitions. Reproduced by permission from United States Institute of Peace.

within and between clans together with changing alliances at home, affect how Somalis construct and imagine these categories.

In 2015 Hanaan commented on how she defines *North* and *South*. She said, "North equals Somaliland, sometimes Puntland." Mohamed commented on his notion of North and South via Facebook Messenger. In 2015 he wrote, "*Waqooyi* (North) is usually referred to ppl [people] from Somaliland and *Koonfur* (South) is referred [to] ppl [people] from southern Somalia (sometimes including Puntland area). In Finland, still the majority of Somalis living here are from the South." These examples highlight the geographic and political definitions of the terms.

During a household visit with two female friends in their thirties from different clan backgrounds, I asked Hodan whether she could tell me about a situation where she was discriminated against on the basis of clan. At first, Hodan responded, "No, I don't think so." Then, after a few seconds, she pointed to her friend Ayaan and said, "They [the South] will say I am *qaldan* (wrong, mistaken). She's wrong. Everything is wrong: the language, the culture, and the clock." *Soomaali qaldan* is a derogatory phrase "denoting that the northerners are incomprehensive in the dialect of their spoken Somali" (Eno 2008:42). *Xamaraawi* is comparably derogatory when northerners use it to refer to southerners. *Xamar* is the original name of the city Mogadishu. Many consultants born or raised there preferred the city's original name. In 2015 Mohamed elaborated on the term *Xamaraawi* via Facebook Messenger. He wrote, "The term *Xamaraawi* mostly means person from *Xamar*, but also it means Benaadiri people [a minority group]. If you are in northern Somalia, *Xamaraawi* means all people who came from *Xamar*."

Later that day, Hodan and Ayaan's children, all Finnish-born, had some difficulty communicating with each other in Somali and so they switched to Finnish. When Ayaan spoke to Hodan's children, they could not grasp what she said. Ayaan used words distinctive to the South. Ayaan explained how she viewed the language of the North. She said, "North language is long and more difficult [than the language of the South]. They [northern Somalis] use *de*. Instead of saying *cun* (eat), they [the North] say *cun de* (eat), *kaalay de* (come), *waryaa de* (hey, hi). North language is long! What is *de*? It doesn't mean anything."

In 2015 Hanaan commented on the intelligibility of northern and southern dialects. She said, "In my high school we were a small group of Somalians from North and South and we had Djiboutians who we called Somalians. Because everyone knew that I had both background[s] North and South [she explained that one parent is from the North and the other from the South], so when our North friends didn't understand the South they asked 'Where is Hanaan?' She can translate what the South people were talking about."

Abdi, a male consultant in his mid-thirties and born and raised in Mogadishu, offered an overview of linguistic differences in Somalia. He told me to visualize an inverted triangle superimposed on a map of Somalia. Abdi explained, "As you move from north to south [from the base of the triangle to its tip], the language gets shorter." In Bourdieu's (1986) formulation of cultural capital, culture is a power resource that is cultivated through socialization. Ayaan describes the northern language as long and difficult and the southern language as practical, a characteristic valued by its speakers but considered less prestigious in the North. Northerners tend to believe that the language spoken in the South lacks mythical and aesthetic value (Kusow 2004).

Abdi continued to contrast the North and South by pointing to differences in constructions of time. Abdi explained that southern Somalis see the day as beginning at 6:00 a.m. and northern Somalis see the day as beginning at midnight. In the South, 6:00 a.m. is considered 12 o'clock; using a clock's face as a reference, each number on a clock corresponds with the number directly across. Hence, if the hour hand is on 3, then it is 9 o'clock in southern Somalia. I observed consultants from places such as Mogadishu,

Kismaayo, and Baydhao use this local way of telling time in the presence of friends from Hargeysa, Djibouti, and Burco. Often these occasions led to laughter and friendly banter. Finland follows the 24-hour clock, which is also known as military time.

In 2015 Mohamed commented on telling time in southern Somalia via Facebook Messenger. He wrote, "In Somalia and Ethiopia (I think it is not official) the clock counting starts after sunrise (6AM) that means 7AM is first hour of the day (1 *saac oo subaxnimo,* 1 o'clock in the morning) 1–12. The time keeping continues till sundown at 18:00 and night time's 1st hour starts (1 *saac oo habeenino,* 1 o'clock in the evening) 1–12 and continues till sunrise."

Another way consultants performed North and South was by emphasizing vestiges of colonial influence to create camaraderie within and between clans while excluding others. Consultants performed North and South by speaking colonial languages and listening to music and watching television programs in these languages. Some prepared and consumed colonial inspired cuisine such as imported spaghetti among southerners and pudding among northerners. Somalis are known to drink spiced tea, but at times southerners drink coffee. Coffee was primarily grown in the South. Southerners tended to claim that they were more open and sociable (some used the greeting *Ciao*), like Italians, than northerners, who were stereotyped as closed off and reserved. In the same way, Somalis from Djibouti (formerly French Somaliland) sometimes spoke French when they met and some women favored French cosmetics and perfumes.

The association of North and South with any of the practices just noted is messy. Many consultants moved away from towns and cities in the north for greater education and employment opportunities in the south. There they picked up new local habits and tastes. The same was true for older consultants studying abroad in Italy, France, or England or for those working in the oil-rich countries. What is significant here is when, how, and why such habits and tastes are transmitted, cultivated, embellished, or understated. If North and South are such pervasive constructions in daily life, they must be useful. These practices have effects on social networks and access to capital in its various forms.

These everyday practices build a regional feeling that can help to expand an individual's access to potential networks or social capital beyond clan relatives to larger groupings. In Finland, consultants claimed that there were more Somalis from the South than there were from the North. Therefore, southern Somalis are favorably positioned to build social networks and exchange capital on the basis of the South. Are *Waqooyi* (North) and *Koon-*

*fur* (South) threats to clan cohesion and capital interests? Can northerners expand their networks in novel ways?

Without social support, an individual's connection to North or South may be at stake. An Isaaq woman recounted a spontaneous interaction she had with a group of men from the North at Helsinki's central railway station. She told that one of the men said to the others in her presence, "She is from South because her husband is from South." The man's tactic was to exclude her from North-based networks despite the woman's paternal clan, location of ancestral clan territory, and dialect. It is unclear whether this was due to a personal conflict with the man or her close association with southerners. In 2015 Mohamed commented on his experience of being labeled as both North and South. When he was a student, he moved from the North to study in Mogadishu. There others considered him to be North. During a recent trip to Somaliland, locals there considered him to be South because of his dialect and referred to him as *Xamaraawi.*

## Telling Fieldwork Moments

Key consultants such as Nasra regularly helped me access other Somalis. As Nasra and I rode a bus from Itäkeskus—a shopping center in eastern Helsinki where many Somalis and other immigrants congregate—to pick up her child from school, we encountered two middle-aged women. After Nasra greeted them in the customary fashion of hugging and kissing each other on their cheeks, she introduced me and told the women about my project. We chatted on the bus until our destinations separated us. Before parting, the women agreed to an interview. As Nasra and I stepped off the bus, she said to me, "They are my clan. That's why they said yes [to participate in the research]. They will answer. I don't like clan, but Somalis are like that." Consultants commonly excused these types of culturally intimate actions to me in those terms.

I utilized this strategy of accessing consultants while accompanying key consultants of various clans as they carried out daily activities with the aim of mapping social networks. Besides clan, other social networks formed in diaspora—networks with classmates, coworkers, neighbors, friends, and in fewer cases, Finns—facilitated access to consultants. These moments demonstrated the importance of accessing consultants through their own social networks. The people I worked with commonly accessed other Somalis through people they trusted: clan relatives. Whenever I encountered a new person in the field, I tried to ascertain clan affiliation utilizing the same telling signs Somalis use to read clan. Before I interviewed Jama, a man in his early thirties, I used that method to establish rapport. When he asked me whether I had already met a number of Somalis, I listed the names of about ten of his clan relatives. Realizing what I had done, Jama said to me, "You are smart. You meet Somalis through relatives. This is the way Somalis meet each other."

Because telling is not foolproof, I misjudged the affiliation of several individuals from their social networks and physical appearance. Once when telling went wrong, I falsely inferred from her physical features that the woman I was about to interview was from a minority group. In this case, I thoughtlessly associated physical features (shape of nose and hair texture) with ascribed status, albeit *the front* is perhaps the least reliable telling cue. When anthropologists become embedded in local culture and form close friendships with the people they work with, they can sometimes lose objectivity. It was not that I believed that physical features could validate affiliation. Rather, these stereotypes were so pervasive in everyday speech that I thoughtlessly made that connection. This misstep led me to reflect on how my fieldwork experiences and relationships with consultants can lead to bias and enhanced my understanding of how such stereotypes are circulated.

During interviews, I directly asked consultants to identify their clan (*qabiil* in Somali). Because of the cultural intimacy of clan for Somalis abroad, I was not surprised that many of the people I worked with were taken aback by my frankness. Some consultants were surprised that a cultural outsider was at all familiar with Somali clanship. When I asked Ubax, a female consultant about her clan Hodan, another consultant interjected, "Stephanie knows about clan." Many believed that Finns were in the dark about clan.

Nearly all surveyed individuals, 175 out of the 186 respondents, 94 percent, responded to my inquiry about clan. Many consultants had previously seen me at *aroosyo* or met me when I was with other Somalis. Most consultants seemed to view me as an unbiased observer for two reasons: I was not a Somali affiliated with a clan nor was I a Finn. Because Somalis were aware that I used the same telling signs they use to read clan and utilized clan as reference markers in everyday speech, my social intimacy in the field balanced my cultural distance. Most of the people I worked with answered my question without hesitation. A few others responded to my inquiry by outwardly expressing their contempt for clan. When I asked one young woman in her early twenties this question, she responded in Finnish, "*Ei hyvää kysymys* [Not a good question]" before revealing Dir as her clan family.

Only 11 out of the 186 respondents, 6 percent, chose not to report their clan to me. A young male consultant, just over 18 years old, who refused to report his clan said, "All Somalis ask this. I don't want." Incidentally, a man who was present during the survey later told me that the young man belonged to a clan with little local presence, which could lead to endless questioning about his affiliation. A female consultant who did not reveal her clan affiliation to me said, "Clan does not make sense to me." In response to my question, the initial reaction of one forty-year-old man was to say, "I know where I belong. I do not identify with my clan but my nation." Then, with a clever smile, he casually remarked that since I had already interviewed his cousin, Abuukar, I could easily determine his clan affiliation. Abuukar belonged to the Hawiye clan family.

Not all my inquiries into clan went smoothly. During two separate surveys, I felt uneasy asking a man and woman about their affiliation. Both appeared uncomfortable and acted a bit hostile toward me. The woman mentioned that she had already participated in a Finnish woman's research project. In fact, she addressed me by that researcher's name as a way to link me with Finns in the presence of her relatives. Two of the woman's relatives with whom I had developed close friendships chastised her for doing so. This made the situation all the more awkward. In a number of instances, the people I worked with noted they were skeptical of Finns, especially researchers.

Surveys revealed that the extent of respondents' understanding of Somali clans was relative to their cultural competence or clan competence. As mentioned earlier, those who arrived in the early to mid-1990s legitimized their clan to each other by exhibiting a certain degree of clan competence. Some of those consultants were already skilled at reciting the names of their clan ancestors and the relationship of their clan to other clans and others contacted relatives to acquire this knowledge. Persons reared in rural areas tended to exhibit a high degree of clan competence about their lineage but were less familiar with clans and minority groups outside their home regions. In contrast, young adults, particularly those born in Finland or those who were recent arrivals tended to be familiar only with the name of their own clan or subclan.

Young adults, particularly those who first learned their clan genealogy in Finland, tended to self-identify by their clan or subclan rather than clan family during interviews. This is revealing, because it points to what relatives teach them and what is important in Finland, and likely at home. A few men instigated an elaborate ritual with me, as in the example at the onset of this chapter using telling place names instead of stating their affiliation. Perhaps this was a way to test my knowledge of these associations or a way for consultants to legitimize their own claims. Some consultants could not name the clan family to which their stated clan or subclan belongs. Although I did not include children in my research, this pattern did not seem to apply to the numerous children and young adults who traveled to Somalia or other countries in the Horn of Africa during summer break. There, grandparents, aunts, uncles, and other relatives—both knowingly and unknowingly—impart knowledge of clan genealogies. Hodan, a female consultant, noted the disparity between her two Finnish-born children's knowledge of their clan genealogy as it related to traveling to Somalia:

> AUTHOR: How will you teach your children where they are from?
> HODAN: Muse went to Somalia twice. He learned from his grandmother. He know[s] my tribe. He know[s] everything. She [her daughter] doesn't know anything. I asked her once where she was from. I listed the tribes. She took the last one each time. I did this twice.

In 2015 Nafiso commented that her child learned his clan genealogy and its relationship to other clans during a recent visit with relatives living in another Scandinavian country. The barrage of the clan-related questions that followed the trip took her aback.

Initially, I falsely assumed that collecting clan or subclan data was too intrusive. My survey reflected this oversight. Consultants who glanced at the survey forms as I inquired about their clan may have stated their clan family, as reflected in the survey, instead of how they self-identify. In retrospect, instead of listing clan families by name on each survey form, I would leave this space blank and record only what each respondent chose to report. When I asked consultants who self-identified by subclan why they did so, they commonly told me that to know where a person was really from, "You need to know the small clan [clan or subclan], not the big clan [clan or clan family]. Clans are too big." In cases where consultants cited their subclan or clan, I made note of how they self-identified.

Because the people I worked with knew that I asked consultants about their clan affiliation, several women whom I consider friends asked me to disclose the affiliation of a few individuals I interviewed that they suspected of concealing their ascribed status as Madhibaan or Somali Bantu. During a household visit, a female consultant asked, "Where is Suufiya from? What is her clan? Some people say she is from [name of town]."

Taking a copy of my informed consent form from my handbag, I asked the woman, "Do you remember this form [informed consent form] you signed? I cannot tell you anything someone else has told me. You are not the first person who has asked me about someone's clan. If I tell, no one will talk to me." The woman apologized for the intrusion and dismissed her actions, saying, "Sorry. Somalis are crazy sometimes." The woman may have thought that our friendship would provide her access to the information she desired, but it could also have been a test to verify that I maintained the level of confidentiality I assured.

# CHAPTER 3

# Movement

## Seeking Autonomy

I arrived at the apartment of one of my consultants, Dega, in eastern Helsinki at 2 p.m. on a Sunday afternoon. Dega is an unmarried girl in her twenties. We first met in 2000 when I conducted my master's research in Finland. Dega and I had met the previous day at McDonald's in the city center where she and some of her friends took my survey. Today Dega agreed to introduce me to other friends living at her apartment complex. She placed some calls on her mobile phone and we knocked on a few doors, but no one answered. Dega assumed her neighbors were still asleep, and so we waited on a bench in the courtyard. As we chatted and basked in the warm summer sun, we noticed a Somali girl and a Finnish boy, dressed in T-shirts and jeans, unloading boxes from a van. Dega approached the girl to introduce herself. As we helped the pair move belongings into a single apartment, Dega asked the girl whether she would participate in my research. She agreed to meet with me after she settled into her new place. Because almost an hour had passed since I arrived, I began to think I would have little to no success in accessing new consultants. Besides, I was tired from attending the *aroos* (wedding) held the previous night. Perhaps sensing my frustration, Dega knocked on another apartment door. A young woman, Khadra, opened the door. Her eyes were partially closed. We recognized each other from the *aroos*. Khadra let us in and agreed to the survey. Moments later, another sleepy girl, Hamda, appeared. She, too, had attended the *aroos*. The girl was visiting from Turku, a city of 180,000 on Finland's southwest coast. The four of us sat around the small kitchen table and drank ordinary black Lipton tea (instead of the sweet spiced tea typically served in family households) as we visited and completed the surveys. Then Dega and

I walked upstairs to her apartment. As Dega unlocked her door, Warsame, a neighbor boy, appeared. He had arrived in Finland from Somalia only a year ago. Warsame followed us into Dega's apartment and explained he had just awakened and that his mobile phone was *kiinni* (Finnish term for closed or turned off). Sometime later, Khadra and Hamda joined us along with a slew of visitors, including other neighbors and a few friends from other parts of the city. Dega and Khadra served each visitor a plate of spaghetti and a glass of fruit juice. After some of the visitors completed surveys, we continued to socialize until late that evening.

Nearly all the people I worked with lived in rental apartment housing for low-income people subsidized by Finnish municipalities.[1] Municipal housing is scattered throughout the Helsinki metropolitan area—encompassing Helsinki, Espoo, Kauniainen, and Vantaa—in an effort to promote integration and thereby prevent segregation. Despite the policy, most consultants and other ethnic minorities reside in eastern and northeastern neighborhoods (Vaattovaara and Kortteinen 2003 and map 4).[2] In these spaces, Somalis and other immigrants live alongside pensioners, economically and socially disadvantaged Finns, low-income households relying on social assistance, and the long-term unemployed, including alcoholics.

Finns' everyday speech points to increasing socioeconomic disparity between areas. When Finns in Helsinki meet, one of the first questions they commonly ask is "Missäpäin sä asut?" (Helsinki slang for "Where about you live?") The answer is telling of financial standing, which is somewhat culturally intimate for Finns. Finns rarely ask anyone other than close family about income because it is considered to be a private issue. Increasing social inequality challenges notions of equality. In 2015 Mohamed commented on how this practice is similar to the way Somalis ask about clan. He said, "Like how Somalis ask clan: [through] the back door."

During the fieldwork period, I heard Finnish friends and media outlets use the moniker "Mogadishu Avenue" for *Meri-Rastilantie* (Meri-Rastila Street), the main street in Meri-Rastila, an eastern neighborhood, because of the noticeable presence of Somalis there. In 2006 *Mogadishu Avenue* became the title of a Finnish sitcom about immigrants living in the country. In 2015 Hanaan commented on the current use of Mogadishu Avenue. She said, "Finns and Somalis still use the expression 'Mogadishu Avenue' for Meri-Rastila, Puotila, and Vuosaari." Puotila and Vuosaari are other eastern neighborhoods. The selective migration that drives the increase in ethnic residential segregation within the Helsinki metropolitan area is twofold: ethnic Finns select to live in areas with few immigrants and immigrants select to live among other immigrants (Vilkama 2011). Finland has less residential segregation by ethnic origin than Norway and Sweden (Mannila 2010:27; see also Pred 1997). In 2015 Nafiso commented on Somalis' selective migration. She said, "It is the same. Most of the people want to live [in] the same area."

My social network tracing indicates that neighborhoods are not the basis of clan groups. In 2015 Nafiso suggested that this is no longer the case. She said, "Now some clans live in same areas." I asked her to specify the areas and clans. When I noticed she was hesitant to answer, I told her that I did not need to know. I was just curious. My probing was too intrusive. Even if she had named the areas and clans living there, I would not include that type of information in this book. Doing so could give readers the impression that some groups are more clannish than others and be a reason for discord among groups. I have worked to avoid causing discord in my fieldwork and this book. Still, the change that Nafiso suggested adds local places as another dimension to telling.

The apartment complex where Dega lived, known locally as Kandahar, had become a destination for young Somalis. Remarkably, Somalis living

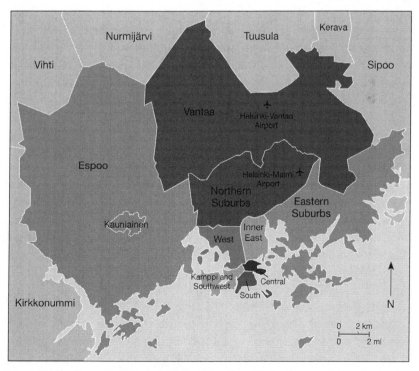

Map 4. Helsinki metropolitan area. Most Somalis reside in the east and northeastern suburbs.

there selected Kandahar, a place not linked with Somalia or Finland, to symbolize their residence. Residents coined the term Kandahar during the NATO invasion of Afghanistan in 2001. At that time, national and international newscasts regularly reported on the heavy aerial bombing of Kandahar, a city in southern Afghanistan, and told of the chaos and destruction that ensued there. As Amina, one woman resident explained, "It [the label Kandahar] just stuck." Since Kandahar also is notorious for being a Taliban center, occupants may make this connection and use the name ironically (Markus Hoehne, personal communication, November 10, 2012).

Although the association between the city of Kandahar and the apartment complex was never fully explained to me, consultants commonly disclosed the following parallels between Kandahar and apartment complex: chaos, destruction, and danger. The nearly constant movement of people in and out of the complex at all hours rendered chaos. This flux included official residents along with visitors who passed by, congregated, or sought temporary refuge. The long-term destruction of the bordering road and sidewalks by Finnish work crews added to feelings of chaos. And some residents suggested that danger loomed in their immediate surroundings. When residents walked home from the nearby metro station, they passed bars and other adult entertainment where they often encountered drunken Finns. Warsame, the boy I surveyed at Dega's home, revealed a deep scar just above his eye that he received late one evening as he walked to his home in Kandahar. He alleged that a drunken Finnish man struck him with a glass beer bottle outside a bar near the apartment complex.

I did not again encounter the girl I met who was moving into the complex, nor do I know whether she moved into the apartment alone or with the Finnish boy. It is probable that her move, like the movement of other Somalis to this complex, was a mixture of chance and strategy. Various circumstances led young Somalis to this complex: conflict with parents and relatives, absence of parents or close relatives in Finland, and divorce. Divorce was fairly common among the people I worked with.[3] A few consultants, married in their late teens or early twenties and divorced after a year or two of marriage, resided there. A female consultant who lived near the family of a boy I interviewed at Kandahar explained his move to this complex. She said that his parents "kicked him out of the house [family apartment] because he was drinking [alcohol]. He now lives in Kandahar."

Young unmarried Somalis living with parents or other relatives moved to the complex or took temporary refuge with residents as a strategy to gain autonomy. Hamda, the girl who attended the *aroos* and was visiting Helsinki for the weekend, explained, "I study and get things done in Turku. I come to Helsinki for fun." Unbeknownst to her parents, when Hamda escapes to Helsinki, she tends to stay with friends at Kandahar instead of with her older siblings. From Kandahar, Hamda moved about more freely than she did in Turku.

One evening, I decided to venture into Helsinki's nightlife with a few girls from Kandahar. The girls selected Tiger (referred to locally as *Tiikeri*, the Finnish word for tiger), a nightclub in the city center, for Thursday R&B (rhythm and blues) night. We met in front of the club around 10:30 p.m. and followed Khadra past the longline at the entrance. At the door, Khadra greeted the bouncers by name and flashed passes to cover our entrance. The bouncers checked our identification to verify that we met the eighteen-year-old minimum age requirement for that night (on weekends the minimum age was higher).[4] In 2015 Hanaan, Nafiso, and Mohamed commented on the popularity of Tiger and another club, Gloria. They all agreed that both clubs are still trendy hangouts. Two newer clubs, Club Namu and Maxine, in Helsinki's city center, are other hot spots.

Inside, the girls joined friends of both sexes who included other Somalis, other immigrants, and Finns. About twenty were in the group. Shortly after we entered, a few of their Somali girlfriends noticed me. They greeted me by kissing my cheeks in the fashion that is customary among girls and women. Then they asked me not to tell their siblings or parents that I saw them there. I agreed and said, "OK, as long as you don't tell them that I was here dancing with you." Most of the girls, like other club-goers, wore heavy makeup and dressed in halter-tops or low-cut shirts with tight jeans or short skirts. A few dressed more modestly in jeans and long-sleeved tops. Every so often the girls assembled on the dance floor to dance to the latest tracks from artists like Ashanti, Beyoncé, and Sean Paul. At times, they replicated provocative choreography from the artists' music videos. Some of the group drank alcohol, mainly beer and cider with the free drink tickets that Khadra scored from the Finnish DJ she was dating, and smoked cigarettes. Others drank water or soda. One girl claimed that a few of the boys smoked marijuana and chewed *qaad* earlier that evening. *Qaad*, also written as *qaat* and *khat*, refers to the leaves or twigs of the Catha edulis plant native to East Africa and the Arabian Peninsula. Men (and sometimes women) chew *qaad* in East Africa, Yemen, and throughout the diaspora for its mildly intoxicating or stimulating effect. *Qaad* is an illegal substance in Finland.[5]

For their Finnish contemporaries in Helsinki, late-teens and twenty-somethings, the same behaviors, with the exception of chewing *qaad*, are commonplace. (It is possible that Finnish friends use *qaad*.) Young Finns tend to travel freely in the city at night, intermingle outside school, and form intimate relationships with little interference from parents or other relatives. They meet in the city center; attend movies and concerts; frequent cafés, recreational facilities, pubs, and nightclubs; host parties at homes and summer cottages; and drink alcohol. During my year as an exchange student in the country (1990–91), it was customary for me to congregate with peers at the marketplace on weekends or attend house parties to drink alcohol. I recall seeing classmates staggering from intoxication at the cobblestoned marketplace. The police were present to monitor the situation but seldom interfered. The sale of alcohol is prohibited to persons under the age of eighteen, but alcohol consumption among teenagers is ubiquitous.[6]

Hamda was not present at *Tiikeri* that evening. If she had been staying with friends in Kandahar she might have joined us. Hamda claimed that such freedoms—hanging out with friends in the city, mixing with boys, and patronizing nightclubs—were impossible for her in Turku,[7] where she lived with her parents and siblings. Still, when Hamda moved about in Helsinki, she was watchful. She claimed that gossip could easily move through clan networks (and presumably any other active social networks) to her parents in Turku.

I, too, was hesitant to move in these circles and frequent those venues. Because I spent most of my time with women my age, in their thirties, or with older women at their homes, I was privy to women's everyday gossip. Girls and women's behaviors were routinely discussed and scrutinized. A few women in the community, nicknamed "Somali BBC," were known as zealous gossipers. Even when I visited places like *Tiikeri*, I limited my dealings with men and dressed conservatively, yet stylish, in a long skirt or jeans and long-sleeved top. I refrained from drinking alcohol even when consultants drank alcohol. Even though some consultants did not care whether I had a glass of cider, I knew that others would not be so accepting. I did not want to put my standing in the Somali community at risk. I feared jeopardizing valued friendships, knowing my behavior could reflect positively or negatively upon others—and on my research project. Likely, male anthropologists in the same field context would face less social scrutiny based on the body and feel less pressure to manage their reputations (Gifford and Hall-Clifford 2008:26).

The social behavior and living situation of the young Somalis residing in Kandahar was neither typical nor exceptional for the people I worked with. The diversity among consultants was tremendous. Shandy (2007) notes this same problem in trying to describe her typical Nuer consultant in the United States. Many consultants between the ages of eighteen and thirty-seven frequented nightclubs and, like the group at *Tiikeri*, some drank alcohol or chewed *qaad* while others strictly observed Islam's prohibition on alcohol and other intoxicants. A significant number of unmarried consultants lived separately from parents, immediate family, or other relatives, the result of a number of factors: absence of parents and close relatives who were deceased or living elsewhere, divorce, a choice to live independently from family, or expulsion from the family apartment. A few consultants who lived alone relished their privacy and personal space. Others lived with Somali friends, and a small number lived with Finns or other immigrants. Still other people I worked with lived in family households of five to twelve persons. Family households, like those in Kandahar, were in flux. Households in Somalia and in the diaspora adjust to the movement of family members and friends (Helander 1991; Tiilikainen and Robleh 1999). Temporary movements were associated with the arrival of newcomers, visitors from abroad, marital problems and divorce, traveling spouse, sickness, birth of a child, and intergenerational conflicts.[8] Although most municipal apartment housing is designed to accommodate small Finnish nuclear families, large Somali family households make do with the space by covering bedroom floors with twin-sized mattresses and utilizing sofas as beds.

Clothing choices varied widely among consultants and even within families. Some girls and women wore a *xijaab* (headscarf covering the hair and neck) or *jilbaab* (a head wrap worn with a long, loose hooded cape in a solid color falling from the head to the chest, waist, or knees and worn with a matching skirt or dress). Few women donned the *niqab* (a veil covering the face). Many of the women I worked with maintained that these Islamic-styled head coverings were not a part of Somali culture (see also Akou 2011). They claimed that only the *shaash*, a head wrap women wear to signify they are married, was traditional. Some women from the South wore a distinctive *shaash* made from silk "specially imported from India with a red and black pattern" (Luling 2002:68). Still other girls and women chose not to cover their hair and wore the same clothing styles as their Finnish counterparts. Some teens and twenty-somethings created their own trends by wearing tight ankle-length skirts with fitted long-sleeved tops paired with *xijaab* and high-heel wedge shoes. The clothing styles of boys and men were less distinctive. Notable exceptions were the *kufi*, a rimless cap, primarily visible on Fridays when men visited mosques, and *macawis*, a saronglike skirt that falls to the ankle, that older men wore at home with a button-down shirt. Luling (2002) notes that men commonly wore a variety of Somali and Western styles in different settings during her fieldwork in southern Somalia in the 1960s.

All the people I worked with identified as Muslims. As with any religion, their religious interpretations and everyday practices differed greatly. I recall one late cold winter evening when a female consultant drove me and a few other women in her minivan to a Somali party at Gloria, a music and theater venue in Helsinki's city center. As we drove near the venue we noticed small groups of men standing at each street corner near the venue's entrance. They sported lengthy beards and *kufi* and covered their long white *macawis* and flowing tunics with winter parkas. When the driver parked the car, she immediately locked the car doors. My fellow passengers seemed tense and laughed somewhat nervously as we waited until they felt confident to make their way past the men. The men were trying to dissuade others from entering the alcohol-free dance party. The women declared that the men's behavior was not a part of their culture. Before we could enter the party, a *sheekh* (learned man of Islam) stopped one of the women in our group and the two engaged in conversation for nearly half an hour. He lived near her family apartment and knew her family well. After we paid the twenty-euro entrance fee, we joined other partygoers from their late teens to early forties as they danced and sang along to the featured Somali singer from London.

## Dispersion and Collective Interests

I first met Dega in 2000 while I was conducting research for my master's thesis. At that time, I frequently visited the apartment where her mother and unmarried siblings lived. Although Dega did not live with her family, she occasionally spent a day or two at the family apartment. The space was crowded and afforded her little privacy. Dega could not come and go as she pleased and was expected to help with domestic duties: caring for younger siblings, nieces, and nephews, cooking, cleaning, and serving guests. Aside from my chance meetings with Dega, I had little contact with her.

Dega's mother disapproved of her unmarried daughter living independently, and she did not encourage me to meet her outside the family apartment. She considered Dega's move to Kandahar (as some other consultants did) as deviant because it challenged her notion of Somali family and gender norms. Unmarried boys and girls are expected to reside with parents or other elder relatives until marriage. Dating should be avoided and virginity before marriage was emphasized and expected of girls. Parents commonly expressed their concern that unmarried daughters risked a tarnished reputation that might affect their prospects for marriage. Surely sons encounter some risks even if parents vocalized less concern. I took note of two girls who lived independently from their parents for a few years and returned to their family households in 2003. Upon their return, they began to don the *xijaab,* and one of the girls started to attend mosque. Shortly thereafter, both girls married Somali men.

In 2015 Hanaan commented on her own experience of living separately from her family. She said, "Even though my parents know that I am trust-worthy and wouldn't do anything that is forbidden in my religion and culture, they are not happy or approve that I moved away at the age of 29. 'You are a girl and it will affect your marriage when you want to get mar-ried.' I am still close to them and still in the family. They still say that there is a room for me when I want to return home." Hanaan commented on the notion that living alone, especially for girls, is deviant and can damage a girl's reputation. She said, "It is still the same. I am independently living so I need to be quiet and not integrate with other Somalians my age. Not all Somalians know that I live alone. They still believe that I am living at home. I will not say until I am asked."

Visits from relatives and friends living abroad, rites of institution such as *aroos, ciid* (holy day, religious holiday), or the arrival of a new wedding or travel video prompted Dega to stop by and, in some cases, stay at the family apartment.[9] Family pressure to participate in these family occasions, the work of integration that uses and builds social capital among kin, also influenced her involvement. As Bourdieu (1998) notes, the family "is one of the key sites of the accumulation of capital in its different forms, and its transmission between the generations . . ., safeguard[ing] its unity for and through this transmission" (69). Bourdieu's thesis suggests that dispersion away from family households, key sites for reproduction of capital, places the family at risk. By extension, does such dispersion place the continual construction of clan at stake?

Because youth are regularly exposed to Finnish society at school, they tend to learn the Finnish language and culture faster than their parents (Alitolppa-Niitamo 2000; Alitolppa-Niitamo and Ali 2001; Tiilikainen and Robleh 1999). In this context, parents compete with Finnish schools, me-dia, and other institutions as agents of socialization (Alitolppa-Niitamo 2004:54). Through this socialization in Finland and relationships with Finns, immigrants, and other Somalis, youth learn about the freedoms and social benefits the Finnish welfare state offers.

The value placed on equality guides Finland's Nordic welfare model. Everyone is entitled to the same rights and responsibilities. This principle is embedded within the country's progressive tax system. The more a person earns, the larger a percentage of federal and municipal taxes the person pays. Even fines for speeding tickets follow a progressive system.

Tax revenues support society and public services in a plethora of ways, such as free healthcare and education, efficient public transportation, child benefits, maternity and paternity leaves and allowances, unemployment allowances, and housing benefits. In 1906 Finland's Parliament was the first in Europe to grant women the right to vote and the first in the world to give women the right to hold office.

Finland's historical commitment to gender equality continues today and manifests itself in daily life. Women hold many high-ranking positions in education, industry, and politics. Mothers and fathers commonly take paid leave from work after the birth of a child. Single mothers and fathers can live comfortably with benefits from the state. Gender equality extends to dating practices. Finns prefer to pay their own way on dates. The practice is so common that there is not a particular Finnish word or phrase for the English phrase "going Dutch."[10] Many consultants witnessed the election of the country's first female president in 2002. President Tarja Halonen was elected for two consecutive terms and held office from 2000 to 2012. In 2015 Hanaan commented on the political aims of a local Somali woman. She said, "A woman in Finland is running for president of Somalia." The woman's bid for the country's first female president has earned her media coverage in BBC News, *the Harvard Gazette*, the *Boston Globe*, the *Marie Claire* fashion magazine, and various Somali online news sites.

Dega's move away from her family's household was not exceptional. It had become increasingly typical of her generation. My interviews and tracing of social networks provide ample evidence for this. About half the consultants who had never been married lived apart from parents or older relatives. Nearly two-thirds of them were boys. Young, unmarried Somalis utilize their Finnish cultural competence to live on their own or with friends. By Finnish cultural competence, I mean knowledge of the social welfare system and the ideas of autonomy and gender equality. From the age of seventeen, Somalis and other permanent residents studying in Finland are eligible to receive their own monthly housing allowance. Nonstudents qualify for a monthly housing allowance at the age of eighteen (KELA 2013). In 2015 Hanaan commented on this trend among younger Somalis. She said, "Quite the same. Few girls live away from families. Mostly boys."

Dega's mother felt also her living apart was deviant because it challenged the notion that families collectively share responsibility for property and substance (Helander 1991:21). In Al-Sharmani's (2004) terms, Somalis in Cairo live as interdependent transnational families, that is, "making collective decisions about who lives with whom and where, relatives across nation-states share the burdens of securing livelihood, the rearing of children and younger siblings, and providing care for elderly and the invalid in the family" (154). With her move, Dega gained financial independence, keeping all earnings from her cleaning job. In contrast, siblings residing at the family apartment contributed their income to the household. Dega's individual interests did not conform to those of her family. Dega defied Somali family norms by ignoring transnational economic obligations such as sending the remittances that cultivate dispersed networks.

Dega's mother managed the household's pooled resources from salaries along with monthly allowances and child benefits. In addition to receiving housing benefits for low-income persons and unemployment allowances, Dega's mother received child benefits. Monthly child benefits are paid from birth until a child's seventeenth birthday. Child benefits are proportional to the number of children in a family and therefore can be significant for large families. It is important to note here that a number of people I worked with did not plan to have large families. They felt that raising children in Finland was expensive and difficult especially for those without extended family members nearby. Childcare subsidies support home care, municipal daycare, and private daycare for children until they begin school at seven years of age. In addition to using these monies to cover household expenses, Dega's mother regularly sent funds to assist kin elsewhere, in particular to those residing in Somalia.

In 2015 Hanaan commented on the tradition of children providing financial support to parents. She said, "Majority of people in Somalia have big families—guarantees you have more of a pension in older age especially when you don't have an official pension system. So when we move to Europe people who are my age and even younger as well continue the same habit that was back home to this day: helping parents financially. Even though us older kids live by themselves or having their own kids. We all tend to support our parents monthly." Hanaan commented on how this financial obligation sets her apart from her friends. She said, "It happened to me many times when I am in a group of friends that decides to take a trip together. I say that I am not able to join because I support financially my parents. For them it's weird because already at the age of eighteen they are independent. That support comes from the parents not the kids to parents. After several years of friendship, they now understand and they accept it." Hanaan described her friends as multicultural. She said, "My friends are quite international friends. Through my work and studies I have gained a lot of friends around the world, but my closest friends are Finns because I went to school with them. I have friends from Poland, Norway, Nigeria, Russia, [and] Estonia. As noted earlier, Hanaan lives separately from her family. It is interesting that Hanaan continues to honor her family financial obligations in spite of her independent living situation. Perhaps this is one reason that she was "still close to them and still in the family." Besides, she was thirty years old, completed her bachelor's degree, and held a good job. This was not the typical situation for those living at Kandahar.

The practice of sending remittances is widespread in diasporas. For Somalis it plays a critical role in sustaining life in the Horn of Africa and dispersed social networks. Remittances sent from relatives abroad are indispensable for those facing everyday insecurity in places like the Dadaab refugee camp in Kenya (Horst 2006). Some consultants were apprehensive about discussing remittances with me because critics cite refugees and immigrants as strains on the welfare state. As one man said, "You are not Finnish. I can tell you. Yes, I send money." Somali refugees in Dadaab refugee camp displayed a similar suspicion and hesitance about questions on receiving remittances because they feared their already meager resources could be cut (Horst 2006:28–29).

Most consultants reported sending remittances to spouses and close relatives.[11] Fewer mentioned that they sent funds to clan relatives. Even if they send money directly to close relatives, consultants realized that some of the funds would be shared with more distant relatives, including clan relatives. For example, in Somaliland, "the regular mobilisation of transfers for collective purposes and the recirculation of remittances through local networks and clan economies" are evident (Lindley 2010:141). These monies help pay for daily necessities, weddings, medical care, education, compensation, travel, business ventures, and migration, legal or otherwise, to join family members in Finland or to move to other choice destinations in Africa, Europe, North America, and Islamic countries. Another result of these transfers is maintenance of clan networks. "Many Somalis would be shamed if they did not support their relatives: one survey respondent [in London] said he would be 'struck off the family list'" (Lindley 2009:49). Besides remitting to networks in Somalia, consultants also sent funds to other countries in the Horn, the Middle East, Gulf States, and the Arabian Peninsula. When consultants stated where they sent remittances in Somalia, some named telling places instead of simply stating Somalia. Remittances were sent informally through *xawilaad*, a global Somali transfer system or by phone, or through formal wiring services such as Western Union.[12] Some of the people I worked with sent money at regular monthly intervals and others sent money occasionally or only during critical moments of need.

Dega's move is one instance of movement at the everyday local level and is illuminating for Somalis' movements on both small and large scales. Movement of young Somalis away from family households as well as global scattering of individuals and families challenges transmission of social capital, which threatens clan unity and exchanges of capital in all its forms. This example at the individual level is informative for more general cases. Like Dega, scattered Somalis waver between individual interests and collective family interests. Like Dega, unmarried consultants who moved away from family households did not remit funds. That behavior differs from that of the vast majority of consultants I surveyed.[13]

Al-Sharmani (2004) notes, "although maintaining interdependent transnational families is crucial for the survival of family members, it has its tensions and challenges because of the competing interests and dreams of individual members" (151). Research among Somalis in London and Minneapolis reveals the financial strain of remittances for senders and how these obligations influence and often limit their employment and education choices (Horst 2006; Lindley 2009, 2010). The pressure of sending money to family members in need is cause for marital strife (Lindley 2009, 2010). One married couple I worked with explained that because they affiliate with politically unaligned clans, each set of relatives accused them of sending more funds to the other spouse's family. Although the couple claimed these allegations did not strain their marriage, it created tension between each spouse and the spouse's family. Each spouse's family viewed any support of the other in-laws as support for a rival clan. In addition to sending money to close relatives, Somalis in London contribute to *qaaraan* (clan assistance) "for individuals and social projects in their hometown" (Lindley 2009:47). Somalis in Dadaab refugee camp contributing to *qaaraan* related this practice to *sako* (*zakat* in Arabic), the Islamic requirement to give alms (Horst 2006:103–4).[14]

It is important to note here that most of Dega's immediate family resided in Finland. Hence, it is probable that comparable families are in a favorable position to build and maintain social capital with more distant kin through transfers of economic capital. They conceivably had fewer problems making ends meet than their counterparts in London and Minneapolis without the safety net of the Finnish welfare state. Still, some consultants shared their difficulty in providing for themselves and their family in Finland. Helsinki is one of the most expensive capital cities in Europe. Only twenty-seven consultants, 15 percent, reportedly received funds from abroad. Most funds came occasionally from close relatives, including siblings and parents, for an *aroos* or at times of need. Others received funds from a spouse or fiancé and, less commonly, from more distant relatives such as cousins and unrelated friends.

Movement to places like Kandahar pit unmarried Somalis' individual interests against collective family interests. By collective family interests, I mean strategies that integrate family members and build and transform various forms of capital among local and dispersed kin. An arduous challenge of diaspora is integration of kin and unity of collective interests when kin live in various host societies where they attend school, go to work, form relationships, and, in some cases, marry outside their community. When young Somalis are primarily socialized in Finland and live separately from family households, integrating and solidifying collective interests presents an ostensible challenge.

## Liminality and Reproduction: Kinship as Usual?

It was a cold, dark weekday evening in December when I visited Amina, who lived in the building across the courtyard from Dega. I called Amina on my mobile phone from outside her building to let her know that I arrived. As we spoke, she shouted to me from her apartment window and threw a key to open the building's main door. Once inside, I noticed that both Somali and Finnish names were common on the occupant list posted near the stairwell. I walked up the stairway toward the apartment and rang the doorbell. Moments later, Nuura, Amina's roommate, opened the door. Nuura was dressed in a long-sleeved knit shirt, ankle-length denim skirt, and a *xijaab* of silk magenta with golden threads. She led me to Amina's bedroom, where Amina was sitting at her computer. Amina was not wearing a *xijaab* or a long skirt. She wore jeans and a long-sleeved top. Like Dega, Amina agreed to introduce me to other Somalis living at the same complex.

Soon after I arrived, Amina knocked at her neighbors' door to invite them over to take my survey. But the neighbor boys and their friends were on their way out for the evening. I recognized a few from weddings and discos. A few agreed to participate in the survey another time, but most turned me down flat. Sometime later, Mohamed, Nuura's boyfriend, arrived. He joined us in Amina's bedroom and agreed to the survey. Before we finished, Mukhtar, another boy, arrived. As had occurred in Dega's apartment, there was an informal candidness among the boys and girls. Awhile later, Xabibo, a young married woman arrived. She wore *xijaab* and clothing similar to Nuura's. Xabibo walked around the room to greet everyone individually. When my turn came, she imparted a curt *hei* (hello in Finnish). Then she headed straight toward Amina's computer and opened Paltalk. Paltalk is a free videochat service that features audio and visual communication, instant messaging, and file sharing. As Xabibo chatted with a man in Toronto in

Somali, the others in the room erupted into laughter. Oblivious to anything funny, I asked, "Why is everyone laughing?" Amina answered, "All people make fun of Abgaal." "Why?" I asked. Amina said, "Their language. People don't know [that] clans have their own language dialect."

After the laughter subsided and Xabibo ended her online socializing, she sat down next to me on Amina's bed. Xabibo was under the impression that I was Finnish until Amina explained who I was. Once Xabibo knew I was American and not Finnish, she warmed up to me and agreed to take the survey. She exclaimed, "All Finns are racist!" Xabibo, who lived outside the complex, interacted with Finns when necessary: at her cleaning job and while shopping. I gave her a copy of the informed consent form. As Amina looked it over, she read Abdi M. Kusow's name aloud. I explained that Kusow was a Somali professor on my doctoral committee in the United States. Then Mohamed, Nuura's boyfriend, asked me whether I knew the meaning of Kusow. "Round, like a ball," I answered. I met a few men who had the nickname of *kusow*. In most cases, the nickname *kusow* was given to them as children to denote their round or stout physique. Mohamed smiled, confirming my answer. "Abgaal?" Xabibo inquired. "Why does everyone think that he is Abgaal?" I asked. I got this response a lot when Somalis read the informed consent form. Amina explained that it is because of the "ow" ending in Kusow, and she offered the following examples: Stephanow (instead of Stephanie), Aminow (instead of Amina), and Marko (a common Finnish male name). Then Amina asked, "Is Kusow Abgaal?" "No," I replied. "Hawiye?" Xabibo asked. "No," I replied. "Daarood?" Mukhtar asked. "No. He is from Baydhabo," I said. "Oh, Raxanweyn," Amina said. "Yes," I confirmed. The group looked surprised.

In a seemingly liminal space such as Kandahar, where young Somalis are physically separated from family households, these individuals formed personal relationships irrespective of clan affiliation. They also tended to interact more frequently with Finns and other immigrants on a personal level than most other consultants. This space may be particularly conducive for young Somalis to question rights and obligations toward family and clan alongside ideas of autonomy and equality. Despite the noted freedoms associated with Kandahar, tenants and visitors could not escape telling. The tension between individuality and clan affiliation and associated status claims is underscored in the everyday mixed-clan setting just recounted. As among the English working-class boys in Paul Willis's (1977) classic work *Learning to Labour*, these young Somalis continue to socially construct boundaries of clan and clan status despite exposure to an opposing ideology, here ideas of autonomy and equality.

Xabibo sat only a few feet away from the others in the small bedroom, barely acknowledging the laughter or disparaging remarks as she chatted with a male relative on Paltalk. I observed similar friendly posturing and jockeying in other mixed-clan settings. Xabibo and her male relative displayed their clan competency by using a common dialect. Xabibo's use of the Abgaal dialect is indicative of her personal investment in her clan's cultural capital, which is critical in telling, and creating a clan feeling without face-to-face interaction. This skill is fundamental in perpetuating clan distinction.

When Xabibo read Professor Kusow's name, it triggered a lively exchange in which the group tried to decipher Kusow's affiliation by using their various degrees of clan competence. All were born in Somalia, but most emigrated from the country at a young age (ages five, seven, eight, ten, nine, and twenty). Only one departed Somalia and entered Finland in the same year. The others spent a number of years waiting with relatives in places like Kenya, Ethiopia, Syria, and Russia to secure passage to Finland or another Western country.[15]

Interest in Professor Kusow's clan affiliation was certainly common. Almost every individual who read my informed consent form inquired about that affiliation. A handful of consultants were personally familiar with Kusow and a few had read his work on the Somali diaspora. In some of these works, he identifies his clan. In most cases—as the foregoing example illustrates—consultants mistakenly identified Kusow's clan as Abgaal, a clan of the Hawiye clan family. My use of Baydhabo, a telling place, pointed to the Digil Mirifle clan family and tested the group's knowledge of an unrelated group. Perhaps Xabibo's focus on Kusow was a tactic to associate her and her clan with his acquired status and cultural capital in the form of a U.S. doctorate and professorship.

Many consultants were surprised to learn that a Somali achieved this status. The age, social class, and educational level of consultants partly explain their reactions. During fieldwork, I observed consultants using the title *doktoor* (Somali for doctor) for the few persons holding a bachelor or master's degree. Most were older adults who obtained university degrees in Italy and France. At the time, there was only one Somali man that I knew of pursuing a master's degree in Finland. There were no Somali professors, which was still the case in 2015. As mentioned in the previous chapter, the number studying at Finnish universities has increased considerably since my fieldwork period. Only one Somali has obtained a doctorate at a Finnish university. The SSIA has held two congresses in Finland: 1998 and 2015. The congresses certainly helped to increase familiarity with Somali academicians holding prestigious professorships around the world in places like Canada, the United States, Denmark, Sweden, England, Italy, Australia, Somalia, and Qatar. Many Somalis follow their work, and visiting scholars often meet with the larger Somali community during conferences.

During surveys, Amina, her roommate Nuura, and the four visitors self-identified in the following ways: Abgaal; two as Daarood; Ogaadeen; and two as Isaaq. The three consultants who affiliated with the Daarood clan family used strategies to make known the divisions among them. After Amina, a twenty-one-year-old girl, self-identified as Daarood; Aweys, a twenty-two-year-old boy, self-identified as Ogaadeen, a clan of the Daarood clan family. Then, when I asked Mukhtar where he was born, he said, "We are from Bosaaso, but we lived in Mogadishu." Moments later, he tagged "Puntland" onto his response. Bosaaso is a port city on the Red Sea in northeastern Somalia. Since 1998, this northeast region has been a part of the self-declared autonomous Puntland State of Somalia. A Harti clan federation (a division of the Daarood clan family) composed of the Majeerteen, Dhulbhante, and Warsangeeli clans established Puntland in 1998 (Hoehne 2006).[16]

It is likely that Amina's home internet access made her apartment a popular destination for young Somalis. Many family households I visited had internet connections, but few young consultants had such connections. Those without home access used their friend's or family's internet during household visits or made use of Finland's rich technological environment. Free internet was readily available at schools, public libraries, internet cafés, and kiosks. When I visited the Cable Book Library near the central railway station, I routinely observed men wearing headphones and sitting at computers listening to BBC Somali and checking Web sites for political developments in Somalia.[17]

The people I worked with used the internet for many of the same reasons as other migrants and dispersed groups: identity politics (Trandafoiu 2013); cybernationalism (Bernal 2004, 2005); cosmopolitan connections (Christensen 2012); belonging and identity exploration (Mainsah 2014); leisure, politics, romance, and other strategic dealings (Miller and Slater 2000), and maintaining connections with dispersed friends and family (Al-Sharmani 2004). It is an affordable way for dispersed family members to "exchange their news, have discussions, resolve conflicts, and make or influence decisions about use of family resources" (Al-Sharmani 2004:151). In this way, the internet becomes not only a global space where families and clan relatives meet to make collective decisions about allocation and use of family capital, but also a space to identify sites for accumulation and transformation of capital in its various forms.

Paltalk was the most frequented site where the people I worked with met for real-time interaction. Somalinet.com and MSN messenger also were popular Somali discussion sites. Still, not all consultants used Paltalk. Some thought such practices were a waste of time and pointed to its addictive effects. A few men and women were rumored to spend up to ten hours a day on Paltalk. Some chat rooms were organized into broad topics such as Islam, parenting, music, gender, or particular communities such as for Somalis in London whereas other chat rooms linked to clans (e.g., Qolka Dhalinta Reer ia La Bashalal No Cay [Ogadenia youth chat room—have fun no insults], Djibouti Qolka Kala Danbaynta Raga Iyo Dumarka [Djibouti chat room where women defer to men], and Somaliland My Home Sweet Home.[18] Some consultants I observed chose to frequent clan-related chat rooms and others preferred chat rooms for Somalis with distinctive tastes, such as for Arabic- or French-speaking Somalis.

Even though consultants could interact online without constraints of clan, they used Paltalk's various communicative features to tell clan in ways similar to those used in face-to-face interactions. Consultants used Paltalk's audio feature to tell clan through clan dialect or another language that kin typically shared. Djibouti Somalis may speak or write in French during real-time interaction in an effort to maintain distinction. At the same time, their use of French cultivates likeness among individuals from other clans who have ties to Djibouti. Illiterate Somalis and those with limited writing proficiency can use the audio option. Web cams offer another performative dimension to online telling: gestures, physical appearance, and dress. Instant messaging allows interlocutors to display clan dialect or local terminology. Some young Somalis—particularly those limited in reading and writing the Somali language—preferred chatting in another language, usually English, French, or Arabic. Those educated in Finland might chat and write in Finnish. File sharing of distinctive photos, Somali *heeso* (songs), and video clips are other telling strategies.

As with telling in person, online telling is open to obfuscation. Telling is ambiguous because it is based on a mixture of myth and reality. Variance in social transmission of clan competence and personal investment in such cultural capital obscures telling. And anyone can enter chat rooms and mask her or his clan. Because social networks tend to link groups of individuals with clans, the rooms that individuals enter tend to reveal clan affiliation.

During interactions, consultants used screen names to protect their identity. Kandahar residents and visitors were no exception. Individual anonymity is deemed essential because online chatting is not considered socially acceptable, especially for women. The internet offered great autonomy, especially for individuals like Xabibo who lived in a family household. At Amina's apartment, she engaged in online connections without the knowledge of her family. At the family apartment of a divorced woman and her children, large groups of women congregated after evening Finnish classes to use Paltalk or observe others using Paltalk without the knowledge of their spouses or families. For Turkish women in Stockholm, the internet presents new spaces of belonging free of social pressure and monitoring (Christensen 2012:899–900).

Another tactic consultants employed to reveal clan more explicitly was to use telling screen names; that is, the strategic use of word(s) to denote clan affiliation (place, region, distinctive term, and so forth). For example, screen names such as Xaayow or Queen Djibouti point to particular clans. Telling screen names are amplified efforts at distinction in the diaspora, and several of the unmarried female consultants employed this tactic. It is plausible that these consultants self-identified by clan because affairs online may result in marriage and relocation.[19] It is important to note that in one case, I noticed a girl using a screen name telling of her mother's paternal clan rather than her own paternal clan. Perhaps the girl utilized more than one screen name or felt more affinity toward her mother's paternal clan. She might consider her mother's clan to be more prestigious or useful than her own. I did not observe unmarried boys when they chatted online, however it is possible that they, too, used telling screen names. The internet presents Somalis with a unique opportunity to maneuver freely among Somalis around the world, and online interactions present young Somalis with yet another liminal space to question clan membership alongside individuality and equality and to imagine other possibilities. Although the internet offers them a chance to interact without restraints of clan, they tend to tell clan. Through telling, Somalis use and develop clan competence. Even though telling constrains individuality, young Somalis recognized clan as a useful resource. Clan networks can open up new possibilities for marriage, movement, and exchange of capital.

In 2015 Hanaan commented on changes in access to technology and use of social media. She said, "Now everyone has a smartphone, more laptops, tablets, and computers instead of TV. They are less at libraries. Now [they are] at home." In regard to social media, she said, "The social media has changed. A lot of people communicate through Facebook, Viber, and Skype." These social networking platforms can be used on smartphones, tablets, and computers. Mohamed added that WhatsApp is popular. WhatsApp is a messaging app for smartphones. According to Nafiso, some people form their own groups on Facebook, and she notes that it is becoming an important space for Somalis to meet their future spouses. Some of my friends who participated in my research regularly use Instagram. Instagram is another social networking app. Its users edit and share photos with friends and interested followers.

## Journeying within Clan Networks

Somalis are modern refugees whose movement is driven by resettlement expectations and channeled through social networks (Kusow 1998; see also Abdi 2015). Instead of waiting in refugee camps for a chance to resettle in the West, they strategically make use of their own networks to devise paths to Western countries (Kusow 1998:124–125). Their strategy is not surprising when one realizes that less than one percent of the world's refugees find resettlement in a third country (UNHCR 2016). There were 19.5 million refugees worldwide at the end of 2014, an increase from 16.7 million in 2013 (UNHCR 2015). In most cases, irrespective of the location from which consultants departed, immediate and extended kin helped finance and assist with their migration. Mothers, aunts, grandmothers, and sisters sold their *dahab* (gold jewelry) and male relatives offered cash for consultants' migration. Relatives imparted critical information for the journey.

The mass exodus of Somalis in the late 1980s and early 1990s is unprecedented in Somalia's history in both scope and scale, but movement of Somalis away from the country was widespread even before the civil war. The country's colonial linkages with England, Italy, and France (in Djibouti) served as pathways for work and study in those countries. Some of the older people I worked with were students at Italian universities and a few younger consultants reported that their parents had studied in Italy or France. In the mid-1960s, the oil industries in Saudi Arabia and the Gulf States began to draw migrant workers (Lewis 2008:57). A number of consultants were born or raised in the former colonial countries. Others were also born outside Somalia: in Yemen; the bordering countries of Djibouti, Ethiopia, and Kenya; and Russia. President Siyad Barre's close relationship with the former Soviet Union facilitated scholarships for a few consultants to attend Russian universities. In the 1980s, a number of Somalis settled in Canada and the United States for educational opportunities. Many of these migrants provided information and resources for others' movement (Horst 2006:145).

Some of the people I worked with strategically used marriage to move to Finland, a safe and desirable location, where they could improve their life chances and those of their families. It was not unusual for individuals to marry kin to facilitate their legal entry to Finland. Several women I worked with had arranged marriages with clan relatives soon after the outbreak of the civil war. Marriages arranged through clan networks offered a swift passage out of the Horn and other transit countries to the West. In some cases, marriage was clearly a strategy to position individuals in a Nordic welfare state in pursuit of family interests to strengthen kin ties, send remittances, and initiate family reunification.[20] The Finnish education system, ranked number one in the world, is another draw.

Some female consultants who married for the prospect of migration mentioned that under different circumstances, they would not have entered into arranged marriages with close clan relatives. Parents and other family members pressured them to marry for their own safety and the welfare of their family. Men likely experienced similar pressure to marry. The women did not specify whether they married a parallel cousin or more distant clan relative. What they did make clear was that if not for the civil war, they would have had more autonomy in their decision of when they married and whom they married. In chapter 4, I discuss tensions between individual choice and family interests in regard to spousal choice and how and why marriage patterns are changing. Some arranged marriages did not last long. A few married again within their clan and the others chose to remarry outside their clan and community.

Somalis in Finland and in other Nordic welfare states are in a favorable position to build and maintain social capital among kin. Because their basic needs are met by the state, they are overwhelmingly remittance senders rather than recipients of funds from abroad. This flow of economic capital through clan networks solidifies collective interests and reaffirms rights and obligations among kin. Remittances are critical for persons whose basic needs are not provided by the state and whose life chances are few. In addition to aiding daily survival, Somalis use remittances for migration to the West, both legal and otherwise.

Warsame, a man in his twenties, had recently been "carried" to Finland from East Africa when I first met him 2003. By carried, I mean illegal migration via a carrier. A carrier is an entrepreneur working in the global Somali informal economy, and the carrier transports people across nation-states (Farah 2000:77–85). By necessity, a carrier's social network spans the globe. Carrying is financially and legally risky for both carriers and clients, but the practice is a viable option for persons without legal means to migrate.

Warsame pointed to the considerable price his family paid for him to be carried. He said, "My mother and brother paid five thousand euro[s] to send me to Finland. It's a lot [of money] for [in] Somalia." In this example, social capital is converted into economic capital and political asylum, a form of cultural capital in its institutionalized state. When Warsame's family in Somalia and elsewhere sent him to Finland, they invested in his future, and by extension, their own. From Finland, Warsame sent monthly remittances to his mother. Perhaps in the future Warsame's mother, siblings, or a new bride from his clan or his mother's clan may join him in Finland through family reunification or because of family ties. It is important to note that during my interview with Warsame he stated, "I had everything there [in Somalia]. I could do whatever I liked." He missed his family living there and the ease with which he navigated daily life. In Finland he struggled with learning Finnish, obtaining an education, gaining employment, and coping with Finnish winters and xenophobia. Warsame was the victim of the attack near Kandahar mentioned earlier in this chapter. Other young Somalis in their twenties who had immigrated to Finland much earlier than Warsame often called him "Fresh" in English. Fresh carried the same connotation as FOB.

Finland's social welfare policies encourage Somalis' movement and global networking. Residents also are free to spend considerable periods of time outside Finland. In order to receive social security benefits, individuals must maintain a primary home and residence in Finland and spend most of their time in the country (KELA 2013). Reduced rates on domestic and international travel are available for children and other full-time students. Travel is more restricted for persons without Finnish citizenship. Those individuals can apply for an alien's passport or refugee travel document in place of a national passport to travel to and from Finland "provided they contain no remarks indicating unverified identity" (Directorate of Immigration 2006:1).

At times, a few consultants' frequent and, in some cases, prolonged travel to other diaspora communities and to the Horn impeded my research, especially my goal to survey 300 consultants. Ease and frequency of travel is significant for maintaining dispersed social capital. More than half the consultants cited travel and sharing photographs, second only to phone calls, as practices they use to maintain social networks with friends and family living abroad.[21] Survey data indicate that 43 consultants, 23 percent, had traveled to Somalia; 33 of them made that trip only once. Besides mentioning visiting relatives as motivation for their trip, a few noted other reasons: owning a home, paying respect to a parent after the other parent's death, circumcising a son, and marrying a mother's paternal clan relative. Most of the people I worked with, 138, or 74 percent, had not traveled to Somalia. Five of them had plans to travel there in the immediate future and a few stated they had no interest to ever travel to Somalia. Five consultants did not respond to the question.

In 2015 Nafiso noted that the number of Somalis traveling to Somalia has increased significantly since 2011. That year, Turkish Airlines added a direct flight from Istanbul to Mogadishu. Before that time, there were no direct flights to Somalia from Europe. Hanaan mentioned other reasons for the increase in travel. She said, "The older ones and a lot of people doing development and health projects in Somalia. The older ones travel to Somalia to spend several months at a time [there]."

Clan networks, formed and maintained in the diaspora, are channels through which many commodities sold in the Somali informal economy move. When Fatima, a woman in her mid-thirties, traveled at least once a year to the Middle East to visit her relatives, she purchased goods for her own consumption and for resale or rental to other Somalis in Finland. Fatima's primary clientele were her paternal clan relatives and those of her mother's clan. In purely economic terms, Fatima profited little from these transactions. Any profits offset some of her travel expenses. Fatima's travel and economic activities offered some relief from her daily routine as a wife and mother of a large family. A notable profit is that her travel and informal economic activities build and maintain clan-based social capital at home and abroad. And many of the goods that she sells enable others to perform clan distinction through distinctive lifestyle choices.

Like other consultants who traveled to and from Finland, Fatima tended to move by way of clan networks. Consultants commonly said, "Somalis never stay at hotels," meaning that wherever Somalis travel, clan relatives would likely put them up. Journeying within clan networks is a socially acceptable way for unaccompanied women to travel long distances. Raxima, a woman in her late forties, reported that "In the [19]50s, women started to be traders. Before, it was only men. Now some religious men do not like women to be traders and [to be] traveling, but they [women] still do it." Lodging with relatives protects women and their kin against salacious gossip that could otherwise tarnish the women's and their family's reputation.

Even Somalis with minimal contact with Finnish society recognized freedoms the Finnish welfare state offered them. As Somali youth used their Finnish cultural competence to live independently from family households, other Somalis used their knowledge of the Finnish social welfare system to maneuver in the Somali diaspora. In some cases, this competency supported lifestyles otherwise unattainable. Some Somalis in Finland used travel as a strategy to expedite family reunification procedures and engage in plural marriage. [22] Hautaniemi (2007) describes the family reunification case of a Somali woman who filed a family reunification petition for her husband residing in the Horn. As she waited for a decision, the woman traveled to the Horn to visit her husband, and she was pregnant when she returned to Finland. Then she reapplied for family reunification. I am aware of similar cases (and, possibly, the same case described by Hautaniemi) in which female consultants traveled to visit their husbands and returned to Finland pregnant.

Although polygyny (a man married to more than one woman) was and continues to be fairly common in Somalia (Lewis 1962; Markus Hoehne, personal communication, November 10, 2012), I was aware of only a few men in Finland with a local wife and other wives dispersed in various nation-states. These husbands maintained their polygynous marriages through regular, prolonged travel. Female consultants often claimed that they disapproved of these marriages. Plural marriages, like clan, were culturally intimate. Finland's state-sponsored marriage is monogamy. Islam permits men to marry up to four wives if they are able to give each wife equal financial support and treatment. One female consultant told me that her neighbor's husband had three wives living in different countries. She said, "He is always traveling. This is not Islam. He uses social welfare to have three wives. This is no good." As mentioned earlier, prior to the civil war in Somalia, plural marriage was most common among older men with status or wealth (Lewis 1994:29).

## Dispersion, Integration, and Clan

Movement of Somalis to Finland presents new possibilities. A number of those who arrived in Finland as adults in the early to mid-1990s quickly embraced a Finnish lifestyle. These women and men made use of opportunities available to them: classes in the Finnish language, higher education, work training programs, multicultural centers, and so forth. Few Somalis take full advantage of these opportunities.

During an in-depth interview with Shukri, who was an exception, I asked about her interactions with other Somalis in the early 1990s when she lived in a Finnish refugee center.

> AUTHOR: Did they ask you about your clan?
> SHUKRI: They didn't say. But I was going to school to learn [the] Finnish language, to town, to disco. I made myself Finnish friends and went out from them [stayed away from other Somalis]. I just came to sleep. I did not depend on them for anything. They were always talking clan, and they lost a lot of time to these things.

Shukri immersed herself in Finnish society, made her own decisions, and formed relationships with Finns. Shukri did not preoccupy herself with clan politics. She worried about the welfare of her parents, other family members, and friends engulfed by Somalia's civil war, as did the other people I worked with. Perhaps Shukri's inclination to welcome new opportunities can be explained by her clan's small presence in Finland. Assuming this reading, she was self-reliant because she had little potential access to local clan networks. Yet I observed some individuals across clans, including those affiliated with the two largest clans in Finland, integrated into Finnish society. Shukri and a few others who eagerly embraced a Finnish lifestyle and enjoyed individual success during the fieldwork period did not experience the atrocities of the civil war firsthand or to the extent that others did. Some had already lived outside Somalia when the war broke out and others fled the country before the country's collapse or at least early on in the conflict.

These exceptional individuals, like Somali youth who lived separate from family households, stood out from the majority of Somalis, who were unemployed and had little contact with Finnish society. They tended to form social networks with Finns and other groups. In some cases, they dated, married, or cohabited with Finns or other foreigners. Some of the women dressed in Western clothing. At times, they were spokespersons for the Somali community on Finnish radio and television, and their success was reported on Somali Web sites.

On occasion, clan relatives pressured such individuals to resist a Finnish lifestyle. Lul, a woman in her thirties, told me that some of her male clan relatives came to her home and told her to wear a *xijaab*, leave the Finnish boyfriend she lived with, and marry a Somali man. When Lul recounted the incident, she was noticeably upset. The actions of her male relatives compromised Lul's independence. Because of that, she found relationships with them to be problematic. Lul said, "It's difficult with Somalis because they always want something—borrow your clothes, shoes, or money. Be careful because Somalis will try to take advantage of you." Lul felt that other Somalis acted inappropriately when they asked to borrow her personal belongings. Lul cautioned me against becoming too personal with other Somalis because they might try to use me as they have her.

Shukri voiced similar feelings:

> I just don't have time for all the visiting and gossiping. Women go from house to house and just talk. They don't do anything. I am studying. I work. I am a mother. I don't have time for this and don't want to be involved. For Somalis here it's clan, but for Finns, we are Somalis.

Shukri gave precedence to her roles in Finnish society as a student and a working mother and dismissed those spending time "visiting and gossiping." Furthermore, Shukri objected to other Somalis wasting time on clan politics instead of using that time for their own personal development (studying or working).

On several occasions, I observed Shukri ignoring knocks at her apartment door in an effort to avoid unwanted interaction with other Somalis. Although Shukri helped Somalis with various everyday tasks, she did not allow them to monopolize her time. Shukri gave priority to her individual roles and aspirations. Still, at times, clan ties challenged her autonomy. In 2015 Nafiso commented on the idea that other Somalis limit her individuality. She said, "Yes, I think that is true."

When I visited a multicultural center, I met Qassim, who had just arrived in Finland a few years earlier. When I surveyed Qassim, he told me about his work in Somalia and the difficulties he faced securing employment in Finland. Because Shukri was familiar with Qassim's line of work and she was knowledgeable about Finnish society, I suggested that the two should meet. Qassim expressed his interest in meeting with Shukri, but he did not know how to arrange it. I assured him that I could arrange such a meeting. Qassim looked at me doubtfully and said, "Somalis don't help each other."

That evening, I phoned Shukri and I told her about Qassim in the hope of introducing them:

SHUKRI: Who is he?
AUTHOR: Qassim Mohamed.
SHUKRI: What is his clan?
AUTHOR: I don't know.
SHUKRI: So, he wants me to get him a job? I got my job.

Regrettably, I called Qassim the next day to tell him that Shukri did not have time to meet him. Why did Shukri inquire about Qassim's clan affiliation? It is likely that she already knew he was not a clan relative. If he were a clan relative he would have known how to contact her, and she would have probably already met him. How could this information sway her decision to meet him? As noted throughout this book, many consultants have friendships with persons across clans. Perhaps Shukri could be swayed to help a nonrelative affiliated with a clan of a close friend, neighbor, classmate, or coworker.

Success in Finnish society or the Finnish formal sector results from an individual's concerted effort and entails a certain finesse with the Finnish lifestyle. I asked Mohamed, who works in information technology, to tell me how he obtained a job.

AUTHOR: Can you tell me about your experience finding work in
Finland?

MOHAMED: There's a lot to say about here. A lot to say! You have
to do everything by yourself. It's not easy.

AUTHOR: What's different?

MOHAMED: If you are a foreigner here and you don't have a social
network, it's not easy to get friends or to get a job. As you know,
it's not enough to apply [for] a job on the internet or [at the]
labor office because the employer wants to know if you are a
trustful [trustworthy] person. I don't know if it's easy, but you
need to have a reference, a Finnish person. It would be better if
the employer knows the reference. It's like a social network.

Finland's ethos of integration emphasizes the role of individuals in becoming
a working member of society (Alitolppa-Niitamo 2001). Such integration
requires individual efforts: Finnish language acquisition; knowledge of Finnish society and culture; education and job training; and contact with Finns
(Sorainen 2003). Although Mohamed met such requirements, he considered
his social networks with Finns to be *the reason* for his current position.
Engaging social networks was problematic for some of the people I worked
with because a number of them had little contact with Finnish society, and
few had personal relationships with Finns. Nearly half the consultants were
unemployed. Most of the people I worked with could not find work for lack
of education and Finnish language skills (three were illiterate in Somali). It
is important to note here that those who identified as unemployed included
thirty-three housewives, some with young children, fourteen students, seven
working in the informal economy (videographer, tailor, two henna artists,
computer repairer, *qaad* seller, and clothing and jewelry seller), and one
pensioner. Some consultants working in the Finnish formal sector were employed in the following jobs: daycare worker, practical nurse, teacher aide,
engineer, computer technology, translator, security, bus driver, Somali language teacher, social worker, and janitor. One notable transformation is men
holding cleaning positions because cleaning is typically considered women's
work in Somali culture. A number of employed consultants complained that
they were offered only temporary contracts to work on multicultural and
research projects rather than permanent positions.

In 2015 Hanaan commented on the difficulty of gaining employment. She
said, "If the person who hires you is under forty-five years old, your chance
to get equally hired with a Finn is good. But if they are older than that,
you don't have a chance to get hired in that position if there is a Finnish
candidate. That happened to me several times." She explained that Finns

under the age of forty-five tend to be more accepting of foreigners. Those raised in the Helsinki area likely went to school with Somalis and other foreigners. They had more experience with diversity than older Finns.

Lul, Shukri, and Mohamed spent more time cultivating networks with Finns and like-minded Somalis than they did with other Somalis. Often they avoided meeting places for Somalis, late-night phone calls, and late-night visits. Although they disregarded many norms followed by other Somalis in Finland and formed social networks with persons outside the Somali community, other Somalis did not consider them outcasts. Their Finnish cultural capital made them useful to others. Somalis—relatives and nonrelatives—regularly called upon Lul, Shukri, and Mohamed to assist with their dealings with Finnish authorities and institutions (hospitals, schools, and so forth).

Despite strategies to restrict the influence of other Somalis in their everyday lives, these women and men occasionally visited clan relatives and unrelated friends, and they participated in collective clan gift-giving and rites of institution. One of these individuals used clan ties to gain entry to Finland (marriage with a clan relative). Lul and Shukri tended to participate in weddings of clan relatives and the weddings of close friends affiliated with other clans. Unlike many other women, Lul and Shukri did not attend countless weddings of those they considered to be strangers.

Despite Lul, Shukri, and Mohamed's strong exposure to Finnish society, they tended to construct clan and make clan status claims just as other Somalis did: through telling, stereotyping, contesting clan, and blaming others who are clannish. These three adults assigned value to their rights and obligations toward family and clan alongside Finnish autonomy and gender equality just as younger Somalis did. It would be a mistake to contend that the experiences of these two groups are profoundly different from migrants before them. It is likely that Somalis living abroad before the civil war in former colonial countries, the Gulf States, Russia, and North America experienced comparable pressures, uncertainties, prospects, and wavering loyalties as they navigated life abroad.

# CHAPTER 4

# CELEBRATION

## Ritual Contests

Hodan, Kadijah, and I spent the entire day preparing for an *aroos* (wedding). For about seven hours we listened to music, watched a wedding video, chatted, drank *shaah* (a Somali spiced tea similar to chai), snacked on Somali and Finnish foods, and primped. We applied a face mask of *qasil* (powder from leaves of the gob tree mixed with water) to clean our skin, took turns using a bonnet hairdryer to set large rollers, fashioned elaborate updos, applied nail polish and heavy makeup, draped our wedding clothing over some chairs so that the incense burning underneath could infuse the cloth with its scent, dressed, and adorned ourselves with gold bracelets, rings, necklaces, and earrings—except I wore fake gold. We were especially excited to wear our new *diric* (Somali women's dress worn at weddings and other special occasions) purchased from Hodan and Kadijah's female relative who had recently returned from Somaliland. A *diric* is a loose fitting dress made from a light, almost transparent fabric. We wore long, opaque skirts called *googgarad* underneath our dresses along with *garbasaar*, coordinating scarves draped around our shoulders. Hodan selected a dark purple bra to wear underneath her light gray and nearly transparent *diric*, a relatively common practice among women at *aroosyo* (weddings). Before we could display the latest dresses to other partygoers, we had to wait for Kadijah's brother, Ismail, to drive us to the wedding. After placing a series of phone calls to Ismail over a span of several hours, he finally arrived. Ismail was late because few Somalis own cars and he and his friends had spent the evening chauffeuring clanswomen from various places in Helsinki and Espoo to the celebration in Vantaa. When Hodan, Kadijah, and I arrived at the wedding held at a youth center gymnasium after 11 p.m., guests were still arriving, and the bride was nowhere in sight. Inside the party, women sat impatiently among their clanswomen, waiting for the bride to arrive and the party to begin. The space was elaborately decorated with colorful Arabian-style carpets and gilded furniture for the bride to sit on while she watched partygoers dance. The walls were covered with curtains in rich blue and purple silk fabrics and lined with multicolored and mismatched seating pillows. Vibrant red silk flowers adorned the curtains, and silk plants were positioned near the bride's seating. Metallic decorations hung from the ceiling (see figure 2). Once we heard that the bride had arrived, a few hundred women—most of them wearing *diric* with coordinating skirts and scarves in a kaleidoscope of colors from pastel tones to jewel tones and *dahab* (gold jewelry)—formed two lines at the entrance while young male DJs played Somali music and the male videographer started to film the activities.

Figure 2. *Aroos* (wedding celebration), Helsinki, Finland, 2001. This *aroos* took place in the common area of a municipal apartment complex. The girls and women wear *diric* with coordinating skirts and scarves and *dahab* (gold jewelry). Women are expected to wear a new *diric* to each wedding. The male videographer (in the far left corner of this picture) is among the few men permitted to attend these women's gatherings. Photograph by author.

The bride and her bridesmaids entered as a procession wearing *guntiino* (similar to the Indian sari) and elaborate sets of gold jewelry with intricate *cillaan* (henna) decorations on their hands, arms, and feet and walked between the two lines of women.[1] Then we formed a circle around the bride and her bridesmaids. Next, the bride's and groom's female relatives took turns entering the circle to greet the bride and dance with her. After that, the bride and her attendants sat down on ornate Arabian-style chairs. The DJs silenced their music so that a middle-aged woman could lead the partygoers in *buraanbur* (women's praise poetry) with her hand drum in singing, clapping, and dancing sequences. Hodan, Kadijah, and I stood on the periphery of the circle with some of their clanswomen. As we clapped in tandem with the other women to the unchanging rhythm of the drum, Hodan clapped offbeat (as if she were unfamiliar with this sequence) and said, "It's boring. It's all *buraanbur*, and there are no North dances." Sometime later, loud voices emerged from the front of the circle, and the *buraanbur* and filming stopped. Some of the bride's and groom's female relatives argued and pushed each other. Male relatives manning the door stepped in to help resolve the conflict. Upset by the dispute, the bride started to cry, and the party came to a standstill. While we waited for the celebration to resume, Hodan and other women told me the women were fighting because one clan "had too many verses" during *buraanbur*.

The fight during a women's wedding celebration is an example of what Moore (1987) refers to as a *diagnostic event*: "a telling historical sign visible in fieldwork" (730). A spontaneous event of the kind is diagnostic because it "reveals ongoing contests and conflicts and competitions and the efforts to prevent, suppress, or repress these" and "how local events and local commentary on them can be linked to a variety of processes unfolding simultaneously on very different scales of time and place" (730–31). On the surface, the fight during *buraanbur* is telling of a conflict between the bride's and the groom's kin. *Buraanbur*, a women's oral poetic genre, is considered to be women's serious genre—a form that is "most valued by official standards" (Kapteijns 1999:21). Kapteijns's historical research on Somali women's oral literature in northern Somalia reveals that this poetic genre, as it was performed at *aroosyo*, was known to be a source of tension between clans. As Kapteijns writes:

> Women also considered their own family and clan background, both on their father and mother's sides, of great significance. They analyzed it in great historical detail in songs of the *buraanbur* genre performed at weddings. The *buraanbur jilaysi* was especially devoted to praising the clan or clan section

(of their fathers) and could lead to quarrels (and even walkouts) between the families of the bride and groom. (25)

*Buraanbur* remains an integral part of Somali wedding celebrations worldwide. Its ritual performance establishes perhaps the only socially acceptable context to display and celebrate clan publicly. During *buraanbur*, partygoers sing poetic verses to praise the bride and groom's families and perform dance sequences that visually distinguish clans. In addition, some dances performed at *aroosyo* identify participants with specific regions of Somalia.

Even women and girls, claiming to contest the importance of clan in their daily lives, seem to be overcome with emotion as they dance excitedly to represent themselves well as dancers and to represent their clan during *buraanbur jilaysi* dance sequences.[2] These dances are commonly learned while watching wedding videos at home, attending *aroosyo* or at household celebrations where *buraanbur* may be performed, including engagements, farewells, and welcoming parties. Although Hodan clapped offbeat during *buraanbur*, she eagerly participated at her kin's weddings by clapping along to dance sequences honoring her own clan. Hodan was often too shy to dance in the middle of the circle for other women; she preferred dancing in pairs or larger groups to Somali, Egyptian, and Western R&B dance music commonly played at *aroosyo*.

Often girls and young women (ages sixteen to thirty) complained to me that *buraanbur* was boring. Somali girls and young women who frequent Finnish discos or youth centers, along with those who learned the latest dance routines from videos on European MTV, prefer to showcase their talents to other partygoers when DJs play Western music. Songs like *Get Busy* by Sean Paul and *Crazy in Love* by Beyoncé featuring Jay Z were all the rage among this group. Celebrants who deem *buraanbur* boring accept its practice because, in time, they will represent and praise their lineage at future weddings of clan relatives.

It is during these displays of cultural competence that clan ties are reaffirmed and reinforced. The practices promote a clan feeling. When a woman publicly tells that another woman is her patrilineal cousin by participating in *buraanbur*, they effectively legitimate kin ties, which lays the foundation for building social capital in the clan.

Less than a week after the *aroos*, I wanted to gather additional local commentary on the conflict, and so I visited a family related to one of the newlyweds. When I told Hibo, a daughter in the family, that I attended a wedding the previous weekend, she asked, "The Daarood wedding?" "Yes," I said. Hibo replied, "I heard it was crazy. The two clans were fighting." "Yes, the bride and guests arrived late," I said. Hibo's mother, Rahma, commented, "Yes, our culture. Not in Somalia, but everywhere else everyone is late. I don't know why. I decided I am not going to anymore wedding[s] because of the late [hour] and clans. At all my children's wedding[s], I didn't have songs for one clan but for both people getting married."

As I told Rahma and her daughters about the fight at the wedding, I pointed to Hibo and said jokingly, "Her clan had too many verses and the others became angry." Rahma laughed, and Hibo joined in the laughter, saying, "Those women are crazy." Then Rahma told her husband, Ahmed, who is Daarood, what I said, and he laughed too. (Rahma belongs to another clan family.) "In Europe, in Finland, clan is like this, but not in Somalia," Ahmed stated. "I thought you would all be at the wedding because they are Daarood," I said. Rahma replied, "Father and Abdi [her son] went to the men's wedding [marriage contract], but we [Rahma and her daughters] would not go to the women's wedding. The family is close to ours [close clan relatives], but they are no good. The mother is no good. She is always talking [gossiping], and their children [are gossiping] too." Hibo and her father excused the culturally intimate event to me, a cultural outsider, by distancing themselves from the event and excusing the women's actions as distinctive of Somalis living in Europe. Rahma's claim of having songs for the clans of both spouses indicated her awareness of social conventions for these rituals at weddings.

The bride's and groom's families trace their ancestry to two distinct lineages, and they clashed over one clan's alleged dominance in the *buraanbur*. Conflicts at weddings are not uncommon. Although the foregoing conflict resulted from a clash between two clan families during the *buraanbur* ritual, arguments over gossip and men commonly surface at wedding celebrations. This gossip often pertains to salacious gossip about scandalous behaviors such as wearing immodest attire, drinking alcohol, and engaging in alleged affairs. Because *aroosyo* are significant community events, they offer an opportunity to challenge and, in some cases, resolve disputes with the backing of clan relatives in the presence of representatives of various clans.

Although *buraanbur* is considered a suitable platform to commemorate clan and clan relationships publicly, one clan family's tactic to monopolize the ritual pushes the boundary of what is deemed socially appropriate. That is, individuals and groups should not publicly reveal how very much clan means to them, as it falls outside social convention. Even though diaspora Somalis often go to great lengths to construct clan boundaries on the ground, they view clan as an embarrassment before outsiders. At a deeper level, the conflict between the two families reveals past and ongoing struggles spanning the Somali diaspora: clan hegemony, clan status claims, and the ongoing civil war in Somalia.

Through the social practice of *buraanbur*, Somalis realize and reaffirm clan relationships and make clan status claims. In this way, kin exchange the various forms of capital. During *buraanbur*, obvious groupings of individuals are telling of clan affiliation and social networks or social capital in the clan. This is especially true of those who enter the circle to dance in response to verses praising a particular clan. Affiliated groups of individuals are linked with symbolic capital in the forms of prestige and recognition through use of a prestigious clan name or reference to an important ancestor. When Somalis demonstrate knowledge of the singing-clapping-dancing sequence and clan history, evident in poetic verses, it suggests a personal investment in clan competence, or cultural capital. Use of clan dialect reinforces clan hierarchy relative to language use as both cultural capital, in the form of specific cultural competence, and symbolic capital. The women's economic capital is evident by the size and quantity of the 21-karat or 24-karat *dahab* they display. A number of women admired my *dahab* at the *aroos*, and a few, skeptical of my claim that it was only gold-plated, appraised its value by feeling the weight of my necklace in their hands.

Incidentally, the group of women accused of trying to control that particular *buraanbur* ritual occupies a higher position in the clan hierarchy (at least according to the lineage narrative) than does the family who contested their tactics. For that reason, it is plausible that the clan's effort to dominate the ritual was a strategy to legitimize their status claim. The other clan's contestation over the ritual may not be simply a matter of which clan sung more verses. Rather it may be a challenge to clan hegemony and clan status claims.

Conceivably, the clanswomen's challenge to women from the other clan who tried to monopolize *buraanbur* felt that their clan had more prestige than the other clan did. Moreover, this clan had a larger number of residents in Finland. The group's potential access to local clan networks was greater. None of my consultants mentioned this reading to me nor did they offer a translation of the poetic verses that prompted the fight. My language skills in Somali limited my understanding of the event (especially how it linked to current political events and divisions at home).

Excerpts from interviews provide some insight into how an event, such as the eruption of a fight during *buraanbur*, relates to ongoing and past struggles. As I filled out the survey of Cali, a man in his mid-thirties, he shared his insight into ongoing contests and competitions among Somalis that span time and place. He said, "After the war and now, clan is more political. No one wants to be ruled and controlled." Then he added, "Some people are into clans, and others are not."

During an in-depth interview with Hodan, the woman I stood next to during *buraanbur*, I questioned her about clan.

AUTHOR: Tell me about your clan.

HODAN: They are racist a little.

AUTHOR: Against whom?

HODAN: Against others because there was not equality [were not treated equally] before when there was this president [Siyad Barre]. Now they [members of her clan] want to be by themselves. They have a scar, even if they tell them. They have these things in their mind. The people were killed. They will say, 'You don't know anything.' But they are good people. Like in Hargeysa, people were raping. There were so many things! Those people are still alive. Their grandmothers and children were raped! There are a lot of bad things in war, in North and also in South.

Hodan's discourse captures the freshness of Somalis' scars incurred by Siyad Barre's regime and wartime atrocities. These scars have yet to fade from memory. They continue to mark and divide Somalis. Hodan says, "Now they want to be by themselves." Indeed, her clan family initiated secession from the rest of Somalia in 1991 and became part of Somaliland. Nongovernmental organizations tend to herald this region as Somalia's safe haven, which is a source of her clan's pride.

Diaspora Somalis from her clan tend to invest in and visit Somaliland. Hodan's northern clan is positioned favorably in the clan hierarchy according to the lineage-based model (prestigious clan dialect, Arabness, nomadic tradition, and so forth). Her clan legitimizes their position through their success at home, distinctive lifestyle, and increasing tendency to prefer marriage with close relatives. Because Hodan's words are culturally intimate, she plays down her partiality to her clan by considering the "bad things" that occurred in the South—albeit as an afterthought. Conceivably, this addendum is a tactic to appear not to be into clan or "racist" against other clans in my presence.

Through the discourses of Cali and Hodan, they linked ongoing contests, conflicts, and competitions to the civil war and clan hegemony (clan's power as an ever-present feature of daily life and clan status claims). Moreover, the conflict during *aroos*, coupled with Cali's insight, attests to the disputed relevance of the clan system and state-sponsored clan hierarchy in the diaspora. Furthermore, Cali points to the prevalence of clan hegemony. He said, "Some people are into clans and others are not."

Although Somali associations are a seemingly explicit effort of Somali men to perpetuate clan divisions in diaspora, the *buraanbur* ritual—as it is performed at *aroosyo*—is a similar attempt by women to institutionalize clan ties (at home and abroad). As Kapteijns (1999) writes:

> Many aspects of relations between kin groups were determined by men, who solved disputes and decided on communal matters in male assemblies. However, women, whose networks of relatives, neighbors and friends by necessity spanned more than one kin group, could have enormous influence. During weddings, ceremonial enactments of the rights and obligations of existing and now-to-be-created kinship bonds, women asserted their voices. Using the literary vehicle of the *buraanbur*, they praised "their" groom or bride, their ancestors and famous kinsmen, their history, perhaps special skills or feats associated with their group, and so forth. They did this so competitively that one of the families would at times walk out in anger. [59–60]

Women predominantly rely upon kin to carry out *aroosyo*. For some women, however, unrelated friends (especially neighbors, coworkers, and classmates) also play an integral role in everyday social networks. Women must skillfully balance these relationships at *aroosyo*, an arduous task because of the cultural intimacy of clan. During the *buraanbur* ritual, participants strengthen bonds among kin and initiate horizontal links among clans. Efforts to integrate and celebrate tribe can escalate into competition among clans of dissimilar status and taste. Some clanswomen may view horizontal links among clans as a challenge or threat to group boundaries and clan status claims.

## Rites of Integration

Like other rites of passage such as birth and death, marriage marks an individual's transition from one status to another, and it is a significant site for building and maintaining social capital in the clan. *Aroosyo* constitute the main community event in Finland, where Somali women of all ages meet to socialize (see also Bjork 2001).[3] In other rites of passage, participation is individually defined with close relatives and friends, and these events are not considered community events. Most consultants deem *aroosyo* acceptable venues for girls and women to congregate.[4] Women celebrate through the night until the early morning hours while their husbands, relatives, or friends care for children. As one female consultant said, "Tired women dance like crazy. You see an old woman who barely walks, and she dances all night!"

McMichael and Manderson (2004) portray women's celebrations among Somali immigrant women in Australia as sites to maintain well-being and to share community life. They write:

> Social events, religious gatherings, and celebrations play an important role in women's lives, promoting interaction, shared time, and a sense of well-being. They support the continuance of Somali culture, community life, and hospitality, and provide shared spaces and community life. [96]

*Aroosyo* bring together hundreds of women from various ages and across different clans. Although an *aroos* cultivates a shared sense of *Soomaalinimo* (Somaliness or being a Somali) among celebrants, the focal point of an *aroos* is maintenance of clan networks and integration of kin. A female consultant claimed, "Women come to weddings to be against clanism [clannishness]. In Finland, no one cares about clan. We are wiser now." Yet moments later, the same consultant asserted, "You have to go [to *aroos*] in order to represent your clan."

As Kusow (1998) notes, "Somali society is highly gender segregated and does not allow women to publicly associate merely for sociability purposes. Thus, women get together and share information through wedding ceremonies" (55). At *aroosyo*, girls and women tend to associate closely with clanswomen, making clan networks visibly observable. This is particularly evident when women visit before the bride arrives and during *buraanbur*. Often, regular meetings among clanswomen are complicated because of family, educational and employment obligations, dispersed subsidized housing, and inclement weather conditions. At other times, some girls and women dance in mixed-clan groups with friends.

Kusow, a Somali male sociologist, conducted his dissertation fieldwork in Toronto, Canada. During that time, Kusow was discouraged from attending women's gatherings, including women's wedding celebrations. As Kusow (2003) writes:

> A wedding celebration consists of two ceremonies held at different times and sometimes at different locations, one for the men and another for the women. The only men allowed to go to the female gathering are those who operate the videocamera or provide musical entertainment, and they tend to be relatives of the bride or the groom. [597]

Because of Kusow's status as a cultural insider, entry to women's celebrations of relatives is feasible. At times, male kin monitor the door and step in during disputes.

Because Somalis in Finland consider *nikaax* (the wedding contract) to be a man's event, I did not attend one. I did observe numerous contracts on wedding videos. Despite these seemingly rigid divisions of gender, a Finnish woman attended a marriage contract on at least one occasion. In this case, the bride's Finnish mother asked the groom's family for permission to attend the contract between her daughter and the daughter's Somali fiancé. Although the groom's female relatives privately criticized the Finnish woman's presence at the *nikaax*, at least they tolerated it. (In retrospect, I might have asked close friends whether I could attend a marriage contract of their kin. It is possible to imagine that my outsider status, like that of the Finnish mother, may have excused my presence at the all-male event). The Finnish family did not involve the Somali family in wedding planning and preparation. The bride's family served typical Finnish food or *voileipäpöytä*, a traditional buffet featuring rye bread, butter, cheese, smoked salmon, cold cuts, fruit, salads, and *karjalanpiirakka*, a small pie of rye crust filled with rice and typically smeared with a mixture of hard-boiled egg and butter, in place the of individually served paper plates of Somali cuisine that are routinely served. Unlike most of the Somali weddings I attended, Finns and Somalis of mixed genders attended the celebration.[5] The Finnish guests arrived to the wedding on time, at 7:00 p.m.; most Somali guests arrived late, at 10:00 or 11:00 p.m., and most Finns had left the party before the majority of Somali guests arrived.

In the Somali tradition, each plate of food tends to include goat meat or mutton with potatoes, *bariis*, rice seasoned with cinnamon and cardamom, pita bread, *canjeero* (crêpe made from corn or sorghum flour), or *muufo* (doughy bread made from sorghum or cornmeal), *sambuusi* (a triangular pastry of Indian origin—*samosa*—filled with seasoned meat, onions, and vegetables or tuna), lettuce, cucumber, and tomato salad, and a banana. Fruit juice or soda is also served. Later in the evening, each woman is served another plate with an assortment of sweets such as cookies, cakes, and *xalwad* (confection made from ghee, sugar, spices, and cornstarch).

Female kin of the groom exerted their influence in decorating the space. In an effort to preserve the clan's influence in this marriage and among kin, the groom's female relatives collected money from clan relatives to purchase wedding gifts such as gold jewelry sets for the bride. They also arranged a separate women's party for the bride and female clan relatives.

As the number of marriages between Somalis and Finns increases, rights and obligations among clan relatives may change. My survey sample recorded seventeen marriages between Finns and Somalis.[6] It is worth mentioning here that Finns married to Somalis tend to purchase goods and services through the Somali informal economy. For example, Leila, a woman in her early thirties, purchases Islamic-style clothing from shops in Dubai, United Arab Emirates, during regular trips to visit her fiancé. Leila buys these goods to resell in Finland. Her primary clientele are Finnish women married to Somali men and who have converted to Islam. Indeed, marriages between Finns and Somalis open up new possibilities for exchanging capital.

As stated earlier, male relatives of both families, including local men of the clan and those living in other diaspora communities—and some unrelated friends—meet for *nikaax*. The *nikaax* ceremony commonly takes place in the afternoon, prior to the women's evening wedding celebration. In general, the groom's family, particularly immediate kin, pays *nikaax* costs. In some cases, more distant clan relatives and friends affiliated with other clans help with the costs of food, refreshments, gasoline to transport attendees, and the videographer. Friends and relatives of the groom who own cars typically provide transportation.

In contrast to women's celebrations, *nikaax* tends to be a more intimate event. It is a ritual gathering of the bride's and groom's male clan relatives. According to Bourdieu (1977), these official kin (official because their relationship follows rules of patrilineal descent) "are reserved for official situations in which they serve the function of ordering the social world and of legitimating that order" (34).

Men's gatherings are more subdued and formal, following religious codes, than women's wedding parties. During *nikaax*, the presiding religious leader, usually a *sheekh* (learned man of Islam), reads verses from the Qur'an that relate to married life. Next the leader asks the appointed male representative from the bride's family whether she consents to the marriage. Then the *sheekh* asks the groom whether he accepts the marriage as well as the amount of *meher* requested by the bride, which she will receive in the event of divorce.[7] This agreed-upon sum is usually in the form of cash. If divorce occurs, the wife may demand that her husband pay *meher*. The immediate relatives of the groom and, less commonly, his extended relatives might assist with the payment of *meher*. After the two families agree on an amount, the groom and male representatives of both families shake hands and formalize the marriage.[8] The groom's male kin present a monetary gift known as *sooryo* (bride wealth) to the bride's male kin, usually a clan elder. The bride's clan elders in attendance receive most of the gift and return about 10–15 percent to the boy's clan.

Women's wedding celebrations held in the evening after the men's *nikaax* were the most popular type of celebration. Mixed-gender celebrations in the evening were becoming more popular during the fieldwork period and were favored by young Somalis. I attended one religious celebration for women only (without music or video recording). This occasion was significantly smaller than other *aroosyo* but still included the *buraanbur jilaysi* dance sequences. It was a type of celebration rare in Finland. Hoehne observed men and women celebrating together at *aroosyo* in Somaliland and noted that different religious orientations may account for the difference (Markus Hoehne, personal communication November 10, 2012). Other researchers have documented greater religiosity among Somali diaspora populations in Toronto, England, and Finland (see Berns McGown 1999; Tiilikainen 2003, 2007).

In 2015 Hanaan commented on some of the changes since the time of my fieldwork. She said, "Nowadays women go in groups because a lot of women have their driver's license and cars. You can find both [women-only celebrations and mixed-gender]. Depends on family. Women's only is more common." Hanaan commented on a recent wedding experience. She said, "I went to a wedding of a close Somalian friend. I rarely go to weddings unlike my older sisters. I never felt so [much of an] outsider in my community of Somalians. The bride and groom were a different clan than I was and the majority of guests were from their clan. When the wedding was going on I felt so invisible. No one came to talk to me and my sister. The worst thing was when the party finished. People were driving each other and we had to call [a] taxi."

## Marriage Taboos and Spousal Preference

One notable role of kinsmen partaking in *nikaax* is to legitimize the clan lineage of the bride and groom. Legitimation is sometimes deemed critical for marriages with persons living in distant diaspora communities. In these cases, the possibility of masking clan ascription is believed to be greater. A female consultant told me the following story, which highlights the role of men in the clan in maintaining clan boundaries and marriage taboos in the diaspora:

> A [name of clan] girl in Finland almost married a *jareer* man from England. He came to Finland and met for the contract. It [the *nikaax*] was canceled because they found out he was *jareer*. They asked about his background, and he said the clan of his master called Xassan. He said he was the clan of his master, but people found out he was *jareer*. Everyone talks about clan. Father said he would not go there [to the *nikaax*]. They [male relatives of the girl] said that it would be bad for the children because they would be *jareer*. They look different.

This story indicates a successful attempt on behalf of the girl's male relatives to impose marriage taboos with Somali ethnic minorities. This taboo is based on the idea that Somali Bantus fall outside the social boundary of Somaliness. The girl's male relatives justify the taboo by pointing to the rules of patrilineal descent. Any children fathered by a Somali Bantu man will be recognized as Somali Bantu. Lacking the support of the clan's men, the *nikaax* and marriage were canceled.

Despite the prevalence of marriage taboos, marriages between the so-called majority clan families and minority groups occur (including marriages with minority men). Consultants reported three marriages between the so-called major clan families and Somali ethnic minorities in Finland. Verifying the potential bride's and groom's clan affiliation prior to marriage is a priority for kin. For example, during a household visit with Abdirizak, a male consultant, and his family, I asked about the importance placed upon legitimizing clan. I asked, "So, do people in Finland check the background of potential spouses?" "Yes, but now small clans can marry the big ones," he replied. Then, he added, "The northern and eastern clans do not like to marry other clans though."

In the above context, small clans refer to minority groups. Abdirizak, who is affiliated with a minority group, is married to an Isaaq woman. His reference to northern and eastern clans surely points to the dominant clans in those areas: the Isaaq (also the Gadabuursi and Ciise, Dir clans) in Somaliland and the Harti clan federation, a division of the Daarood clan family including the Majeerteen, Dhulbahante, and Warsangeeli clans in Puntland.

The following excerpts from in-depth interviews offer some insight into individual preferences and familial expectations in the choice of a spouse:

> KHADRA (ISAAQ): Some men from my clan got together in one home in Rastila [neighborhood in East Helsinki] and called my mother in Yemen to tell her that I could not marry my husband because he is Daarood. She said [her mother said] to the men, "Why did you not win my daughter? She must have found a good man."

> ASHA (ISAAQ): My father wants me to marry an Isaaq. I don't know for me. I marry for love, but not Hawiye.
> AUTHOR: Why?
> ASHA: I don't like them. I don't understand their culture, their language. They are different people. I think they are cold people.

> AUTHOR: How did you meet your spouse?
> HODAN (ISAAQ): I meet him in Helsinki.
> AUTHOR: How? Where?

HODAN: I meet him through one of his cousins. He is a relative. The same tribe. He is not [name of subclan].

*THEN SHE HELD UP HER RIGHT HAND AND BEGAN TO USE HER FINGERS TO COUNT THE LINEAGES SHE SHARED WITH HER EX-HUSBAND.*

WE HAVE SEVEN [LINEAGES] IN COMMON. WE HAVE THE SAME GRANDFATHER.[9]

I STARTED TO WRITE THE SUBCLANS IN MY NOTEBOOK.

HODAN: You are writing this down?

*SHE STOPPED RECITING THEIR COMMON LINEAGES.*

AUTHOR: OK, I will just listen.

*I PUT DOWN MY PEN AND PAPER AND LISTENED TO HODAN CONTINUE HER RECITATION OF THE SEVEN COMMON ANCESTORS SHE AND HER FIANCÉ SHARED. THEN SHE NOTED OTHER PERSONS I WAS ACQUAINTED WITH WHO SHARED THIS SAME GENEALOGY.*

AUTHOR: Does your family ask you when you will marry?

MOHAMED (MAJEERTEEN, A DAAROOD CLAN): No, never.

AUTHOR: No?

MOHAMED: Yes, I remember when I visited Kenya in 1995, my mother was there. She didn't even ask me when I was going to marry, but some of my relatives living there said that if I go back I can call them, and they can arrange the best lady.

AUTHOR: Whom might your relatives choose for you?

MOHAMED: I think from the same clan, a young lady who is close to them [a close clan relative]. I don't know exactly, but anyway.

AUTHOR: How did other Somalis react to your choice in a spouse? [Farah married a Finn.]

FARAH (GADABUURSI, A DIR CLAN): My mother—she reacted to my marriage. She told me that my kids would not be mine and that it would be difficult with another culture. My grandmother also reacted the same way. Some Somali friends told me to take it slow and think again.

AUTHOR: How did other Somalis react to your marriage?

AYAAN (HABAR GIDIR, A HAWIYE CLAN): Nobody know [knew]. We made [a] secret marriage in Somalia with [a] *sheekh*. We did not tell until after we were in Finland. We keep [kept] it secret because my ex-boyfriend want to marry me, and he was from me [my] same clan.

AUTHOR: How did you meet your husband?
HAMDI (OGAADEEN, A DAAROOD CLAN): Ethiopia. My husband's
mother and my father are brother and sister.

Among Somalis, marriage is more than a union between two people. It is also a tie between two families and two clans, which is one reason that consultants' families, sometimes including more distant clan relatives, commonly exert social pressure or act as go-betweens to influence the marriage. Interview excerpts point to tensions between individual choice and family interests and make clear that consultants' families prefer marriage with clan relatives.

Prior to the civil war, anthropologists described distinct marriage patterns among northern and southern clans. Helander (1991) notes, "In the north it is often seen as preferable that the spouse is a member of another clan. The marriage will then also serve to create a form of alliance between two previously unrelated (and therefore potentially hostile) groups (23). Lewis (1994) explains why exogamy, marriage outside of the kin group, is the rule: "The primary lineage is normally, and the dia-paying group always, exogamous, because these units are already so strongly united that marriage within them is considered to threaten their cohesion" (51). "In the south . . . the preferable marriage is with a close relative. Father's brother's daughter/son is often depicted as the ideal person" (Helander 1991:23). Lewis (1994) notes that for the Digil Mirifle, endogamy, marriage within the kin group, is the norm and included patrilineal and matrilineal cousin marriage.

Since the civil war, Hoehne (forthcoming) notes a shift from exogamy to marriage with close relatives in northern Somalia. He argues that more rigid notions of territory and descent now characterize the north and notes Somalis in the diaspora illustrate this in their investments in clan territories. This change in marriage patterns was becoming evident among some consultants affiliated with northern clans as with the woman sharing seven common ancestors with her fiancé. Although most of the people I worked with chose their own spouses, kin often influenced their choice. Some consultants preferred marriage with close relatives and others, in all clans, married against kin interests. Although Somalis in Finland marry outside their clan family, clan, subclan, and increasingly their community, the most favorable spouse tends to be a clan relative with shared tastes.

Al-Sharmani (2004) notes that with the exception of minority clans, most Somalis in Cairo report that a potential spouse's clan affiliation is unimportant. I did not find this to be the case in Finland. One explanation of this disparity may be the desire of many Somalis in Cairo to migrate to the West to increase their life chances (Al-Sharmani 2004, 2007; Kroner 2007). For some individuals, the prospect of westward movement may trump marriage taboos or clan preference (even marriage with minority clans).

In 2015 Hanaan commented on being single in her thirties. She said, "Mostly, my age people have two or three kids. Personally, I don't regret anything—that I am single. I progressed with my studies and have career and have traveled the world. In my opinion, at this age is the age that I could think about settling down. I know who I am, what I want in life, and with whom I want to share it." Hanaan commented on her own preferences in a spouse. She said, "When it comes to me, the least thing I would think about is clan. Most of my friends are foreigners so most of the Somalians I meet are the same clan as my parents, mom's or dad's. It doesn't really matter. To have a marriage it will mostly be through friends or family friends. But personally, it does not need to be Somalian, but a Muslim man: educated, good person from a good family, family-oriented, and open-minded. If a man is open-minded, he usually drinks alcohol and everything else." Hanaan explained that this last point makes it difficult for her to find a suitable husband.

## Keeping Up Appearances

Like Finns, Somalis prefer to arrange weddings during the summer, a period when the sun is visible at day and night. In contrast to Finns, however, Somalis tend to invite hundreds of guests to their celebrations.[10] Most Finns wed at a church and hold a small reception to follow. Couples living in cities often opt for a civil ceremony. Since Somalis tend to marry after a brief engagement, wedding celebrations are often prepared in haste. In some cases, the bride's and the groom's families may have only a few weeks to prepare a wedding. It is vital to have social networks in place so that social capital can be accessed swiftly to assist with wedding planning, preparation, and implementation. Male and female relatives and, in some cases, friends from different clan backgrounds, assist with the many tasks necessary to host a wedding, which include renting space for marriage contract and *aroos*; making and delivering invitations or personally inviting guests; preparing food; decorating; serving food and refreshments; transporting guests; cleaning up; and offering gifts. Among clan relatives, support is institutionalized through tacit rules of reciprocity.

Following rules of balanced reciprocity or reciprocal exchange of equal value (see Sahlins 1972), the family mentioned in the beginning of the chapter was obliged to assist relatives. Despite Rahma's claim that she would no longer attend weddings, "because of the late [hour] and clans," Rahma and her daughters took me as their guest to a wedding of the girls' clan relative. At the *aroos*, we received preferential seating and we were served food and refreshments before nonrelatives were served. Rahma's daughters helped the bride's family with planning the *aroos*, preparing food, decorating the space, and cleaning up after the event.

Incidentally, a few weeks before the celebration, the bride's mother visited these clanswomen in order to end an ongoing feud. The mother did so in hopes that they would assist with wedding preparations and participate in the celebration. As with any relationship, kinship ties are unstable. Somalis must maintain and sometimes mend clan relationships. During the celebration, the bride and her mother posed for a photo with Rahma and her daughters. This still image, featured on the wedding video, illustrates the strength and unity of clan ties and presents such ties as stable.

Despite Rahma's paternal ancestry, she tended to associate with her husband's clan relatives rather than with her own paternal clan. It is unclear whether this was Rahma's choice, a result of her lack of acceptance among her clanswomen, a consequence of marrying a man from a different clan, or a combination of these factors. As a teenager, Rahma left the home of her paternal clan, in the North, to live in Mogadishu. Prior to the outbreak of Somali civil war, Rahma, along with her husband and children, called Mogadishu home. There, she and her family occupied a high social position. Before emigrating to Finland, it is also plausible that Rahma had less in common with her clanswomen, who lived primarily in the North (or outside Somalia), than she did with women from her husband's clan and other women who called Mogadishu home, especially those who were part of the city's elite.

According to survey data, Rahma actively maintains social networks with clan relatives in Somaliland, Djibouti, and in other diaspora countries by telephone, travel, and videos. To a lesser extent, she sustains these connections through her own social networks in Finland by sharing news. She has been unable to garner support from women of her paternal clan who reside in Finland. Because Rahma did not use social networks among her paternal clan in Finland, she did not have access to them.

In contrast, Rahma's association with the paternal clan of her husband and children is what Bourdieu (1997) identifies as a practical relationship. It is used, maintained, and cultivated. It is notable that her husband's paternal clan relatives (the same clan as the children) access the couple's children through Rahma rather than her husband. This is yet another example revealing clan networks as flexible and highlights the significance of affinal relationships, which are ties through marriage. Cawo M. Abdi

(2015) comments on her own affinal relationships and other links across clans: "My own position as someone whose clan is different from that of her children, and many of her own family members (cousins, uncles and aunts, grandmother, great aunts, etc.), puts me in a position to be able to identify and have linkages with multiple Somali clans and regions. All Somalis in fact have such expansive kinship linkages that almost always crosscut clan lines" (25).

The following excerpt from an in-depth interview with Shukri, who appeared in the previous chapter, elucidates clan networks as flexible. It points to differences among clans in terms of potential access to social networks and the integration of its members.

> SHUKRI: Sometimes I help them [my clan] when they call.
> AUTHOR: What kinds of things does your clan ask your help with?
> SHUKRI: If there is a girl or boy getting married [from] my clan and the clan try to buy gold or something. If it's two hundred euro or something, they divide, and they say that I pay twenty or fifty euro.
> AUTHOR: Did you receive gifts of gold when you married?
> SHUKRI: When I married, I get it, yes. Not only [from] my clan, but friends from different clans.
> AUTHOR: Who helped you with your wedding?
> SHUKRI: It was another clan. Five percent was my clan. One woman who lives in Myyrmäki [a neighborhood in Vantaa] did all the cooking. She is [name of subclan].
> AUTHOR: Why didn't your clan help you?
> SHUKRI: They [my clan] are like that. I don't know.
> AUTHOR: Are there any people here [in Finland] from your clan?
> SHUKRI: They are few. They are not a unit.
> AUTHOR: Why not?
> SHUKRI: I don't know.
> AUTHOR: Are other clans like a unit?
> SHUKRI: Yes, most of them. My clan is not over 50 [persons in Finland].

Shukri explained that clan relatives did not support her marriage because they were unable to act as a collective as other clans do. When she married, a friend from another clan cooked food for her *aroos*. It is unclear when and how Shukri cultivated this relationship and whether she reciprocated this exchange. The presence of Shukri's clan is small Finland ("not over fifty"). Shukri's potential access to social capital among kin is less than it would be for a person from a larger clan. And because her clan is small in Finland, I do not identify her clan by name. Shukri acknowledged that relatives contacted her to contribute to wedding gifts for clan affiliates. This is a reciprocal exchange that cultivates clan ties.

When Shukri married in the mid-1990s, it is probable that few of her clan relatives resided in Finland. Along with her Finnish cultural capital and prestige accumulated in Finland (symbolic capital), Shukri has networks among Finns and immigrants living in the country (social capital). She has access to potential social capital outside her clan and the Somali community. These connections, along with her Finnish cultural capital, make her particularly useful as a cultural broker for other Somalis, including nonrelatives needing assistance in their dealings with Finns and Finnish institutions.

Shukri revealed that it was risky to assist nonrelatives. In fact, she recounted numerous instances when she lent money and goods to people outside her clan and they failed to reimburse loans or return her belongings. On one occasion, Shukri lent a set of *dahab* to a woman to wear during a celebration. She did not return Shukri's jewelry and claimed it was lost. Perhaps this woman did not consider herself obligated to return the jewelry to Shukri, a nonrelative and member of a clan with few affiliates in Finland. The woman was aware that whether the gold was lost, stolen, or simply not returned, it was unlikely the incident would affect her own kin networks. The woman's clan is large Finland. Still, it is also possible that the woman borrowed gold because she lacked social capital among clanswomen. Shukri's example underscores not only the flexibility of clan networks in the diaspora but also the greater uncertainty of reciprocity from nonrelatives and of efforts among individuals like her to cultivate networks outside the Somali community.

Shukri is married to a non-Somali, educated and employed in the Finnish formal sector, and was more interested in garnering social capital among Finns. I met with Shukri as she was preparing to attend an International Women's Day celebration. The celebration was held at a multicultural venue in the center of Helsinki. She groomed herself meticulously as if she were attending an *aroos*. That is, Shukri dressed in *diric*, covered her hair with a coordinating scarf, and wore a new set of gold jewelry. She had purchased these items during a recent trip to Somalia. Although Shukri and some other Somali women regularly wear European clothing at home, at work, and during leisure time, they commonly don headscarves and sometimes *diric* when they make public appearances among Finns (for television, newspaper and magazine photographs, cultural events, and speaking engagements).

Shukri said, "Many Finnish women working with foreigners will be there" [at the celebration], and she told me that was why she was eager to attend. Before Shukri left her apartment, she was sure to place a stack of business cards in her purse. Unfortunately, I was unable to accompany Shukri to the party because I had more interviews scheduled.

## Performing Distinction

In most cases, clan networks are vital to successfully carrying out a wedding. The subtleties of these networks are evident in informal economic activities related to *aroos*. In addition to assisting with wedding tasks, relatives often pool economic capital. They purchase wedding goods (cultural capital in its objectified state) and services from the Somali informal economy. In addition, the bride's and the groom's families often buy merchandise——such as clothing, decorations and crafts, and gold jewelry——from relatives working in the informal sector. Families may borrow or rent goods such as patterned

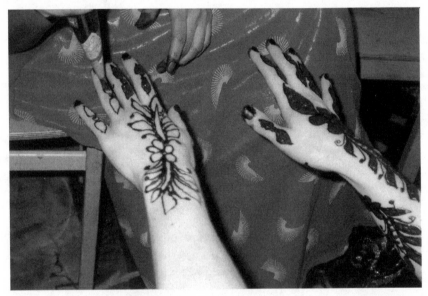

Figure 3. *Cillaan* (henna) application in preparation for an *aroos*, Vantaa, Finland, 2003. A consultant applies henna to my hands for *aroos* at her apartment. She used a piece of uncooked spaghetti to apply black hair dye to create the design before filling it in with red henna. The artist used a cone-shaped bag similar to a piping bag used to apply icing to cakes to apply the henna. At the time, black nail polish was fashionable to complement the henna style. The artist's fingertips are dyed with red henna. This is an everyday style. Some aging women and men use henna to cover gray hairs. Men use it to dye graying beards. Photograph by author.

rugs, ornate fabric to use as wall coverings, and Arabian-style furniture to decorate the space from the informal sector. Families also purchase services from local Somalis as well as from Somalis living in other diaspora communities. These include services of henna artists, videographers, DJs, poets, singers, and hair and makeup artists. Clan relatives in Finland commonly host performers such as singers visiting from abroad.

When Somalis visit relatives in other diaspora communities, Somalia, and other countries in the Horn, they often buy commodities sold in the informal economy. In turn, Somalis resell some of these items to kin in Finland as well as to friends across clans and neighbors. Relatives in the Horn and other diaspora countries also mail commodities for resale in Finland. When Somalis travel within clan networks, it helps them build and maintain otherwise dispersed social capital. Through transactions within the informal economy, various forms of capital convert into other forms.

It is important to note that not all clans have affiliates in Finland who provide the aforementioned goods and services. A case in point is that only two men (one affiliated with a majority clan and the other a minority group) serve as the primary videographers for wedding videos in Finland. On numerous occasions, I observed transactions between nonrelatives; and, in some cases, the family prefers the skills, personality (cultural capital in the form of competence), and merchandise of nonrelatives.

In *Distinction*, Bourdieu (1984) argues that French social classes distinguish themselves through lifestyle choices such as art, clothing, education, food, music, leisure activities, sports, and household decoration. Because each class possesses distinct social spaces in which individuals learn to appreciate specific tastes, distinction is transmitted through socialization. Correspondingly, Somalis in Finland make and encourage distinctive lifestyle choices in an effort to legitimize and transmit social differences between clans.

The appropriation of cultural goods is one strategy of distinction that Somalis use to maintain clan boundaries and notions of clan hierarchy in the diaspora. A number of cultural goods exchanged in the Somali informal economy enable women to perform clan distinction in relation to other clans at *aroos*. During the fieldwork period, 2003–04, I observed an example of this distinction. I noticed some women wearing a *diric* style that they referred to as "Djibouti-style." That is, Isaaq and Ciise (a Dir clan associated with Djibouti) women wore this style, and it was distinguishable from other *diric* because of its extra-large cut and longer sleeves. The *diric* (see figure 2) was brought from Djibouti to Somalia in the 1970s and it is now widely popular among Somali women (M. Abdullahi 2001; Akou 2011). I did not see any women wearing this style of *diric* during my earlier fieldwork (2000–2001).

Samiira, a female consultant from Djibouti, noted that the women there (and from Djibouti) prefer a different henna style than women in the South. She said, "Henna in Djibouti is less decorative, simple, elegant, just black." Like the telling screen names that young Somalis employ during their online interactions that I discussed in the previous chapter, the appropriation of a Djibouti-style *diric* is a product of what I call an amplified effort at distinction in the diaspora.

The wedding tradition of *xeedho* is symbolic of northern clan families. Women in East Africa commonly make the container by hand. Somali women in Finland purchase the container during their travels or they order it through the mail for their own use or for resale in Finland. The outer container is shaped like a woman's body and dressed in cloth; the container contains *muqmad* (also called *oodkac*), dried meat, butter or fat, dates, and spices and it is covered with leather and decorated with shells. *Muqmad* is recognized as traditional food of the northern pastoralist, traveler, and warrior; "Muqmad was and remains the part of the wedding gift offered by the mother at the wedding of her daughter" (M. Abdullahi 2001:146–47).

The outer container is cunningly tied shut with a string to make it cumbersome to open. During wedding festivities, men from the groom's family try to disentangle the string and open the lid without spilling its inner contents while family and friends jeer them. The care the men take in opening the container represents the care the groom takes with his bride and the protection his kin is expected to extend to his new family.

Although I did not see men participating in the *xeedho* tradition at any wedding I attended in Finland, I observed it in wedding videos sent from other diaspora communities and viewed in consultants' households in Finland. In the past, only the groom's male relatives could open the container on the night of *todobo-bah* (end of seven), which marked an end to the seven-day wedding period. More recently, the tradition has taken on new variations, including separate containers for women and substituting desserts for the *muqmad* (M. Abdullahi 2001).

On one occasion, I joined a bride's female relatives to share *muqmad*. This effort at distinction is a strategy northern clans use to continue their association with pastoralism. As established earlier, Somalis who favor the lineage narrative consider a pastoral lifestyle more prestigious than any other mode of production such as agriculture or fishing. It is in the interest of northern women to consume cultural capital that symbolically legitimizes their high status (at least among their kin). Such consumption of this cultural capital may be especially critical if southerners outnumber northerners in Finland, as many consultants claimed they did.

Similarly, I attended a wedding celebration in another Scandinavian capital city that united two southern Dir families. There, guests ate food distinctive of the South, and they feasted on *daango* (popcorn), and *bun iyo cambuulo* (a plate of boiled maize and beans served with roasted coffee beans in ghee and sugar); and drank Somali coffee. Southern Somalis consume coffee more than northern Somalis do. In the North, Somali tea is the preferred beverage. Thus, *bun iyo cambuulo* and coffee are telling of southern cuisine and southern clan affiliation. This cuisine reflects distinction in regional produce and in taste and, in Bourdieu's terms, "in 'showing off' a life-style" (Bourdieu 1984:79). When I shared food with women at *aroosyo*, women from the South commonly told me they eat the banana that accompanies their other food with their meal whereas women from the North told me that they eat the banana after they eat their meal. Sharing distinctive food integrates clan relatives or groups affiliated with the same regions because it creates a clan feeling. Furthermore, these practices are symbolic of clan status claims.

Often, during *aroos*, clan relatives of the bride and groom present distinctive gifts such as *xeedho*. Brides might receive sets of gold jewelry from immediate relatives as well as collective gifts from clan relatives. According to C. Ahmed (1995), jewelry "is often passed on from mother and grandmother (on the maternal side), and women seem to receive a great deal of wealth at their weddings" (164). It is common for women to purchase gold in Dubai and resell it through the informal economy in Finland. Gold jewelry is considered to be a woman's property and asset. It is portable wealth that provides security (Bjork 2001; see also Akou 2011). In moments of crisis, it is often sold to help their immediate family and other kin.[11] The women that I worked with in Finland and Milwaukee, Wisconsin, typically kept their gold secure in hard cases with a combination lock. When some of the women I worked with had extra money, they invested it in gold jewelry.

Fardowsa, a girl in her early twenties, proclaimed that "Clan is good. For weddings, they help and give a lot of gold and gifts." Grooms often purchase sets of gold jewelry for their new wives. One female consultant explained to me that when her fiancé asked her how much gold she desired, she responded, "two necklaces with earrings and rings and a full arm of gold bangles." The design of the jewelry is less important than its weight or value. A wedding necklace remains the bride's property for life (Lewis 1986). Occasionally, at an *aroos*, a bride's mother, clan relatives, and her mother's paternal clan relatives formally present collective gifts of gold to the bride. For example, at one celebration I attended, clan relatives gave a bride more than five sets of gold jewelry. In addition to gift giving among official kin, gifts are strategies to cultivate networks with practical kin.

In one case I observed, a group of unrelated women formally presented a bride with a set of gold jewelry during *aroos*. The emcee announced that the gift was from Djibouti and noted that, like the groom's family, the women identified Djibouti as their home. In this public context, the acceptance of the gift not only constrains the couple to reciprocate but also extends reciprocal obligation to members of the groom's clan (see van Gennep 1960). One interpretation of this tactic may be that it is a means of building social capital and exchange the various forms of capital across clans, since the groom's family will likely reciprocate the gift at a future wedding. This attempt to create horizontal links between the two clan families was met with opposition.

Earlier that evening, the bridesmaids ignored a woman who presented a gift on behalf of Djibouti. Remarkably, she was the same woman who tried to enter the circle to dance with the bride. The bridesmaids, acting as "custodians of the limits of the group," recognized that "Through the introduction of new members into a . . . clan . . ., the whole definition of the group, i.e., its fines, its boundaries, and its identity, is put at stake, exposed to redefinition, alteration, adulteration" (Bourdieu 1986:250).

The woman was upset by the bridesmaids' assumption that, as a member of another clan, she had no right to dance with the bride. She related the incident to the groom's sister, who was a close friend. After hearing the story, the groom's sister took the woman's hand and led her into the circle to dance. In that way, the groom's sister showed that although the woman was unrelated, the woman was her friend and was justified in her actions. The groom's sister may have been aware that the woman would later present a gift to the bride. At times, wedding videos feature the presentation of gifts. This depiction exemplifies active social networks (social capital) and their relationship to economic, cultural, and symbolic capital.

In 2015 Hanaan commented on distinctive practices at weddings. She said, "At *aroos*, they have different dances in the North and the South. Not *buraanbur* (they dance the same style during *buraanbur*). Djibouti-style *diric* (caftan-style dress) is still going on. Usually worn by North but now the South use it, too."

## Watched Weddings: Capital and Circulation of Videos

Wedding videos document an important rite of passage, and they serve as a record of the event. According to consultants, wedding videos became popular in Somalia in the 1980s as Somali expatriates lived, worked, or studied in distant places such as the former colonial countries, the former

Soviet Union, the Middle East, India, and elsewhere. Before this time, photographs served as primary documentation for weddings.

Men working in the informal sector professionally film and edit these videos. According to one male consultant who filmed wedding videos, in 2003 he charged 200 euros (about 275 USD in 2003) per film. Videographers work within an established genre and know the expectations of viewers. Each video, approximately three hours long, fits onto a videocassette, which makes circulation easy and includes footage from *nikaax* and *aroos*. DVDs replace videotapes if dispersed family members own DVD players. Video clips from weddings are posted on YouTube and Facebook and sent by smartphone. Irrespective of the space and place that the wedding occurs, each video communicates the same message: a union forms between two clans, two families, and two individuals. Significantly, Somalis use videos to construct clan boundaries and clan hierarchy through visual representations that legitimize clan affiliation through ritual acts such as *nikaax* and *buraanbur*.

During the fieldwork period, I observed that consultants regularly watched wedding videos in households with family and friends. They tended to play videos repeatedly, not played once and put away. Videos are rewound and fast-forwarded, and viewers pause the video if there is some question about a specific person (question of clan affiliation) or to further examine a dance style, favorite song, or an attractive man or woman. Sometimes, viewing videos is an interactive event. Girls and women sing along to the videos, and they respond to poetic verses by clapping, snapping fingers, calling, and dancing to poetic verses honoring their clan (Bjork 2001).

In this context, youth are socialized in marriage ritual, custom, and cultural tradition as a child's first exposure to weddings is often through videos. Cultural competence is transmitted as youth observe acts of integration such as the *buraanbur* ritual and collective gift giving. They learn to tell clan through names, language, appearance, social networks, and distinction strategies. Notably, in most cases, videos portray clans as integrated, unwavering units as the various forms of capital exchange among kin. In the struggle for capital in its various forms and clan distinction, it is in the interest of individuals to circulate visual representations of weddings. Because each exchange is in itself the work of integration, these videos display solid clan networks.

The production, transnational circulation, and viewing of wedding videos are social practices that link otherwise dispersed networks on a global scale (Bjork 2001). One example demonstrates the value of these videos in the diaspora: during my fieldwork in Milwaukee, Wisconsin, in 1999 I

Figure 4. Videographer filming at an *aroos*, Vantaa, Finland, 2003. The male videographer working in the Somali informal economy films the *buraanbur* ritual at an *aroos* held in the common space of an apartment complex. Photograph by author.

met a recent Somali bride who was dissatisfied with her wedding video. The woman arranged a second *aroos* merely to film a new video. The bride recognized that the potential return from her video outweighed the extra costs and effort of the filming.

Through circulation of videos, Somalis maintain dispersed social networks and form new networks through marriage. According to survey data, half the respondents use videos to maintain contact with family and friends living abroad in a number of ways.[12] Videos enable viewers to see how relatives and childhood friends have changed over the years. Some use these videos to identify a potential marriage partner among the guests shown. Men commonly select prospective wives from the eligible girls and women shown in wedding videos (Al-Sharmani 2004; Bjork 2001).

It is important to note here that not all women and men consider *aroosyo* suitable places for girls and women to congregate because it is well known that men view videos in groups, sometimes while chewing *qaad*, to watch women celebrating at *aroos*. Because these men's viewing practices are well known, women know where to position themselves for inclusion or exclusion in videos. Women who dress in Islamic dress that typically covers the body except for face and hands commonly avoid "the stage" during *aroos*.

The selection of marriage partners is mediated through modernity and access to information technology, which includes mobile phones with camera and video capabilities, video recorders, email, and social networking sites. Within this context, diasporic Somalis maintain mobile social capital in two ways: first, the production of wedding videos for worldwide distribution and consumption, and second, people migrate because of the circulation of wedding videos.

In 2015 Nafiso, Hanaan, and Mohamed commented on how technology use has changed since the fieldwork period. Nafiso and Hanaan noted that DVD and smartphones have replaced videocassette tapes. In 2016 Mohamed added the following by Facebook Messenger. He wrote, "Wedding videos are not so popular as before, but women watch nowadays DVDs, smartphone videos, Facebook, and YouTube clips. And also they use smartphone applications to share wedding images."

# CHAPTER 5

# CRISIS

## It's Tribe Things

On a weekday afternoon, Layla, Farhia, and I met at Robert's Coffee, a popular Finnish coffeehouse chain at the Itäkeskus shopping center. Itäkeskus (referred to locally as *Itis*) is located at the Itäkeskus metro stop in East Helsinki. *Itis* is the largest mall in Scandinavia. Its location is convenient, near the metro and in close proximity to many consultants' neighborhoods in the eastern part of the city. This together with its culturally diverse patrons attracted many of the people I worked with. Although some establishments, like Hesburger, a Finnish fast-food chain, were known as meeting places for men of particular clans, Somalis across clans met at the mall. Over coffee and *korvapuusti*, a rich Finnish roll flavored with cardamom and cinnamon and sprinkled with pearl sugar, Layla talked about her upcoming wedding to Nasir. He was living in Belgium. The couple initially planned to arrange their wedding in Finland, but Nasir was concerned about the going rate of *nikaax* (wedding contract) there. Layla consulted with Halima, a female relative, about the cost because Halima's son, Yusuf, had recently married. Yusuf's *nikaax* cost 1,600 euros (about 2,200 USD in 2004). This amount covered food, water and soft drinks, gasoline to transport guests, and a videographer to film the wedding contract. Layla voiced unease about the cost. She was concerned about telling this to Nasir. Still, Farhia advised Layla to ask her fiancé for "much more money than is needed. He is educated. He must be [a] rich man." After chatting for an hour, we left Robert's Coffee. It was nearing the end of the school day and Farhia had to catch a city bus to her children's school. As we walked toward the bus stop, Farhia's mobile phone rang. Farhia took the phone from her jacket pocket, glanced at the incoming number, and returned the phone to her pocket. "It is someone from Somalia to ask for more money," Farhia said. After Farhia boarded the bus, Layla and I walked toward the metro station. Layla told me about her recent phone call with Nasir. He told her he could not afford a large wedding. After we said goodbye and hugged, Layla boarded the metro traveling east to her apartment, and I boarded the metro traveling west to my apartment near the University of Helsinki. The next day, I returned to *Itis* to meet another consultant for an interview. Walking through the mall, I ran into Layla, who told me that her wedding plans had again changed. Nasir and a few of his male relatives will travel to Helsinki for a small wedding held at Layla's family's home. "I have not told my relatives because they will be upset and [they will] not understand," Layla said. Layla and I agreed to meet for coffee later that afternoon. When we met, Layla told me that her wedding plans had changed again. Nasir decided that they should not celebrate their wedding because a male clan relative of theirs had died. Layla justified Nasir's decision, noting that the relative was "an important man in Somaliland politics."

Layla's and Nasir's families approved of the couple's marriage. The couple's clan had a relatively small presence in Finland. Their clan relatives continued to move to Finland—typically through marriage and family reunification—but a substantial number also had emigrated from Finland. Interview data suggests that these individuals generally moved to England or Somaliland to join more sizable numbers of their kin. Their clan and other northerners have colonial links with England and a long-established migrant community there. In the early 1900s, migrants from British Somaliland, a British protectorate from 1887 to 1960, settled in Cardiff, London, and Liverpool to work as seamen and traders (see El-Solh 1991; Lewis 1994, 2008). Because the clan's size was small in Finland, affiliates had fewer chances to celebrate clan than members of other clans.

According to the people I worked with, most Somalis in Finland were from the South and belonged to one of two clan families. Since *aroosyo* constituted the only communitywide event and the only appropriate occasion for consultants to celebrate clan publicly, these occasions tended to be highly anticipated by northerners. At the *nikaax*, male clan relatives legitimize the lineages of the bride and groom. At *aroos* women honor clan and clan relationships during the *buraanbur* ritual (Somali poetry sung only by women). In the opening passage of the previous chapter, Hodan, a woman affiliated with a northern clan, voiced her dismay at attending yet another "boring" wedding of southerners when she stated, "There are no North dances."

It is predictable that Layla's family and her clan relatives in Finland wanted to arrange a large *aroos*. Layla's relatives in Finland expected Nasir's family living in Belgium and some of the couple's clan relatives in other European countries to participate in the celebration. Such an event would present clan relatives in Finland with an exceptional opportunity to integrate kin and to accumulate and exchange capital among local and dispersed kin. Layla's presumption was convincing when she said her relatives "will be upset and [they will] not understand" if she had a small wedding at her family's home.

The death of a revered male clan relative freed Layla from disclosing her new wedding plans to relatives. The death absolved Nasir from paying for a wedding contract. I did not have a chance to meet Nasir and to ask him why he could not finance a large *nikaax*. It is plausible that Nasir's lack of financial capital correlated with his lack of clan social networks. My observation and interview data suggests that clan relatives commonly pooled resources and labor for *nikaax* and *aroos*. I did not have an opportunity to ask Nasir whether clan relationships were important to him. Regardless of Nasir's viewpoint, he used clan. Nasir met Layla through clan relatives, and he canceled the wedding event because of a clan relative's death. Nasir demonstrated his obligation toward his clan by publicly recognizing the passing of a prominent relative.

During an in-depth interview, Sahra, a female consultant who is affiliated with the Isaaq clan family, shared her insight about her rights and obligations toward clan or tribe:

Tribe, people need tribe when something is happening—for wedding or sorrow—when someone died. Actually, it's like you have to. I have to. Maybe if there is a Hawiye [a clan family] who dies, I don't have to go. If he is Isaaq and his father died, I have to go and say I am sorry. *It's tribe things* [emphasis added]. I don't know. Unless you know the person [who died].

Sahra's comments underscore that an individual's access to social networks or social capital in a clan results from an individual's continual effort to maintain that access. Sahra understood that disregarding the death of a clan relative would affect her potential access to clan networks. Not only did Sahra feel less sentiment toward nonrelatives, she believed that networks with nonrelatives were less useful than networks with relatives. It appears that Nasir also recognized these "tribe things."

Because the deceased male relative had prestige among Layla's clan family, it is not surprising that Nasir decided to cancel the wedding celebration. Not only was the man a close clan relative, he also was "an important man in Somaliland politics." Since 1991, the Republic of Somaliland has acted as a de facto state (Hoehne 2009). Consultants affiliated with the Isaaq clan family took pride in Somaliland's autonomy and relative peace and stability. Its flag featured prominently in a number of consultants' apartments.[1] When other people I worked with referred to Somaliland, they intended it to be telling of the Isaaq clan family, the largest group residing there. Hoehne (2009) notes that this reading is what Somaliland politicians want to deny. They work to downplay the Isaaq's dominance and promote an inclusive Somalilander identity that includes Dir (Gadabuursi and Ciise clans) and Daarood (Dhulbahante and Warsangeeli clans), as well as the Isaaq clan family (Hoehne 2009:264). Despite national holidays, an anthem, and a flag, locals tend to view themselves as northerners or members of particular descent groups.

During an interview with a male consultant in his mid-thirties affiliated with the Gadabuursi clan, I mentioned that I rarely heard anything about his clan other than that they marry Isaaq and live in the North. He responded, "They don't tell you that we are the president? Isaaq are racist sometimes." At that time, Dahir Rayale Kahin, a member of the Gadabuursi clan, was Somaliland's third president (the first two presidents were Isaaq). He was the vice president to the second president, Maxamed Xaaji Ibraahim Cigaal, and succeeded the president, who died in office. Puntland politicians refer to the people of Somaliland as Isaaq rather than Somalilanders and Somaliland politicians refer to Puntland as Majeerteen, a clan of the Daarood clan family, the largest group residing there (Hoehne 2009:265).

It is plausible that Nasir's decision to call off the wedding celebration was not only out of respect for the deceased man's family. This timely crisis presented an opportunity for Nasir to build social capital among kin. Nasir's decision appeased the couple's relatives and it integrated kin by fostering clan sentiment. Perhaps this was also a tactic to position Nasir with the well-respected and well-connected family that had strong networks in Somaliland and with other relatives in the diaspora.

Farhia, the woman who ignored the incoming call from Somalia, explained how the prosperity of an individual or a family correlates to social networks. Farhia said, "If rich people die, people bring food, a camel. If poor people die, no one comes." Rich people are rich because they have networks; poor people are poor because they lack networks; and therefore, it may be more useful to maintain networks with rich people than it is to maintain networks with poor people. Also, I wonder whether Nasir would have held a small wedding at Layla's family home if the deceased close relative had lacked the prestige and social networks that they imagined.

During the fieldwork period, I visited two households with friends to offer condolences after the death of immediate family members. One of the deceased lived in Finland and the other lived in Somalia. I noticed women across clans stopping by to visit and pay their respects. The majority in attendance were female clan relatives who answered the door, prepared food, and served food and drinks to visitors. In 2015 Hanaan commented on clan members' obligations when someone dies. She said, "Yes, that's true. This still exists. When a close relative dies in Somalia, the people who visit and say condolences are from my parent's clans even though they [Hanaan's mother and father] are from different clans." Hanaan's example indicates that obligations extend beyond one's paternal kin and include ties formed by marriage.

## I Don't Need Them. I Have Everything.

If I would have had a chance to ask Nasir about his decision to cancel the wedding celebration, it is unlikely that he would have mentioned anything about clan obligations or clan networks. Because the people I worked with considered clan to be culturally intimate, they would likely consider such a response to be uncouth. I would suppose that Nasir would have told me that he had no choice but to cancel the celebration because it was conventional to do so.

Consultants rarely divulged that they made use of clan. When the people I worked with did account for their use of clan, they routinely maintained that such use was out of their control. They blamed *other* Somalis for the ubiquity of clan in daily life. Consultants tended to gloss over their own use of clan and to dwell on other Somalis' use of clan. This tactic distances oneself from appearing to be into clan and it implicates other Somalis with being clannish.

Simons's fieldwork in Mogadishu during the country's collapse reveals that when Somalia's state institutions failed to provide security and resources for its citizens, Somalis "found themselves falling back on lineage and clan members they knew they could trust" (Simons 1994:820). This was especially frustrating for Simons's Somali colleagues at the World Bank's Central Rangelands Development Project (CRDP)—many of whom were young, university-educated males who took pride in their self-reliance. As ideal citizens, they "believed in what they had been taught in school: the value of nationalism, the merit of honest work, and the evils of nepotism" (Simons 1995:6). They, too, resorted to using clan ties.

My aim in this chapter is to explore consultants' use of local clan networks in the face of everyday crisis. I focus on consultants who are successful in the Finnish formal sector and embrace a Finnish lifestyle in ways more apparent than others do. They consider themselves independent and uninfluenced by clan in much the same way as Simons's colleagues in Mogadishu. These consultants were either born in Mogadishu or relocated to the capital city for higher education. There they learned the state's ideology in school. This chapter also investigates the group's frustration with other Somalis' use of clan, and, less commonly, their own manipulation of clan networks.

During in-depth interviews with these consultants, I asked them whom they called upon when they needed help. I intentionally omitted the terms *clan* and *tribe* from my question because I did not want to sway responses. The interviews focused on networks with local Somalis rather than Somalis at home or living elsewhere. The following excerpts illuminate why some of the people I worked with refrained from calling upon clan relatives in moments of everyday crises:

> AUTHOR: When you need help, whom do you call?
> SHUKRI: The first, it's a friend. I have one best friend, Ali, and the second is my brother. Mostly, I don't call anyone [any other Somalis] for help because then they will want something. Most of them don't need help. On weekends, I like to rest.
> FARAH: I call my friends if I need money—a loan. I say that I can pay [my friends] back then. My friends are from different tribes [clans]. I loan them money if I trust them to pay [me] back.
> NUR: *I don't need them* [other Somalis]. *I have everything* [emphasis added]. I have a job and a family. I call my [non-Somali] wife.
> ASHA: Sister, father.
> HUSSEIN: I am usually with Finnish [Finns] and other foreigners. This is who I call if I need help.
> MOHAMED: Shukri, Nur, friends—friends in Turku. There's no one or two persons. I just call. There's a lot of people.
> AUTHOR: When you need help, do you call anyone from your clan?
> MOHAMED: Never. I don't know them [clan relatives in Finland] by name, but I didn't have a chance to meet them [or] to live with them. We don't have the same background. Most of them are from different places.

None of these consultants mentioned asking local clan relatives for assistance. Because clan is culturally intimate, the omission was predictable. The people I worked with tended to exert much effort to not appear clannish or to be into clan. Farah was the only individual to broach the topic of clan. Farah reported that his local network consisted of friends from "different tribes." Mohamed did not consider his connection with clan relatives in

Finland until after I directly asked him whether he called upon those relatives for support.

Besides the cultural intimacy of clan, these consultants considered themselves to be self-reliant. They all possessed a command of a Finnish lifestyle, worked in the Finnish formal sector, and spoke Finnish fluently. They were always punctual for our meetings. This was rarely the case with other consultants. A few displayed cosmopolitanism through their openness to intercultural interaction, education, and employment opportunities. Cosmopolitanism as a form of cultural competence or "built-up skill in manoeuvring more or less expertly with a particular system of meanings and meaningful forms" enabled them to exchange capital with Somalis, Finns, and other groups (Hannerz 1990:239). Only a few of them pointed out others' clans, and such instances were rare. These individuals denounced other Somalis preoccupying themselves with clan issues and not making use of new opportunities in Finland: free education, employment, and relationships with Finns and other foreigners.

It is appropriate here to restate Farah's quote, which was cited in the introduction: "Tribe is one of those things that make unprogress." Farah, like many of the people I worked with, deemed clan to be antiquated and unfitting for life abroad. Consultants embracing a Finnish lifestyle tended to equate clan with constraint. As Shukri stated earlier, those who dwelled on clan issues tended to pass on chances for building Finnish cultural and social capital in the forms of Finnish cultural competence and social networks with Finns.

Shukri and Nur candidly characterized social networks with most local Somalis to be limiting. She refrained from requesting help from other Somalis because they would expect at least a mutual exchange. Shukri viewed exchanges with most local Somalis as seemingly endless cycles of reciprocity that limited her autonomy. She relied on her siblings and best friend for support. Because Nur had what he wanted, a permanent job and a family, he did not view practical relationships with other Somalis to be useful. When Nur faced an everyday crisis, he relied on his non-Somali wife.

Shukri and Asha asked immediate relatives for help. Farah, Hussein, and Ali did not have immediate relatives living in Finland. Since Farah, Hussein, and Mohamed arrived in Finland without close relatives, they have always lived independently from family. This may have compelled the men to seek social networks with other Somalis who were in a similar position or to look for networks with persons outside the Somali community. It is possible that these men felt less pressure and came across fewer occasions to maintain clan-based social networks than did those living in family households. They were not averse to calling upon all kin in times of crisis. The pool of kin to seek assistance from was narrower, consisting only of immediate family and occasionally extended family. They felt it was not in their best interest to ask more distant clan relatives for help for the reasons discussed in this chapter. Perhaps some were averse to using clan relationships because they recognized this is how clan gains currency.

Farah, Hussein, and Mohamed appeared to feel greater affinity toward Somalis with similar backgrounds in their premigration experience, migration experience, and lifestyle abroad than they did toward local clan relatives. Farah and Mohamed reportedly lived in mixed-clan neighborhoods where they formed friendships with neighbors and classmates across clans. An anthropologist conducting fieldwork in Mogadishu from 1986 to 1987 did not observe separate quarters for different clans (Bhoola 1989:46). Hassan, a male consultant born and raised in Mogadishu, portrayed those from Mogadishu as a collective that disregarded clan:

> AUTHOR: When you first arrived in Finland, how did Somalis relate to one another?
> HASSAN: We people from Mogadishu did not care about clan. We, from South, speak same language. We act as Mogadishu.

Whether Hassan and others that "act as Mogadishu" were less inclined than Somalis from the North to engage in clan politics is unimportant. "There did grow up a generation of young urban people to many of whom clanship meant little, or who were committed to rejecting it" (Luling 2006:476). What is critical is that Hassan and others like him sensed a *Mogadishu feeling* with local Somalis that crosscut clans as opposed to a clan feeling with local clan relatives. For Farah, Hussein, and Mohamed, affiliated with three different clan families, this feeling also outweighed political configurations in Somalia but did not transcend the notion of North and South. Consultants who lived in the capital city commonly regarded themselves as more cosmopolitan than those from the North and rural areas.

During Barre's regime, the National Security Service closely policed Mogadishu residents and arrested and detained government dissidents and clan sympathizers (see Lewis 1994, 2002; Samatar 1988; Simons 1995). In response to everyday surveillance, Mogadishu residents concealed clan telling and devised new, evasive ways to talk about clan (Simons 1995:7). It is likely that Somalis in the North did the same to avoid overt displays of tribalism. Barre's regime weakened the North by concentrating aid and trade in the South (Lewis 1994:177). Growing dissension in the North was met with harsh military rule and surveillance. Supporters of the Somali

National Movement, an Isaaq-led opposition group, were harassed and imprisoned (Lewis 2008:68).

Consultants from Mogadishu tended to characterize themselves and others from the capital city as nationalistic and those from the North and rural areas as clannish. Despite this, each former Mogadishu resident who participated in an in-depth interview recalled an incident prior to the civil war during which another Mogadishu resident asked, "Where are you from?" Farah moved from the North to study at Somali National University in Mogadishu. He proudly stated that he knew all the Somali clans. Farah said, "I learned when I went to Mogadishu to study. Everyone wanted to know where I was from so I learned." Although most consultants from Mogadishu reported that they lived in mixed-clan neighborhoods, some of the people I worked with lived in telling neighborhoods. The ethnographic example at the onset of chapter 2 is a testament to this: Ayaan lived in a neighborhood in Mogadishu that was telling of her clan.

When I asked Mohamed whether he ever called local clan relatives for help, he unhesitatingly answered, "Never." Mohamed explained that he did not know his clan relatives by name because he never had a chance to meet them. Since Mohamed did not grow up near his clan relatives, he did not have the same background as they did. At the end of my interview with Mohamed, I asked him about his clan:

AUTHOR: Tell me about your clan.
MOHAMED: Most of them they are living in Kalabeyr [a town in central Somalia in the Mudug region]. It's near the area . . . now it's called Puntland. Most of them they are living in rural areas. Most of them are nomads. They have a lot of camels. It's peaceful. But the place is not for me. I've been there two times in 1986 and 1988.
AUTHOR: Did you visit this place during your school holiday?
MOHAMED: Yeah, it was my school holiday. I was visiting relatives. I went there to drink camel milk and let's say [eat] a lot of meat.
AUTHOR: Camel meat?
MOHAMED: Yes. And to see what's it like to live there because my father was living [there]. When he was 13, he moved to Mogadishu. Almost his whole life he was living at the city [Mogadishu]. My mother also moved [to Mogadishu] when she was 16 or 18 years old. I don't remember.

Even though his clan is large in terms of numbers in Finland, he was not interested in cultivating networks with them or exchanging capital. It is clear that Mohamed did not feel a *clan feeling* with his clan relatives living in Kalabeyr or Finland. He did not share similar customs with them. He preferred the company and friendship of others from Mogadishu and various clan backgrounds. Perhaps when Mohamed lived in Mogadishu he did not participate in practices that integrated clan members or that cultivated a clan feeling. Mohamed's lack of clan competence may be another reason for his lack of social capital with local clan relatives. If Mohamed had grown up among his clan, perhaps he would have preferred to build social capital with local clan relatives rather than with nonrelatives (then again, maybe not).

In 2015 I contacted Mohamed by Facebook Messenger to comment on his most significant relationships, which happen to be with Somalis from different clan backgrounds. He wrote, "I met Nafiso and other friends when they came to Finland at the refugee reception center. At that time, ppl [people] from same districts or neighborhood used to meet and hang out, as they did not have anything else to do. Even at that time some were keen on clan issues, but there were lot of ppl who are not interested [in] the clan issues at all. Nur, Nafiso, and I were also [with a lot] lot of other friends [we] still keep in touch because we came from the same neighborhood in Mogadishu." In 2016 I contacted Mohamed again to ask a few lingering questions about the associations of some clans and subgroups. He was incapable of helping me to resolve the issues and reminds me of his conscious decision to forgo learning kinship genealogies. There are others like Mohamed who have put forth effort to remain uninformed and indifferent to clans.

Persons affiliated with clans with small numbers in Finland often formed social networks with nonrelatives. Shukri, Nur, and Farah belonged to this category. During an in-depth interview, Farah talked about how few members of his clan lived in Finland:

> AUTHOR: You are the only Samaroon [a subclan of the Gadabuursi, a clan of the Dir clan family] that I have talked with. How many Samaroon live in Finland?
> FARAH: We are small here, about twenty. Most went to England, USA, Canada, and Sweden. People [clan relatives] who came here came from Mogadishu by Aeroflot. It was [not] planned to come here. It was a mistake. There are few men here, maybe five. The women here are married to Majeerteen [a clan of the Daarood clan family] men so I don't go to visit them.

Not only did Farah's clan have a small presence in Finland, several of his male clan relatives had emigrated from Finland, and clanswomen outnumbered clansmen. Perhaps if Farah's clanswomen had married Samaroon or Gadabuursi men instead of marrying Majeerteen men, he might have felt

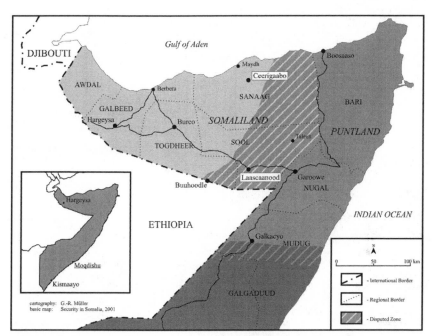

Map 5. Political divisions in northern Somalia: the Republic of Somaliland and Puntland and their disputed border zones. Reproduced by permission from Markus Hoehne, "Puntland and Somaliland Clashing in Northern Somalia: Who Cuts the Gordian Knot?" Crisis in the Horn of Africa, Online Essays. Social Science Research Council, 2007. http://hornofafrica.ssrc.org/Hoehne/.

welcome to visit their homes. Majeerteen men had a large clan presence in Finland and so it is likely that they did not need to expand their networks. The Gadabuursi and Majeerteen clans tend to represent opposing political agendas at home (see maps 5 and 6). Many Gadabuursi are a part of Somaliland and support its secession and most Majeerteen support Puntland and seek to unify Somalia. The president of Somaliland at that time belonged to the Gadabuursi clan, which may have made horizontal links between the Gadabuursi and Majeerteen all that more difficult.

When Farah needed a loan, he relied on friends whom he lived among as an adult or those whom he met during migration. As an adult, Farah moved from his clan's territory in northwest Somalia to Mogadishu. The friends Farah called upon affiliate with different tribes, and a number of those friends did not live in Finland. The clan relatives he maintained close relationships with lived outside Finland. Why might Farah have chosen to rely upon nonrelatives rather than on relatives? Is it credible that Farah

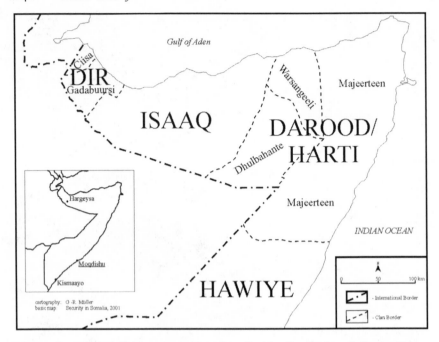

Map 6. Genealogical divisions in northern Somalia. The distribution of clan families (in uppercase) and clans (in lowercase) illustrates the messiness of territorial and genealogical associations. Darood is an alternative spelling for Daarood. Reproduced by permission from Markus Hoehne, "Puntland and Somaliland Clashing in Northern Somalia: Who Cuts the Gordian Knot?" Crisis in the Horn of Africa, Online Essays. Social Science Research Council, 2007. http://hornofafrica.ssrc.org/Hoehne/.

found loans with nonrelatives to be less limiting than loans with clan relatives? Farah exchanged economic capital with a few dependable friends who repaid loans and followed rules of balanced reciprocity (reciprocal exchange of equal value). Farah may have considered these friends as more trustworthy than his clan relatives.

If Farah asks a clan relative for help, the exchange may no longer be conducted on an individual level but rather on a collective level. Simons argues that "success at maintaining and expanding networks also required one to allow oneself to *be* [emphasis in original] taken advantage of" (Simons 1995:117). Individuals who draw upon clan networks must expect other clan relatives to do the same to them. The open-endedness of clan ties makes the relationship especially taxing. In some contexts, an individual may try to manipulate clan ties on a number of levels: clan family, clan, subclan, and so forth. And, as it has been illustrated throughout this book, at times individuals draw upon their mother's paternal clan relatives, North or South, or try to cultivate new groupings such as "Djibouti" and "Mogadishu." Perhaps Farah and others with little clan presence in Finland will come to act as "Somalilanders."

Shukri was an active member of Finnish society. She considered her success the product of her own hard work. Shukri insisted that other Somalis did not need her help in order to achieve success in Finnish society. Shukri said, "Most of them [Somalis] don't need help. On weekends, I like to rest." Shukri affiliates with a clan with a small clan presence in Finland.

I did not ask Shukri to explain why most Somalis did not need her help. Her comment may point to one or more of the following issues. First, most Somalis living in Finland are affiliated with clans that have a large presence in the country. For Somalis affiliated with large clans, their potential access to clan networks was greater than Shukri's. Second, the Finnish welfare state offered Somalis and other refugees and immigrants scores of opportunities for personal development. Third, Shukri valued her free time and autonomy over helping others who were not resourceful.

## Keeping It Underground

Consultants' responses to my question "When you need help, whom do you call?" suggest that they did not maintain local clan networks. Perhaps these Somalis who embraced a Finnish lifestyle considered local clan networks to be of no use to them. Since participant observation led me to believe that the opposite was true, I asked the same consultants another, similar question: "Who calls you when they need help?" Again, I intentionally omitted the terms *clan* and *tribe* because I did not want to sway consultants' responses. The following excerpts offer us another chance to examine these consultants' use of clan:

AUTHOR: Who calls you when they need help?

SHUKRI: Sometimes I help them, my clan, when they call.

AUTHOR: What do they ask you to help them with?

SHUKRI: 'My son is sick, can you call a doctor?' To give a time [to make a doctor's appointment] or go with them to a doctor or if they don't understand it if [it] is a serious sickness. A loan. Money is ended, and they [clan relatives] want to buy food or they have to pay telephone [bill] or they [the phone company] take off [cancels the phone service]. Mother or somebody is sick and going to operation. Something like that. [This conversation was held in English and was occasionally interrupted by Shukri's daughters. This is why the language appears as broken English.]

AUTHOR: Who calls you when they need help?

FARAH: Somalis ask me for a loan or to help them fill [out] some form or to read them a paper they received from the [Finnish] government.

AUTHOR: Who calls you when they need help?

NUR: Everything [everyone]: Job, education, translation, money, school. All [Somalis ask help] for job[s], and even to help for wedding[s]. To rent place [to hold a wedding] or to help decorate it or to give advice—what they can do [for a wedding]. If a singer comes, "Can you take us to the party?" or "Can we use your car?" They [Somalis] want to use you.

AUTHOR: Who calls you when they need help?

ASHA: Money; look for [a] job; school; language [Finnish]. They ask me to make food, [to] make place [decorate wedding space], and [to help with] wedding stuff. Relatives ask other clan problem or something—car ride. If they [nonrelatives] say [that] Isaaq is bad, it's like we are different. We [Isaaq and South] don't understand each other. I don't like South.

ASHA: Clan is also good. If some people [nonrelatives] want to fight me, they bring other women from their clan.

AUTHOR: Why would they want to fight with you?

ASHA: For anything—a man, gossip.

AUTHOR: Who calls you when they need help?

HUSSEIN: Maybe someone from my clan will call or email me about how to get a job or [how] to take a course. I keep it underground like successful Finns. Like Swedish-Finns, they *keep it underground* [emphasis added]. They keep to themselves.

AUTHOR: Who calls you when they need help?

MOHAMED: A lot of people—some hundreds. Most of them they [the requests for help] are technical. Let's say about computers, electronics. And sometimes some of them [Somalis] don't know how to fix it [a computer], [or] install it [software], [or assemble] new furniture.

AUTHOR: Do Somalis ask you to help them find a job?

MOHAMED: Not much, few.

AUTHOR: Do Somalis ask you to help them with Finnish translations?

MOHAMED: Yeah, sometimes translations. Weddings a few times.
Not much. Invitations, arranging a place, that kind of stuff. Not
cooking (Mohamed laughs). I remember only one time some [So-
malis] asked—*not* [a] *relative*—someone else asked [a nonrelative asked], 'We need to collect for [a] wedding gift.'

Unlike the responses to the previous question I asked consultants, this question resulted in nearly all consultants—with the exception of Farah and of
Nur—broaching clan in their response. Surely, I might have provoked more
telling responses if I had tactically inserted the terms *clan* or *tribe* into both
questions, but it was not my intention to compel clan-related statements.
If I had, it might have hindered the candidness of the people I worked with
because it might have inaptly foregrounded the cultural intimacy of clan.

Why were consultants at this interview moment franker about the ubiquity of clan than they were at the previous interview moment? Did my
persistent questioning influence consultants' answers? Did the extra question simply give consultants more time to ponder clan? Or did the cultural
intimacy of clan compel consultants to be more outspoken? I argue for the
latter explanation.

As I expected, these consultants were eager to inform me about *other*
Somalis using clan networks. As mentioned earlier, Somalis tended to gloss
over their own manipulation of clan and to dwell on other Somalis' manipulation of clan. This tactic distances oneself from *other* Somalis who appeared
to be motivated by clan. Still, when consultants assisted clan relatives with
everyday crises, they cultivated clan networks.

Shukri reported that clan relatives asked her for help. Shukri admitted to
helping clan relatives only "sometimes." She participated in collective gift
giving and in *aroos* with her clan. The dialogue in chapter 3 suggests that
Shukri was more likely to help clan relatives than to help nonrelatives. Even
though Shukri's clan was relatively small in Finland, her Finnish cultural
competence, Finnish social capital, and economic capital made her exceptionally useful to clan relatives and nonrelatives.

Interview excerpts revealed that other Somalis considered all these consultants to be useful because of their command of a Finnish lifestyle and,
in some cases, their economic capital. All consultants acknowledged that
they helped other Somalis in their moments of crisis. Almost all consultants
admitted to assisting clan relatives. Mohamed and Asha even admitted to
using and cultivating clan networks.

In the previous section, Mohamed claimed he did not know his local clan relatives. Mohamed stated he did not understand his local clan relatives because their backgrounds were dissimilar to his. It is surprising that Mohamed mentioned an occasion when a nonrelative asked him to contribute money for a nonrelative's wedding gift. Because Mohamed emphasized *nonrelative* in his statement, it is likely that local clan relatives have asked Mohamed to contribute money for clan relatives' wedding gifts or that such a request is uncommon.

Asha was the most forthright about her use of clan. When unrelated women wanted to fight with Asha, she relied upon her clanswomen for protection. I did not ask Asha where other women might instigate a fight with her. Since girls and women commonly brought conflicts to the forefront at *aroos*, Asha could be confronted there. Asha did, however, disclose reasons for such a crisis: gossip and men.

Like many of the other people I worked with who embraced a Finnish lifestyle, Asha limited her interaction with other Somalis. Asha explained why she did this:

> AUTHOR: Tell me about your interactions with and relationships with Somalis in Finland.
>
> ASHA: It's not so close. I can't trust Somalis. I have [had a] bad experience. Sometimes [I visit] their house, wedding, party, discos. Only my sister and some relatives I trust, but not [Somalis who are] my age.
>
> AUTHOR: Why do you not trust Somalis who are your age?
>
> ASHA: Because they talk too much. Some are North and some are South because there are not a lot [of Somalis who are her age] from North [in Finland]. I also have friends from other countries.

I did not ask Asha to recount the bad experience. It is conceivable that Asha's bad experience with Somalis involved gossip. Asha, a girl in her early twenties, was the youngest consultant among those highlighted in this chapter. Although Asha was unmarried, she lived independently from her family's household. Asha did not live in Kandahar, but she enjoyed a liberated lifestyle similar to that of Kandahar residents. Asha dressed in Western-style clothing, drank alcohol, smoked cigarettes, frequented discos, and dated Finnish boys. These lifestyle choices made Asha an easy target for gossip. Asha claimed that Somalis from her age group gossiped the most, which made it difficult for her to trust her peers and made relationships with other Somalis tricky. Participant observation indicated that some of the girls and women who made lifestyle choices similar to Asha's avoided being a target for gossip by keeping their indiscretions more private.

In 2015 Hanaan commented on how alcohol use has changed since the fieldwork period. She said, "Today those who drink show that they drink and don't care. This includes boys and girls, but boys are more showing than girls. I see girls drinking wine, beer, cider on the terrace and not caring what other Somalians would say about them." It is popular to enjoy drinks with friends, classmates, and colleagues on pub, restaurant, and café terraces in the city center or near the seaside during the warm summer months.

Asha enjoyed friendships with Somalis from both the North and from the South. Asha was quick to point out, however, the reason she had any friends from the South. She said, "There are not a lot [of Somalis her age] from North [in Finland]." Asha felt affinity toward her clan relatives, and she claimed that she felt different from Somalis affiliated with other clans, particularly those from the South. Notably, during an in-depth interview with Asha, she revealed that she used her stepmother's southern clan for protection in a crisis. Asha said, "When I was little it was war [in Mogadishu]. My stepmother teach [taught] me her tribe for safety. She was from Mogadishu."

Although Asha had an independent lifestyle, she maintained networks with Somalis in the same way that other Somalis did: visiting households and attending weddings and parties. Only she did so less frequently than others in her age group living in family households. The same was true for the other interviewees emphasized in this chapter. It appeared that clan relatives excused them from daily maintenance of clan networks because they were exceptionally useful in terms of their access to financial capital and Finnish cultural competence. Asha, however, did not possess the capital that Shukri, Nur, and Mohamed had access to (educational credentials and careers).

Somalis regularly asked Shukri, Nur, and Mohamed for assistance when they confronted daily crises. And each consultant complied with many of these requests from relatives and nonrelatives. Still, Nur could not help but think of other Somalis as a burden, and he felt bothered by other Somalis. He explained, "They want to use you." Many of the other people I worked with voiced the same estimation.

Some of the people I worked with even shared their strategies for limiting interaction with other Somalis and avoiding helping them. Mohamed, a single man in his thirties, found it difficult to say no to Somalis when they asked for his help. This was evident from the "some hundreds" that called him when they needed assistance and the lengthy list of tasks he helped with. Mohamed tried to deter these requests for help:

> Sometimes I just close [turn off] the phone and sleep. For example, last night I went to sleep before 9 [p.m.] and switch[ed] off the phone and went to sleep. And sometimes I just mute the phone and then you can see who called last night and when they called. Some [Somalis] call at 11 [p.m.] or 12 [midnight].

Mohamed employed this everyday tactic in order to avoid performing time-consuming tasks for others. For the same reason, Shukri ignored knocks at her door from other Somalis. Gewertz and Errington (1999) note that the new elite in Papua New Guinea employ similar tactics to evade helping less successful Papua New Guineans.

Hussein, an unmarried entrepreneur in his early thirties, employed a similar technique. Hussein tended to frequent places that most other Somalis shunned. Hussein suggested that we meet at Café Vanha for the interview because he planned to meet a Finnish colleague there later that evening. This haunt is a favorite among students at the University of Helsinki. It is located in Vanha Ylioppilastotalo [Old Student House] in central Helsinki and dates back to the late 1800s. Hussein was noticeably the only Somali at the establishment. Most customers were drinking beer or cider with friends. At the time, if Somali girls and women merely entered such a place they could face a crisis, because their reputations might be tarnished by salacious gossip.

Between sips of Lapin Kulta (translates as Lapland's Gold), a popular Finnish beer, Hussein—in casual business attire, a slim-fit button-down shirt tucked neatly into his trousers—said, "I *keep it underground* [emphasis added] like successful Finns. Like Swedish-Finns, they keep it underground. They keep to themselves." Hussein's reference to Swedish-Finns is illuminating. *Finlandssvensk* (Swedish for Finland-Swedish or Finland-Swede), as they call themselves in Swedish, are an ethnic minority in Finland and comprise 5.3 percent of Finland's population (Official Statistics of Finland 2015). Sweden governed Finland for seven hundred years until Sweden was forced to cede it to Russia. Since Finland's independence in 1917, the country has had two official languages: Finnish and Swedish.

When I was an exchange student in Finland from 1990 to 1991, my school friends commonly complained to me about having to learn Swedish at school. Throughout the years, these same friends have imparted a number of stereotypes of Swedish-speaking Finns or Finland-Swedes. They think they are better than other Finns. They tend to be wealthier and think they are more sophisticated. They often demand services at governmental offices and department stores in Swedish. They prefer to keep to themselves and attend Swedish-speaking schools and universities.[2] Perhaps Hussein modeled his behavior after this stereotype. He limited his social networks to people who were like-minded and had what he wanted: financial capital and successful careers. It is fitting then that when Hussein encountered a crisis, he called upon Finns and other nonethnic Finns, but not Somalis.

Dega, a city social worker, also distanced herself socially from other Somalis. She recalled an incident in which a client accused her of favoring clan relatives. She said, "One young man came in [to my workplace], and he said that I only get money for my relatives. I told him that I do not have relatives in Finland—only my husband and kids. He meant clan relatives." Three consultants working as public servants did not respond to my inquiry about their clan affiliation. They maintain (as many Somalis do) that clan does not play a significant role in their daily lives. They contend that their associations were restricted by the watchful eyes of other Somalis, especially their Somali clientele who might suspect them of nepotism.

In 2015 Hanaan commented on a recent work experience in which a clan relative expected preferential treatment. She said, "A guy was asking me to give him a favor to get 'special service' because he is my mom's relative. I told him that since he speaks Finnish, he should go to be served by the Finns [her Finnish coworkers]."

Nur, a school employee, expressed his disillusionment with the current state of Somalis in Finland:

AUTHOR: How do Somalis in Finland relate to each other now?

NUR: Very difficult because most are nomad from countryside. It's difficult to understand them. They say they are from Mogadishu, but they are not. Physically they are in Finland, but mentally they are in another place. They have not [no] interest to be in Finland. There is no community here. Everyone is thinking about tribe [clan], and everyone thinking about himself. There is no self-confidence.

AUTHOR: What do you mean by self-confidence?

NUR: If you do something, they think what does *masjid* (mosque) say? What does tribe [clan] say? What does family say? They talk about bullshit. How this country [Finland] is racist. That's why I don't want to do anything for them. It makes me sick.

Nur's sharp words captured the vital role of the homeland, clan, and mosque in everyday life for local Somalis, particularly in terms of decision making.[3] Distinct backgrounds (*habitus*) in terms of clan, class, livelihood, and residence prior to migration, compounded with the effects of civil war and the current spatial organization of Somalia, have led to further fragmentation among Somalis abroad. Nur struggled with the notion that many Somalis organize by clan or adherence to Islam rather than uniting under a nationalist identity. He was frustrated with Somalis who preoccupied themselves with homeland politics and blamed racism for their lack of success and acceptance in Finland rather than making an effort at integration: learning Finnish, attending school, and gaining employment.

Nur considered himself to be self-reliant. When Nur made a decision, he did not confer with clan relatives or religious leaders. Nur's frustration with other Somalis could also stem from his lack of clan-based social capital. Nur's clan, with its small presence in Finland, did not act as a collective, as did many of the clans with a larger presence. It is conceivable that these circumstances compelled Nur to integrate and build social networks among Finns and other Somalis from Mogadishu. Still, Nur and other individuals employed in the Finnish formal sector commonly reported their dissatisfaction with other Somalis' unwillingness to separate individuals from clans and related interests.

## Everyday Crisis

Excerpts from in-depth interviews clearly demonstrate why many of the people I worked with turned to the few Somalis who had a command of a Finnish lifestyle when they faced crises. Also, the excerpts reveal consultants' tactics to avoid assisting Somalis who requested their help. What is less clear from the passages is why these individuals helped other Somalis and why they cultivated networks with other Somalis. When these consultants encountered an everyday crisis, did they utilize clan networks?

Participant observation of these and other consultants sheds light on how they used clan networks in moments of crisis. Perhaps the most frequent everyday crisis was salacious gossip or other conflicts, including divorce and adultery. The fight at the *aroos* and the earlier excerpt from Asha's interview are evidence of this. I consider gossip to be an everyday crisis because it may affect an individual's potential access to clan networks and networks across clans.

Farhia, a recent bride who once lived independently from her family's household, was a common target of gossip. After Farhia was married, her clanswomen gossiped about her even more. So, in an attempt to abate the gossip, Farhia invited some prominent local clanswomen, along with her sisters, to her home for a traditional feast. Hibo, Farhia's sister, explained that the clanswomen gossiped about Farhia because she did not arrange a women's wedding party when she married.

After the women's visit to Farhia's home, Farhia called Hibo and told her that she spent all her money on the feast. If Farhia was successful in curtailing the gossip and gaining the support of her clanswomen, Farhia's money was well spent. Farhia's hospitality likely cultivated clan networks. It is unlikely that such a gesture would substitute for a rite of integration where relatives exchanged the various forms of capital. Still, Farhia's efforts might have diverted a crisis, that is, the loss of her clanswomen's support.

Other everyday crises such as sickness, medical emergencies, and death called for support. In such cases, extra help was needed to meet daily requirements: caring for children, cleaning, buying and preparing food, paying bills, and so forth. Sometimes clanswomen sold their *dahab* (gold jewelry) in order to offer support to relatives. "Bracelets, necklaces, and earrings are often sold at times of drought, and collections are expanded at times of surplus" (C. Ahmed 1995:180). At other times, relatives living in Finland and other diaspora locations would temporarily move in with the person in need until the crisis subsides. In order for consultants to quickly draw upon such networks, they must be regularly maintained.

In 2015 Hanaan commented on the benefit of having clan relatives nearby to help during divorce or marriage problems. She said, "Sometimes clan is a good thing. For example, when a girl gets divorced she needs her father's clan to support her. If she is abused the elders from both clans negotiate and say what is right and protect her."

When individuals did not have access to clan networks, they might ask nonrelatives for assistance. Hawa, a woman in her thirties, was such an individual. She was from a small clan with small numbers in Finland, and most of her immediate relatives lived in the Horn of Africa. When a close relative of Hawa needed to have a life-saving operation, she called Rukia, a nonrelative who was successfully employed. Hawa cried as she told Rukia about the crisis. Rukia said that she was reluctant to give Hawa several thousand euros to pay for the operation, but she found it difficult to say no to Hawa, and she lent her the money. Although Hawa promised to repay Rukia in an agreed-upon number of installments, when I ended my fieldwork, Hawa had already missed the first payment. It is unclear whether Hawa had offered Rukia similar assistance in the past.

As mentioned in chapter 4, Shukri lent other Somalis her *dahab* and her money on numerous occasions. For the most part, she found such exchanges with nonrelatives to be risky. Still, sometimes Shukri could not say no to Somalis facing a crisis. Shukri, Hawa, and Rukia are affiliated to small clans in Finland. Perhaps Shukri and Rukia's support of nonrelatives were efforts to build social networks beyond their small clan. If Shukri and Rukia encounter a crisis that requires the support of others, they may call upon these networks.

In 2015 Hanaan commented on when it is appropriate to expect assistance from clan relatives and provide support. She said, "In Finland, you need [to be] more proud of yourself and not ask money from clan. If something happens in Somalia, in your clan's area, then they collect money from all around the world from the same clan. When my uncle died in Somalia, all close male relatives collected money for wife and kids. In Finland, you don't need that support because the government and your own work and close family they help you." Hanaan's example of *qaaraan*, clan assistance, illustrates its value as a resource in case of contingency.

## Crisis of Clan Legitimacy

Perhaps the paramount crisis for the people I worked with was a lack of clan legitimacy. Legitimizing clan membership has significant effects on marriage prospects and access to clan capital. To legitimize personal claims to clan membership, consultants used the everyday practice of telling. Still, some individuals were suspected of masking their clan affiliation.

Given the value of clan, some Somalis exerted a tremendous amount of effort toward discovering the clan affiliation of ambiguous individuals. Nuura, a female consultant, revealed that she attempted to unmask the clan ancestry of another consultant. When Nuura traveled to Somalia, she and her female cousin, Hawa, visited Safiya's family in hopes of learning the woman's rightful clan.

Safiya was in Somalia at the same time as Nuura and Hawa, and Safiya was well aware of what the two women sought. Safiya even told me about the incident:

> Nuura and her cousin Hawa are like private detectives. They tried to find out my tribe. They also tried to find out about my relative's wife. They wanted to know who she was [what her tribe was]. Nuura and Hawa came to our home in [name of town].

I am unaware of other cases similar to this one. Because the people I worked with tried to verify the clan affiliation of a potential spouse, this instance was not surprising and it may be more common than I know of. A crisis of clan legitimacy is serious for the individual. Persons suspected of falling outside the social boundary of Somaliness may face social ostracism. The same was true for their children. Such a crisis will not affect one's standing in Finnish society.

## Averting Crisis at Home

Among Somalis in Finland, Nuura, Hawa, and Safiya's trips to Somalia are not exceptional. Roughly a fourth of consultants had visited Somalia, and a few planned to visit within the next year. Often, crises such as sickness (their own or relatives') and death prompted consultants' first trips back to Somalia.[4] Survey data reveal that consultants visited Somalia for the following reasons: to visit relatives, including sick relatives, and to pay respect after another relative's death; to do work-related projects for the Finnish government and nongovernmental organizations; to participate in business ventures; to engage in informal economic activities; to vote, to hold political office; to spend a summer holiday away from school; to be married; to build a home; to seek traditional healing, and to attend the circumcision of young boys. Although it was more common for men to travel to Somalia to marry, a few women embarked on a similar journey to marry a man in Somalia. In these few marriages that took place during the fieldwork period, at least those that I was aware of, consultants married within their own paternal clan or with a person from their mother's paternal clan. Finland's social healthcare system does not cover circumcision procedures for boys because Finns do not have a tradition of circumcising boys. Some private physicians perform circumcisions for a fee, providing both parents consent and the boy understands the procedure.[5] In 2015 Hanaan commented on the status of male circumcision in Finland. She said, "[It's] still illegal in Finland, only for health purposes." She explained that some families travel to Middle Eastern countries to have the procedure performed for boys.

When I asked consultants where they traveled in Somalia, they tended to answer with the following telling places: Afgooye, Berbera, Burco, Bosaaso, Ceerigaabo, Jariiban, Kismaayo, Qorulugud, and Somaliland. Somaliland was the most common destination. Mogadishu was the second and least telling one. When Shukri told me about her most recent trip home in the early 2000s, another reason for visiting particular places became apparent:

AUTHOR: Tell me about your most recent visit home.
SHUKRI: It happens, too many people are coming now here [to Mogadishu]. And then everybody is trying to find their family or who's coming [to meet you]. After that, everybody is trying to find [their] bags. After that, you run away to home.
AUTHOR: Who meets you at the airport?
SHUKRI: My family.
AUTHOR: Which family members meet you at the airport?

SHUKRI: The airport is fifty kilometers from the big town. I think
fifteen men or something come to get me at the airport. They are
security. They come in a truck, and they all have machine guns.
But not the driver; he has a pistol. The first time I was afraid, but
not now. I know them. They are my clan.

As the above passage indicates, clan networks were essential for Shukri's
safety in Mogadishu. Shukri's armed escort was not the standard. The situation she described was likely due to heightened violence. During fieldwork,
consultants' clan affiliation largely determined where they could safely travel
in Somalia. One young woman said, "I was born in Mogadishu but I can't
go there. My clan is not there. They are in Ethiopia." Consultants' use of
telling place names may have been a tactic to legitimize their claims to clan.
It is more likely that the people I worked with stated a telling place name
because they returned to their ancestral clan territory. At that time, many
Somalis in Somalia tended to reside in their clan territory unless it was unsafe
to do so. Consultants tended to visit those territories, and this is where they
received clan protection. Although kin may offer protection because they
feel a sense of duty and obligation toward visiting relatives, it is conceivable
that their need for economic capital is the primary motivation. It may be
that visiting relatives paid kin for their personal security.

In 2015 Nafiso commented on her recent trip to Hargeysa. She no longer
makes regular trips to Mogadishu because her close relatives relocated to
the North. She said, "In Hargeysa [there are] no guns [needed for protection when she arrives]. Before in Mogadishu when it was more dangerous,
yes. Now there is outsider military with guns providing security at the
airport—African Union or AMISON [African Union Mission in Somalia]."

At the Ninth SSIA Congress held in Aalborg, Denmark, in 2004, I met
four Somali men—Cabdinuur, Abuukar, Moxamed, and Caddow—who
traveled to the conference from the Horn of Africa. After we introduced
ourselves to each other, Moxamed asked me about my conference paper. I
hesitantly told the men that I planned to discuss clan in the diaspora. My
mere mention of clan led to the following exchange:

ABUUKAR: Yes, it's good to talk about clan.
CABDINUUR: Yes, clan matters.
CADDOW: I am a professional. I don't need clan.
CADDOW'S COMMENT AMUSED ABUUKAR.
CADDOW: Some people come to the hospital and expect that I serve
them first because they are from my clan. I tell them that they
must wait in line as the other patients do.

AUTHOR: Why did you return to Mogadishu?

ABUUKAR: This is where he is from. He has his clan to protect him there.

AUTHOR: Oh. Is the hospital a safe place? Do you drive a car to work each day?

CADDOW: I have security to take me to and from work.

AUTHOR: Your clan?

CADDOW: Yes.

AUTHOR: So, you could not work safely in Mogadishu without your clan?

CADDOW: Yes.

*The other three men laughed.*

Learning that Caddow used clan ties for his everyday safety is noteworthy. Even more compelling is that my conversation with these Somali men who reside in the Horn of Africa represents yet another culturally intimate moment. Although Caddow used clan daily to travel safely to work, he claimed, "I am a professional. I don't need clan." Such a statement characterizes clan as being antiquated and those that use it uneducated. Abuukar was quick to confirm that Caddow lived among his clan in Mogadishu and that Caddow used clan networks. None of the other three men admitted that they made use of clan. Still, it is likely those men too used clan relatives to avert daily crises. And it is likely they utilized networks with neighbors, coworkers, mother's paternal clan, and networks through marriage when they needed help.

## Crisis and Clanship

Simons (1994, 1995) argues that during the dissolution of Somalia, the structure of clanship was exposed. In the North, however, Somalis found themselves in a liminal state much earlier, beginning in the early 1980s when Barre's promotion of his own clan affiliations was exposed (Markus Hoehne, personal communication, November 10, 2012; Lewis 1994, 2008). Following Turner (1974), Simons (1994) notes that in times of crisis, "the structure of society itself is revealed, embedded, and disembedded" (822). As Somalis found themselves in a liminal state—that is, without security, resources, or government infrastructure—they turned to people they could trust: clan relatives.

In this liminal state of dissolution, clanship was a viable option for Somalis, including those who considered themselves to be self-reliant and to be proponents of nationalism. Simons argues that this liminality, together with communitas (a feeling of intense solidarity and sentiment), accounted for the emergence of clanship. Turner (1969) views communitas and structure as a binary opposition; Simons (1995), however, argues that "both conditions [communitas and structure] are operative but with mutually constructive—and not just opposing—effects" (192).

Simons (1995) notes, "as conditions worsen, individuals increasingly cohere in order to depend on one another because they *know* they can, not because they *think* they should" [emphasis in original] (142). How do Somalis *know* they can rely upon clan relatives? Simons theorizes that, in the case of Somalis, feeling and sentiment that derive from shared "language, common ancestry, custom, and so on . . . has not been adequately considered" in the literature on tribalism (194). Also, the literature does not consider why such feeling and sentiment among clan relatives and markers look like hard structure.

Although Somalis who embraced a Finnish lifestyle used clan as other Somalis did, they tended to do so less frequently. They rarely asked relatives and nonrelatives for help because they believed doing so would escalate into endless obligations. Other Somalis considered them to be exceptionally useful because they had access to economic capital as well as to Finnish cultural and social capital. Other Somalis excused these more prosperous individuals from daily practices such as visiting households. Although Somalis who had a command of a Finnish lifestyle tended to evade the frequent requests of other Somalis for help, they also tended to grant the requests of clan relatives. It is possible that these prosperous Somalis realize that life in the diaspora is uncertain. If they maintained clan networks now, the networks may be useful to them in the future.

In 2015 Hanaan commented on the persistence of clanship and how the everyday crisis of racism can unify Somalis. She said, "At this moment we are in the same situation all over again. We always have different clans, which have problems with other clans. This continues. It never changes. The war starts in 1990s and we are living in 2015 and the same thing continues—like day one. But when the enemy is an outsider, all Somalians are best friends for life—forgetting history of clans and problems they had with each other. When racism comes in front of us, then we forget the clan word."

# CONCLUSION

This ethnography is the first work to consider the role of clan or tribe in the Somali diaspora and the only book that considers women's perspectives in addition to the traditionally recognized men's perspectives on the topic of clan. I sort out reasons why clan is so important in the diaspora, even if many Somalis deny this to be the case. It also underscores changing clan relations and value of clan in Somali society abroad since the state collapse. The practice theory approach employed in this book helps to uncover that what appears to be hard structure is actually the effects of practices achieved on the ground. In the moments of telling, movement, celebration, and crisis, Somalis' use of local and global clan networks is what makes these seemingly habitual everyday practices become a durable pattern that resembles structure—over time and as the result of constant effort.

Through an intimate look at the everyday life of Somalis in Finland, I reveal the cultural intimacy of clan. The people I worked with are embarrassed by the notion that clan in any way affects their life abroad. They routinely blame cultural insiders and outsiders for its persistence as a source of both division and association. Yet everyday encounters point to consultants' habitual, though understated, efforts to construct clan through telling. Telling is a strategy for legitimizing genealogical claims to clan, constructing boundaries of Somaliness, and avoiding faux pas (Bjork 2007b). Although Somalis who arrived in Finland during the early to mid-1990s tended to self-identify by the reckoning of ancestors, the sophistication of telling during the fieldwork period points to an ongoing level of investment in clan competence.

Telling is also fundamental in building a *clan feeling*, an affinity honed through perceived commonality and trust, which is vital for making clan feel real. In this book, I consider clan as a form of social capital. I have shown that clan is not a latent and accruing value. Clan networks must be actively maintained in order for them to be useful. Clan relationships become real and have real effects through clan's utility as a resource. The people I worked with accumulated and exchanged capital in its various forms through local and global clan networks. This challenges the assumption that social capital always decreases with migration and points to the value of clan ties as an investment for Somalis around the world.

The book makes clear that Somalis use clan in modern ways. Somalis' management of capital on a global scale is evidence of the embrace of clan. Lewis argues that "they [Somalis] embrace it [modernity], adopting and adapting what interests them for their own purposes" and deploy Somali kinship "tactically as a multipurpose, culturally constructed resource" (Lewis 1998b:105). The use of clan has real effects seen in social networks, informal economic practices, marriage practices and taboos, migration, travel, remittances, and politics and development in Somalia. Daily life exposes networks as flexible and reveals innovative configurations and uses. Consultants may use clan networks in certain contexts, but they may draw from other networks that crosscut clans.

The book exposes the messiness, as opposed to the abstracted orderliness, of clan. Creating a *clan feeling* and sense of obligation among clan relatives is cumbersome. For Somalis employed in the Finnish formal sector and who embrace a Finnish lifestyle, the effort is particularly taxing. In the diaspora, Somalis encounter ideologies that compete with a collective and hierarchical clan ideology. Also, the people I worked with possess various degrees of clan competency, that is, knowledge of clan genealogies and clan relationships. Individual investment in this cultural capital requires individual and group effort. Some consultants feel more *kinship* with individuals that share similar migration experiences, prior residence, time of arrival in Finland, religious practices, Somali dialect and other spoken languages, and interests than they do with clan relatives. And some consultants are more integrated with their mother's paternal clan than with their own paternal clan, and others feel little to no connection with clan relatives or the larger Somali community.

Mohamed A. Eno's reading of why individuals self-identify in particular ways during particular moments, in Chapter 2, underscores clan identities as flexible and situational. How does an individual feel at a particular moment? Who is considered a clan relative? At what level of segmentation do Somalis feel like a member of a clan? How does identification relate to ongoing status claims? In what ways do these claims link to the size of local groups, local power dynamics, or status narratives? What local and global conditions (relationships, alliances, and oppositions) influence this choice? I have shown that, in some cases, the size of clans in local settings can affect the ways individuals and groups organize. Individuals with few clan relatives can choose from a variety of options as they see fit. They can cultivate networks based on Mogadishu, *Waqooyi* (North) or *Koonfur* (South), build networks with Finns or other immigrants, or create new associations. Plus, the everyday practice of telling can be used to form links across clans.

Strategies to build new associations can be met with resistance. This was evident when a group of women from a northern clan (southerners outnumber northerners in Finland) presented a collective gift of gold jewelry to a bride affiliated with another clan at *aroos* (wedding). The women's public attempt to cultivate association based on Djibouti, a shared previous place of residence, indicates the difficulty of creating and balancing horizontal links between clans. Even though persons affiliated with northern clans have less potential access to clan-based social capital than those affiliated with southern clans, such a public exchange challenges the group's parameters and affiliate's rights and obligations. It is notable that the women did not present their gift on behalf of "Somaliland" given that both clans comprise a significant proportion of Somaliland residents. Associating under the banner of "Somaliland" may have been too culturally intimate in a public setting such as *aroos*, pushing the boundaries of what is acceptable. Such a move could be too boastful because Somaliland is relatively peaceful and stable, which distinguishes it from most other regions in Somalia. It would also indicate blatant support for Somaliland's political agenda, including its secession and claim over its contested border with Puntland. Also, the women were aware that the video of the wedding would circulate widely in Finland, throughout the diaspora, and at home.

It is likely that some of the people I worked with form networks and political identities based on a Somalilander, Puntlander, or nationalist ideology (and, at times, identifying or drawing from numerous categories). I have heard Somalis in the United States identify as Somalilanders, Puntlanders, and Somali nationalists and have noticed friends on Facebook posting, sharing, and liking pages associated with these and other identities such as Jubbalander. (The Jubbaland state of Somalia is an autonomous region in southern Somalia.) These associations are also flexible and situational. Research in northern Somalia indicates that political identities are flexible "due to the common practice of 'climbing up' or 'down' the chain of male ancestors, on which the segmentary lineage system of Somali society is built" with flexibility diminishing amid violence (Hoehne 2006:3). Openness is also evident in political flip-flopping, which is illustrated in a story recounted by Hoehne (2006). One of his male consultants, a member of the Dhulbahante, a Daarood clan that inhabits the contested region between

Somaliland and Puntland, left his position with the Puntland government to work for Somaliland. His decision to switch sides was not only due to political interests. The man's economic interests also figured into the decision. The Puntland government was unable to pay salaries with regularity. This example is illuminating for Somalis around the world and speaks to the novel ways that Somalis construct and use clan. Although this story is fascinating on so many levels, I am left wondering, now that the man switched sides, does he consider himself as *Waqooyi* (North) or *Koonfur* (South)? And how do others view him in various contexts?

The political identities I have noted are further complicated by marriage and migration. In addition to the primary clans that inhabit Somaliland and Puntland, there are Somalis affiliated with other clans that now live there as a result of marriage, internal migration from south to north largely to avoid drought and civil unrest, and returnees. The minority groups that live there face discrimination and have little to no political representation (Hoehne 2014:10–11). Several of the people I worked with traveled to these areas regularly and a few married either their own paternal clan relative or their mother's paternal clan relative there. These ties may strengthen one's affiliation with these territories, its people, and its political aims and form the basis of similar alliances among Somalis in Finland and online.

This book makes clear the ways culture is shared, negotiated, and contested. Somalis share clanship, but the sentiment and meaning clanship evokes is highly individual and situational. *Kinship as usual* is nothing more or less than the interpersonal relations marked by tensions concerning clan affiliation, rights and obligations, changing alliances, and clannishness. Luling (2006) notes, "When it comes to the current violence in Somalia, 'clanship' does not explain the conflict; it does not even explain the various line ups. It does, however, define the possibilities for lining up" (471). Somalis share traditions and, as in any other culture, there are multiple claims to them. Clans jockey for power and prestige by unveiling new forms of distinction and constructing new narratives. My work also shares similarities with Mainsah's (2014) work with young African women in Norway in that the Somali diaspora "articulates a diaspora consisting of cross-border networks and a scoping global gaze involving a diverse range of connections and orientations" (Mainsah 2014:113). Although this is the case for young Somalis living independently from their families in Kandahar, it is also true for the other people I worked with. Their gaze shifts in accord with local and global interactions, associations, conflicts, and future possibilities. One of the more constant beliefs is that people can easily hide their ascribed status in diaspora.

The Somali population in Finland has nearly doubled in the ten years since my fieldwork ended. It is likely that new arrivals to the country will continue to tell clan in order to legitimize their clan affiliation and claim their Somaliness. Telling will continue to transform with varying degrees of clan competence, migration experiences, and shifting political engagements and identity constructions. Future arrivals may emigrate from areas where clan ties are critical for daily life. Some may have used clan networks, their own paternal clan networks, or their mother's paternal clan networks to meet and marry a spouse as a means to enter Finland. When adults and children visit relatives in Somalia, the Horn, and other locations they might learn about clan genealogies and relationships in novel ways, become skilled in new ways of telling, or consume goods they later unveil as *amplified efforts at distinction* in Finland. Tremendous linguistic variation has developed since the country's collapse as a result of groups returning to ancestral clan territories and southern to northern migrations (Kapchits 2010:1). How will these linguistic changes affect telling, clan sentiment, and possibilities for building networks across clans?

My discussion of the Somali diaspora in this book has been limited to Somalis affiliated with the so-called majority clan families. Although a few of the people I worked with identified as belonging to the Benaadiri minority group, their numbers are few and I had less contact with them than with other Somalis. As more minority groups resettle in new locations, they may begin to jockey for power and prestige as they compete with other Somalis for local resources. These groups, too, have their own narratives that anthropologists should record and consider.

Nearly ten years after my fieldwork in Finland, there are still relatively few minorities living there. One pivotal change in the Somali diaspora since my fieldwork in Finland was the highly publicized selection of 12,000 Somali Bantus for resettlement in the United States. Their shared history of persecution as ethnic and racial minorities in Somalia coupled with continued discrimination in Kenyan refugee camps led to their targeted settlement. Unlike Somalis from majority clans, few Somali Bantus possessed global social networks, educational credentials, and financial capital to help them strategize for resettlement in a Nordic welfare state. Yet, like Somalis from majority clans, Somali Bantus are in Kusow's (1998) terms *modern refugees*. They refused to accept further containment in refugee camps and skillfully defined and employed the label "Somali Bantu" and creatively strategized for resettlement in a third country (Besteman 2016:96–99). From 2009 to 2011, I carried out fieldwork among this group in a metropolitan area in the United States.

In May 2003, when the first Somali Bantus arrived in the city, they relied upon a Somali Somali association for food donations and other services. Many of the Somali Bantus I worked with used the term Somali Somalis to refer to Somalis affiliated with majority clans. Some Somali Bantus struggled with this dependency and realized that the Somali Somali association could and did benefit from this dependency: access to grant monies to facilitate their community's integration and impression of a homogeneous and united Somali community. Two years later, the first Somali Bantu ethnic community association was formed despite discouragement from some members of the Somali Somali association. In 2009 a splinter group established another Somali Bantu organization in the city. The new group claimed they disapproved of the older association's collaboration with one of the local Somali Somali organizations.

In August 2009, at one of the new organization's weekly meetings, nearly forty women and men crowded into the living room and kitchen of a modest family apartment. The family apartment also functioned as the group's headquarters, which supporters dubbed "The White House." The space was ornately decorated with gilded furniture, colorful curtains and rugs, handicrafts and ceiling decorations distinctive to the Somali Bantu, and a large U.S. flag. Ahmed, an elderly man, said,

> I am seventy years old. In Somalia, Somali Somalis would not eat or sit with us. They said that we have big noses and kinky hair. They called us names like slave and *jareer*. The government kept us down and did not want us to know anything. Somali Somalis did bad things to us in Somalia. We were happy when the United States government brought us here. There is no discrimination here. We have equal rights. The Somali Somalis wanted to keep us down. They do not want us to be educated. They did not want us to start our own organization. They discriminated against us in Somalia, and they still do this here. I helped start the other Somali Bantu organization. Do you see any Somali Somalis here? There are only Somali Bantus here.

That narrative is not uncommon or limited to private spaces. Increasingly, Somali Bantus perform these narratives in public spaces as tactics to assert their freedom of speech and group distinctiveness and to gain recognition and legitimacy (Bjork 2009; see also Besteman 2016). Besteman (2016) notes that public narratives involving "retelling stories about their marginalization and discrimination in order to make their case met animated opposition from some members of Lewiston's Somali community, who protested that the Somali Bantu label is little more than a strategic marketing campaign based in fictional renditions of history and entrepreneurial motivations"

(Besteman 2016:223). A significant utility of these practices is to cultivate a *group feeling* based on a history of shared injustice and oppression rather than on a shared genealogy (Bjork 2010, 2016).

Kusow and Eno (2015) argue that Somali Bantus and other Somali ethnic minorities "removed from the social boundary of Somaliness do not accept the logic of this stratification system and enact their own formula narratives by shifting the category of stratification and exclusion from an ancestor-based narrative to one constructed on either morality or territoriality" (13). Narratives of injustice and oppression distinguish Somali Bantus and other minorities as peaceful rather than warlike like Somali Somalis (Kusow and Eno 2015:12). Consultants report that they are disengaged from homeland politics. They point out that Somali Somalis sustain fighting through clan militias and the terrorist group al-Shabaab, participate in piracy, and hold more parliamentary seats by quota. Somali Bantus and other ethnic minorities such as the Madhibaan argue that they are the *true* rightful owners of the land as some are indigenous to Somalia and currently work to reclaim their land. They point to the lineage narrative that claims "the founding Somali ancestor came from outside the Somali region and suggest, if that is the case, the descendants are not logically the rightful owners of the land and therefore should go back to their ancestral home" (Kusow and Eno 2015:13; see also Kusow 2004).

At the Tenth SSIA Congress held in Columbus, Ohio, in 2007, I attended the only panel on Somali ethnic minorities. During the discussion, a panelist and a conference observer put forth a cultural-social evolutionary argument as a status claim and counternarrative to the association of northern clans with pastoralism and prestige. They argued that pastoralism is less evolved and less civilized than metalworking and agriculture. Because pastoralists are nomadic and use less advanced technology, they are less evolved and civilized than those who lived in permanent settlements and used more advanced technologies.

Since the Somali Bantus' resettlement was highly publicized by various news outlets in the city where I conducted fieldwork and the group is sizable (about 650 persons), few choose to hide their ascribed status. Some tell they are Somali Bantu by wearing one of their ethnic association's silk-screened T-shirts featuring the organization's logo and name, which includes the words "Somali Bantu" in bold letters. The shirts are a noticeable feature of everyday life in the Section 8 apartment complexes federally subsidized for very low income families where Somali Bantus live alongside Somali Somalis and others economically disadvantaged. The T-shirts help create a *group feeling* and are indicative of a growing movement toward distinction: distinctive from Somali Somalis. Besides the T-shirts, language, social networks, beaded necklaces and bracelets worn by babies and young children, and, in some cases, names, are telling of Somali Bantus.

Diasporic identities, like other cultural identities, are never fixed or complete (Hall 2003). For many Somalis in Finland, it means picking and choosing from a wide variety of cultural forms and wavering between individual and collective interests. The future of Somalia remains uncertain. As political configurations at home play out in the diaspora, being Somali and a member of a clan will mean different things to different people at different times. Hall (2003) argues, "Cultural identity . . . is a matter of 'becoming' as well as of 'being.' It belongs to the future as much as to the past. It is not something which already exists, transcending place, time, history, and culture. Cultural identities come from somewhere, have histories. But, like everything which is historical, they undergo constant transformation. Far from being eternally fixed in some essentialized past, they are subject to the continuous 'play' of history, culture, and power" (236).

As with Somalis in Finland, Somali Bantu identities are situational and strategic. When I visited an association run by majority Somalis, I noticed an older Somali Bantu man there. I asked other Somali Bantus why he was working for this group. Like Hoehne's (2006) consultant in northern Somalia, the Somali Bantu man's decision was motivated by economic interests. The Somali Bantu associations could not pay salaries. Other Somali Bantus visited the same association for employment assistance. How can Somali Bantus compete with majority Somalis for local resources and resist dependency on them, since majority Somalis possess greater access to capital in its various forms, including higher salaries and literacy rates, educational credentials, cultural competence, and longer established social networks in the country?[1]

When Somalis faced uncertainty as the nation-state crumbled, some turned to clan relatives for support. In the same way, clan networks are an efficient way to access capital as long as the situation in Somalia remains precarious and Somalis are dispersed worldwide. If Somalis do not continue to feel themselves members of a clan, or that clan networks have no real effects or usefulness, they will be less likely to make it real on the ground. The same can be said for the relatively new group known as the Somali Bantus.

# NOTES

## CHAPTER 1. CLAN AND CULTURAL INTIMACY

1. The SSIA, founded in 1978, organizes a conference roughly every three years. The first congress was held on July 6–13, 1980, in Mogadishu, Somalia.

2. *Black Hawk Down*, a Hollywood film released in 2001, portrays the *Battle of Mogadishu*, during which nearly 100 U.S. Army Rangers were dropped into Mogadishu by helicopter to capture militia leader General Muhammad Faarax Caydiid. The drop led to a clash with hundreds of Somali gunmen and destroyed two Black Hawk helicopters. This film is told from the point of view of U.S. Army Rangers surviving the mission. Somalis staged protests over the film's debut, including Somalis in Boston, Massachusetts; Milwaukee, Wisconsin; Minneapolis, Minnesota; Los Angeles, California; and London.

3. Many consultants contend that Siyad Barre's divide and rule policy led to the country's collapse.

4. The people I worked with, when speaking in English, routinely used the terms *clan* or *tribe* interchangeably to refer to their patrilineal descent group. In the same way, consultants used the terms *mother's clan* or *mother's tribe* to refer to their mother's patrilineal descent group. It was apparent that consultants defined these terms in various ways that depend on context. First, the terms clan and tribe can refer to a clan family, clan, or subclan. Second, the meaning of these terms, that is, whom they include in these groupings, is fluid and shaped by local and global conditions: active networks and social alliances, personal affinity, and ongoing political divisions and alliances. Third, other terms such as specific clan names and subclan names may be too culturally intimate. In cases where the people I worked with clearly referred to a specific clan family, clan, or subclan, I made note of it in the text unless doing so would jeopardize anonymity. Fourth, the terms *clan* and *tribe* are more inclusive and facilitate potential access and exchange of capital. When I use the terms *clan* or *tribe* or *mother's clan* or *mother's tribe*, I am referring to a consultant's (or their mother's) patrilineal kin group. It can include any group of individuals in diaspora or at home on the basis of various levels of segmentation.

5. One exception was Abdurahman Moallin Abdullahi's (2001) paper, "Tribalism and Islam: Variations on the Basics of Somaliness," presented at the European Association of Somali Studies/Somali Studies International Association's International Congress of Somali Studies held in Turku, Finland, in 1998.

6. From 1930 to 1960, the theoretical school of structural functionalism dominated British social anthropology.

7. See also Evans-Pritchard and Fortes (1940).

8. *Peoples of the Horn of Africa: Somali, Afar, and Saho* is based on library research.

9. In 1955, Lewis began fieldwork in the British Somaliland Protectorate. Lewis relied solely on the accounts of elite men. Lewis carried out fieldwork with the Digil and the Raxanweyn in southern Somalia for three months in 1962 (Lewis 1998a).

10. Luling's (2002) work is the published version of her 1971 PhD dissertation, *The Social Structure of Southern Somali Tribes*. Luling was a student of Lewis.

11. *The Invention of Somalia* developed from papers presented at the 1992 African Studies Association's annual meetings.

12. Helander engaged in a similar contentious debate with Besteman (Besteman 2000; Helander 1998).

13. Shandy (2001) notes that refugee resettlement does not suggest permanent settlement. In her study of Nuer refugees in the United States, Shandy observed the various migrations of her consultants within the country.

14. Somalia represents one of the first African nation-states to collapse after the breakup of the Soviet Union. Prior to Somalia's civil war, few Somalis reached Finland. In the 1980s, a small number of university students (about ten people) entered Finland under bilateral development aid programs. These few Somalis who arrived in Finland prior to Somalia's civil war rarely prompted other Somalis to migrate to Finland (Alitolppa-Niitamo 2000).

15. Forty percent of consultants entered Finland as asylum seekers or quota refugees. Nine individuals did not report their entry status.

16. "The asylum seeker is not tested without his/her informed consent. This is relative, though, as refusing the test automatically leads to a negative family reunification decision by authorities" (Hautaniemi 2007: 128).

17. The following list begins with the year that consultants arrived, followed by the number of individuals interviewed who arrived in Finland that particular year: 1988 (2); 1989 (2); 1990 (43); 1991 (14); 1992 (15); 1993 (30); 1994 (19); 1995 (7); 1996 (10); 1997 (12); 1998 (7); 1999 (2); 2000 (3); 2001 (2); 2002 (4); 2003 (3); 2004 (1); not reported (8); too young to recall year of arrival (2).

18. Olli Immonen, Finnish Parliament Member and member of the True Finn Party, posted the following on Facebook on July 24, 2015: "I'm dreaming of a strong, brave nation that will defeat this nightmare called multiculturalism. This ugly bubble that our enemies live in, will soon enough burst into a million pieces. Our lives are entwined in a very harsh times. These are the days, that will forever leave a mark on our nations future. I have strong belief in my fellow fighters. We

will fight until the end for our homeland and one true Finnish nation. The victory will be ours."

19. I became part of consultants' networks. I helped those following an English language track in their higher education. I assisted their children with English and Spanish homework. I assisted consultants who were in the process of moving or planned to move to an English-speaking country with conversational English. I edited résumés, presentations, reports, and school applications. When consultants dealt with Finns (at daycares, schools, and bureaucratic offices), they asked me to accompany them. Even consultants who spoke fluent Finnish believed that they would fare better with Finns if I, a Caucasian American female, were present. Female consultants—who were close friends—asked me to look after their children and assist with relatives' wedding celebrations and other parties. Some women asked my advice when they made decisions about employment, education, and personal situations.

20. From 2000 to 2001, I enrolled in Finnish language courses at the University of Helsinki. During summer 2002, I attended an intensive Finnish language course at the advanced level. Maintaining my Finnish language skills was complicated by my limited contact with native Finnish speakers during fieldwork. On most occasions, when I met Finns, they initiated conversation in English. There were some places where I could utilize Finnish: shops, restaurants, cafés, libraries, and doctors' offices. Gaining a working knowledge of Somali was more problematic. In 1999, I began learning Somali from an elderly woman and her friends at her apartment in Milwaukee, Wisconsin. During my doctoral research, a portion of my Wenner-Gren grant paid for a Somali language tutor.

## CHAPTER 2. TELLING

1. See Tiilikainen (2007) for an overview of Islamic dress worn by Somali women in Finland.

2. Most scholars affiliate the Sheekhaal with the Hawiye clan family. Some consultants questioned the group's origins and affiliations. The Somali man who approached me at the SSIA congress in Denmark to write a book about his clan self-identified as Sheekhaal.

3. After nine years of *peruskoulu* (compulsory basic education), students follow an academic track (*lukio*) or vocational track (*ammattikoulu*).

4. "Most Gadabuursi members think that they are descendants of Sheikh Maxmuud (nicknamed Samaroon) who, according to them, lived 17 generations ago" (Georgi Kapchits, email to author, March 15, 2015).

5. "The perception of *sheegad* or *sheegato,* in Somali society, varies from one context to another. It depends on who the informant is or which culture s/he hails. It is a phenomenon that takes various shapes and degrees not only across clans and cultures in the country but also one whose manipulation was extended into the Diaspora. For example, in the context of Virginia Luling, she was discussing a

category of Bantu/*Jareer* group that was affiliated to another; so according to her, *sheegat* was translatable as client; in other cases, client is equated to servant or one owned by another, a mild term under which the status of slave is hidden. According to a dominant clan/group in its home area, individuals or small groups that it accommodated and who lived with them for a long time and became part of the 'clan' might in conflict times be separated from the clan and classified as *sheegad* or *sheegato*. There are customary and/or traditional processes that are involved in the acceptance and affiliation of a *sheegat* into the clan or a group dominant in a certain area" (Mohamed A. Eno, email to author, March 13, 2015).

6. Even in the early 1990s, Alitolppa-Niitamo (1994) notes some research participants avoided Somali associations because of a lack of trust and clannism.

7. See also Kapchits (2010) for an overview of Lamberti's (1984; 1986) classification of Somali dialects.

8. Siyad Barre's regime based Somalia's official language on Barre's own dialect, the dialect of the northcentral regions (Eno et al. 2016; Virginia Luling, email to author, May 26, 2008). When the Somali government adopted *Af-Maxaa* as the official language, it disenfranchised *Af-Maay* speakers (also called *Maay Maay*) and Somali minorities (Eno et al. 2016). What's more, the state strategically adopted an official script for *Af-Maxaa* that was unfitting for *Af-Maay* (Mukhtar 2010). For Bourdieu (1991), symbolic capital is the legitimization of power relations through symbolic forms such as language. Barre's regime forced *Af-Maay* speakers to linguistically assimilate through its state-sponsored media, education, literature, and poetry. The regime severely punished and killed dissidents including "many of members of the Af-Yaal, 'the language keepers'" [of *Af-Maay* and *Maay* culture] (Mukhtar 2010:281).

## CHAPTER 3. MOVEMENT

1. Most consultants lived in municipal apartments housing rented to low-income individuals and families in the Helsinki metropolitan area (Helsinki 138; Vantaa 28; and Espoo 14). Five consultants resided outside this area: Turku 3, Järvenpää 1 (a town of 40,000 inhabitants 38 kilometers north of Helsinki), and Jyväskylä 1 (a city of 135,000 inhabitants 270 kilometers from Helsinki in the lake district of Central Finland). I accessed these individuals during their visits with other consultants. One consultant did not report a place of residence. Consultants lived in the following types of housing: rented municipal apartment, 164; row house, 8; student housing, 6; owned apartment, 4; rented house, 2; refugee reception center, 2; and unreported, 1.

2. Vaattovaara and Kortteinen (2003) argue that this new urban differentiation resulting from the development of the information sector in West Helsinki, which has attracted young, university-educated Finns to the area, is a threat to the state's values of equality.

3. Divorce was prevalent in Somalia both prior to Somalia's independence in 1960 and after the country's collapse in 1991 (see Lewis 1962; Simons 1995). Consultants

suggested that divorce is even more common in the diaspora than it was before the civil war.

4. The minimum age at these establishments vary from eighteen to twenty-four. Pubs stay open until 2 a.m. and some clubs remain open until 4 a.m.

5. The regulation of *qaad* in diaspora communities varies. Although it is banned in France, Switzerland, the Netherlands, Eritrea, Tanzania, Canada, the United States, and the Scandinavian countries, it is legal throughout the Horn of Africa, Yemen, and Australia. In 2014 *qaad* was classified as an illegal substance in the United Kingdom. Sizable numbers of Somalis living there supported the ban through public protests and online petitions. Proponents of the ban link *qaad* consumption to social, financial, and mental problems.

6. The minimum age to purchase beer or wine is eighteen and the minimum age to purchase beverages with higher alcohol percentages is twenty.

7. Isotalo's research in 2004 among Somali girls and women in Turku reveals that Somali men and women easily monitor their behaviors and movements because the community is small and others are likely to recognize them (Isotalo 2007). Her consultants believed that they lived more descent and moral lives than their counterparts in Helsinki. They associated the capital city with social ills such as greater individualism, more Somali parties, and nightclubs. Isotalo (2007) notes, "deviations from (re)constructed traditional gender ideals and practices may easily be considered as signs of assimilation to Finnish majority culture—particularly to its non-desirable forms" (188). We must also consider how transnational linkages and cultural forms inform local gender constructions.

8. Any of these circumstances can cause family and friends to spend time at another person's household.

9. The Somali term *ciid* (*eid* in Arabic) refers to the Islamic holy days of *Eid-ul-Fitr* and *Eid ul-Adha*. *Eid-ul-Fitr* or Little *Eid*, signals the end of Ramadan. Ramadan is the ninth month of the Muslim calendar, marked by daily fasting from sunrise to sunset. It is a time of worship and contemplation and serves to strengthen family and community ties. In the evening, families and friends gather to eat and visit. Families and friends celebrate these holy days in mosques and at home. Traditional foods and sweets are served, and children commonly receive gifts. *Eid ul-Adha*, commonly referred to as Big *Ciid,* marks the end of *hajj*, the annual pilgrimage of Muslims to Mecca. Families typically mark this day with a feast.

10. This makes each person feel independent without owing anything to the other. If someone wants to pay for the date, it should be stated beforehand, "Haluan tar-jota/maksaa kaiken treffeillä" (I want to pay the whole date). Otherwise the couple might end up arguing about the bill.

11. Lindley (2010) notes that Somali women are increasingly remittance senders and recipients. "People often prefer to send money to female relatives because they are generally responsible for keeping the home, feeding the family and looking after children. Some people overseas fear that male relatives will spend the money on *qaad* or on marrying a second wife rather than prioritizing the existing family's needs" (63).

12. See Horst and Van Hear (2002) for a discussion of the effects of the *War on Terror* on *xawilaad*.

13. Survey data indicates that 123 (out of 186 total) consultants remit to family members; 49 reported not sending remittances to kin, and 14 did not respond to my inquiry. The vast majority of these funds were sent to relatives residing in Somalia. In fact, 90 individuals reported they regularly remitted funds to relatives in Somalia.

14. Many Somalis abroad give *sako* in the form of remittances to persons in Somaliland during Ramadan and *ciid* celebrations (Lindley 2010:67). Muslims are required to give *sako* annually by contributing 2.5 percent of their cumulative wealth to the poor. *Sako* (*zakat* in Arabic) is one of the five pillars of Islam.

15. At times, when I asked consultants about their age, they said, "My real age or the age on my papers?"

16. Other small Harti subclans also inhabit this area: the Leelkase, Awrtable, and Dashishle.

17. The achievements of affiliated diaspora Somalis also are highlighted on these Web sites.

18. I found these chat rooms at http://www.paltalk.com, accessed October 16, 2006.

19. Another popular site for online matrimonial quests was Somalinet.com.

20. Abdi (2015) argues that Somali migrants seek not only financial resources such as stable income and welfare services but also belonging and community and the benefits of Western citizenship, including the value of a Western passport and education.

21. Consultants maintained dispersed social networks through the following everyday practices: telephone calls, 93 percent; travel, 61 percent; photographs, 61 percent; internet, 60 percent; social networks in Finland (i.e., sharing news), 53 percent; videos, 51 percent; post, 41 percent; and audiocassette tapes, 6 percent. Three individuals did not respond to the question. Because I did not list audiocassette tapes on the survey, it is possible that more consultants used them to maintain networks.

22. Because plural marriage is not permitted by the Finnish state, only one spouse can legally enter the country on the basis of family ties.

## CHAPTER 4. CELEBRATION

1. Brides tend to change their dress two or three times during *aroos*; in general, brides wear *diric*, an evening gown, and in some cases, an Arabian-style white wedding gown.

2. I use the term *girl* to refer to unmarried Somali females; that is, girls who have never been married. For that reason, the category "girls" does not include divorced women.

3. Seventy-eight percent of survey respondents interacted with other Somalis at *aroos*. This was the second most commonly reported place for interaction among Somalis; household visits ranked the highest at 93 percent.

4. Some girls and women do not follow their prescribed gender roles. They freely socialize in public spaces such as cafés, discos, shopping centers, and bars.

5. During the fieldwork period, *aroosyo* were commonly held in public spaces such as youth centers and common areas at apartment complexes. Few weddings were held at hotels and restaurants.

6. This figure does not include previous marriages ending in divorce. According to one male consultant, there were nearly 100 marriages between Somalis and Finns. The Finnish Red Cross led a multicultural family association for Finnish-Somali families. Four consultants reported having spouses from other ethnic groups.

7. In 2016, Mohamed commented on the *meher* tradition via Facebook Messenger. He wrote, "*Meher* is usually paid after the *nikaax* and the groom can decide when he will pay it, but it is compulsory to pay it after divorce. In Somali tradition, women prefer not to receive the *meher* after *nikaax* or during marriage time because they assume that it is easier for the men to get divorce when there is no obligation to pay the *meher*."

8. "Islamic Sharia law does not require a written marriage certificate, but Somali state law that was in force up to 1991 did require a certificate signed by the Sheikh and the witnesses (Family Decree Law no. 23 of 11 Jan. 1975)" (Virginia Luling, email to author, May 17, 2008). In Finland, a couple makes their marriage official under Finnish law by marrying in a civil service.

9. "*Awoow* is the Somali term for grandfather and ancestor. This dual meaning often confuses immigration officials when they interview Somalis" (Virginia Luling, email to author, May 17, 2008).

10. Finns living in the countryside tend to have larger weddings and may invite the entire community.

11. See Loughran et al. (1986) for historical images of women's jewelry with descriptive text.

12. Three individuals I interviewed did not respond to the following question: "How do you maintain contact with family and friends living abroad?" In addition to wedding videos, videos documenting welcome and farewell parties, performances of Somali singers and dancers, and recent trips (to Somalia, the Horn of Africa, or other diaspora communities) circulate through the diaspora.

## CHAPTER 5. CRISIS

1. I did not visit any Gadabuursi households, and so I am unstable to state whether the few Gadabuursi who lived in Finland displayed a Somaliland flag as did many of the Isaaq households I visited. I noted Puntland flags in the households of several consultants who self-identified as Majeerteen, a Daarood clan.

2. Many Finland-Swedes do not fit any of the stereotypes mentioned. A number of my friends and acquaintances feel more Finnish than they do Swedish and some even make their Swedish names sound or appear more Finnish. For example, Peter might introduce himself as Petteri and this is the way other Finns refer to him.

3. In most cases, *homeland* refers to Somalia. In other cases, Somalis may consider other countries as their homeland because some were born and raised outside Somalia.

4. Tiilikainen (2007) discusses why Somali women in Finland travel to Somaliland to seek traditional healers.

5. "The operation requires written consent from both of the boy's parents. The boy must be told of the operation beforehand in a way appropriate to his age. If the boy refuses the operation, it must not be performed" (Infopankki 2015).

## CONCLUSION

1. Most Somali Bantus are illiterate, arrived in the United States with little or no education, lack transferable job skills, experience psychological trauma, face discrimination from majority Somalis and other Americans, and feel pressure to take low-paying jobs in order to meet resettlement goals of self-sufficiency rather than increasing their capacities (Besteman 2012).

# GLOSSARY

| | |
|---|---|
| abtirsiino | Genealogical reckoning or recitation of genealogy |
| aroos | Wedding celebration, marriage |
| buraanbur | Women's praise poetry |
| ciid | Holy day, religious holiday (*eid* in Arabic) |
| cillaan | Henna, also *xinna* |
| dahab | Gold, gold jewelry |
| diric | Somali women's caftan-style dress (also spelled *dirac*) |
| diya | Compensation payment (also spelled *diyo*) |
| Finns Party | Finnish political party with anti-immigrant rhetoric (formally True Finns Party) |
| ina'adeer | Translates as first cousin from paternal uncle's side, also patrilineal cousin (The term has become more widespread since Somalia's civil war and used for political mobilization, denoting clan or subclan relatives.) |
| Itis | Slang term for Itäkeskus shopping mall in Eastern Helsinki |
| jareer | Kinky hair or hard-textured hair, derogatory term for Somali Bantus denoting African-like hair |
| jileec | Soft hair or soft-textured hair, term associated with dominant Somalis denoting Arab-like hair |
| Koonfur | Southerner (*reer* Koonfur), south |
| lukio | Finnish term for high school |
| Madhibaan | Somali ethnic minority, occupational caste group considered socially polluting but believed to descend from the same apical ancestor as other Somalis |
| masjid | Arabic term for mosque |
| meher | Money the husband gives to his wife if the couple divorce |
| Midgaan | Derogatory term for Madhibaan |
| nikaax | Marriage contract (*nikah* in Arabic) |

| | |
|---|---|
| qaad | Leaves and twigs of the plant Catha edulis, which are chewed for its mildly intoxicating or stimulating effect (also spelled *khat, qaat, qat*) |
| qaaraan | Clan-based assistance |
| qabiil | Clan, tribe |
| Ramadan | Ninth month of the Muslim lunar calendar marked by fasting during sunlit hours |
| reer | Family, lineage, ethnic group |
| sako | Islamic religious duty of annual almsgiving |
| sheegad | Adopted member of a clan |
| sheekh | Learned man of Islam (*sheikh* in Arabic) |
| Somali Bantu | Somali ethnic and racial minority group, term coined in 1991 |
| Somali Somalis | Somalis belonging to the so-called majority clans, a term used by Somali Bantus |
| Soomaalinnimo | Shared sense of Somaliness or being Somali |
| Soomaali qaldan | Derogatory phrase for northerners |
| sooryo | Cash presented to bride's male kin after *nikaax* |
| tol | Patrilineal descent or clanship |
| Titanic | Derogatory term for Somalis arriving to Europe by boat |
| uunsi | Incense |
| Waqooyi | Northerner (*reer* Waqooyi), north |
| Xamaraawi | Person from Xamar (Mogadishu), also Benaadiri minority group (*Reer Xamar*) |
| xawilaad | Somali informal global transfer system commonly used for remittance sending |
| xeedho | Container shaped like a woman's body and filled with spiced meat or sweets and dressed in white cloth; part of wedding tradition |
| xeer | Social contract or treaty that binds groups together |
| xijaab | Headscarf that conceals hair and neck worn by some Muslim women (*hijab* in Arabic) |

# REFERENCES

Abdi, Cawo M. 2015. *Elusive Jannah: The Somali Diaspora and a Borderless Muslim Identity*. Minneapolis: University of Minnesota Press.

Abdullahi, Abdurahman Moallin. 2001. "Tribalism and Islam: Variations on the Basics of Somaliness." In *Proceedings of the EASS/SSIA International Congress of Somali Studies: Variations on the Theme of Somaliness,* edited by Muddle Suzanne Lilius, 227–40. Turku, Finland: Centre for Continuing Education, Åbo Akademi University.

Abdullahi, Mohamed Diriye. 2001. *Cultures and Customs of Somalia*. Westport, CT: Greenwood Press.

Ahmed, Ali Jimale, ed. 1995. *The Invention of Somalia*. Lawrenceville, NJ: Red Sea Press.

Ahmed, Christine Choi. 1995. "Finely Etched Chattel: The Invention of a Somali Woman." In *The Invention of Somalia,* edited by Ali Jimale Ahmed, 157–89. Lawrenceville, NJ: Red Sea Press.

Akou, Heather Marie. 2011. *The Politics of Dress in Somali Culture*. Bloomington: Indiana University Press.

Al-Sharmani, Mulki. 2004. "Refugees and Citizens: The Somali Diaspora in Cairo." PhD diss., Johns Hopkins University.

———. 2007. "The Poetics and Practices of *Soomaalinimo*: The Somali Diaspora in Cairo." In *From Mogadishu to Dixon: The Somali Diaspora in a Global Context,* edited by Abdi M. Kusow and Stephanie R. Bjork, 71–94. Trenton, NJ: Red Sea Press.

Alitolppa-Niitamo, Anne. 1994. *Somali Refugees in Helsinki: Focus on Social Networks and the Meaning of Clan Membership*. Report 1994:11. Helsinki: Ministry of Social Affairs and Health.

———. 2000. "The Equator to the Arctic Circle: A Portrait of Somali Integration and Diasporic Consciousness in Finland." In *Rethinking Refuge and Displacement,* edited by Elżbieta M. Goździak and Dianna J. Shandy, 43–65. Arlington, VA: American Anthropological Association.

———. 2001. "Liminalities: Expanding and Constraining the Options of Somali Youth in the Helsinki Metropolitan Area." *Yearbook of Population Research in Finland* 37: 126–47. Helsinki: Population Research Institute, Family Federation of Finland.

———. 2004. *The Icebreakers: Somali-Speaking Youth in Metropolitan Helsinki with a Focus on the Context of Formal Education.* Series D 42/2004. Helsinki: Population Research Institute, Family Federation of Finland.

Alitolppa-Niitamo, Anne, and Abdullahi A. Alí. 2001. "Somalidiaspora Suomessa: Muutoksia, Haasteita ja Haaveita" [The Somali Diaspora in Finland: Changes, Challenges and Dreams]. In *Monietnisyys, Yhteiskunta ja Työ* [Multiethnicity, Society, and Work], edited by Annika Forsander, Elina Ekholm, Petri Hautaniemi, Abdullahi Ali, Anne Alitolppa-Niitamo, Eve Kyntäjä, and Nguyen Quoc Cuong, 134–47. Helsinki: Palmenia-kustannus.

Barnes, Cedric. 2006. "U dhashay-Ku dhashay: Genealogical and Territorial Discourse in Somali History." *Social Identities* 12 (4): 487–98.

Bernal, Victoria. 2004. "Eritrea Goes Global: Reflections on Nationalism in a Transnational Era." *Cultural Anthropology* 19 (1): 3–25.

———. 2005. "Eritrea On-line: Diaspora, Cyberspace, and the Public Sphere." *American Ethnologist* 43 (4): 660–75.

Berns McGown, Rima. 1999. *Muslims in the Diaspora: The Somali Communities of London and Toronto.* Toronto: University of Toronto Press.

———. 2004. "Tranformative Islam and Shifting Gender Roles in the Somali Diaspora." In *Putting the Cart before the Horse: Contested Nationalism and the Crisis of the Nation-State in Somalia,* edited by Abdi M. Kusow, 117–33. Trenton, NJ: Red Sea Press.

Besteman, Catherine. 1991. "Land Tenure, Social Power, and the Legacy of Slavery in Southern Somalia." PhD diss., University of Arizona.

———. 1995. "The Invention of Gosha: Slavery, Colonialism, and Stigma in Somali History." In *The Invention of Somalia,* edited by Ali Jimale Ahmed, 43–62. Lawrenceville, NJ: Red Sea Press.

———. 1996a. "Representing Violence and 'Othering' Somalia." *Cultural Anthropology* 11 (1): 120–33.

———. 1996b. "Violent Politics and the Politics of Violence: The Dissolution of the Somali Nation-State." *American Ethnologist* 23 (3): 579–96.

———. 1998. "Primordialist Blinders: A Reply to I. M. Lewis." *Cultural Anthropology* 13 (1): 109–20.

———. 1999. *Unraveling Somalia: Race, Violence, and the Legacy of Slavery.* Philadelphia: University of Pennsylvania Press.

———. 2000. "A Response to Helander's Critique of 'Violent Politics and the Politics of Violence.'" *American Ethnologist* 26 (4): 981–83.

———. 2012. "Somali Bantu in a State of Refuge." *Bildhaan* 12: 11–33.

———. 2016. *Making Refuge: Somali Bantu Refugees and Lewiston, Maine.* Durham, NC: Duke University Press.

Bhoola, Furhana Ahmed. 1989. "Household Structure, Decision-Making, and the Economic, Social, and Legal Status of Women in Mogadishu, Somalia." PhD diss., Michigan State University.

Bjork, Stephanie R. 2001. "Watched Weddings: Circulating Videos and Transnational Community-Building amongst Somalis in Finland." Master's thesis, University of Wisconsin—Milwaukee.

———. 2007a. "Clan Identities in Practice: The Somali Diaspora in Finland." In *Somalia: Diaspora and State Reconstitution in the Horn of Africa,* edited by A. Osman Farah, Mammo Muchie, and Joakim Gundel, 102–13. London: Adonis and Abbey.

———. 2007b. "Modernity Meets Clan: Cultural Intimacy in the Somali Diaspora." In *From Mogadishu to Dixon: The Somali Diaspora in a Global Context,* edited by Abdi M. Kusow and Stephanie R. Bjork, 135–57. Trenton, NJ: Red Sea Press.

———. 2007c. "Diasporic Moments: Practicing Clan in the Somali Diaspora." PhD diss., University of Wisconsin–Milwaukee.

———. 2009. "We Are Somali Bantu! Reclaiming a Stigmatized Identity in the Diaspora." Paper presented at the Annual Meeting of the American Anthropological Association, Washington, DC, December.

———. 2010. "Circulating Identities among Somali Bantu in the United States." Paper presented at the Annual Meeting of the American Anthropological Association, New Orleans, November.

———. 2016. "The Politics of Somali Bantu Identity in the United States." *Bildhaan* 16: 80–92.

Bourdieu, Pierre. 1977. *Outline of a Theory of Practice.* Translated by Richard Nice. Cambridge, UK: Cambridge University Press.

———. 1984. *Distinction: Critique of the Judgement of Taste.* Translated by Richard Nice. Cambridge, MA: Harvard University Press.

———. 1986. "The Forms of Capital." Translated by Richard Nice. In *Handbook of Theory and Research for the Sociology of Education,* edited by John G. Richardson, 241–58. New York: Greenwood Press.

———. 1991. *Language and Symbolic Power.* Translated by Gino Raymond and Matthew Adamson. Cambridge, MA: Harvard University Press.

———. 1998. *Practical Reason: On the Theory of Action.* Stanford, CA: Stanford University Press.

Burton, Frank. 1978. *The Politics of Legitimacy: Struggles in a Belfast Community.* London: Routledge and Kegan Paul.

Caldwell, Melissa L. 2004. *Not by Bread Alone: Social Support in the New Russia.* Berkeley: University of California Press.

Carsten, Janet. 2004. *After Kinship.* New York: Cambridge University Press.

Cassanelli, Lee V. 2010. "Speculations on the Historical Origins of the 'Total Somali Genealogy.'" In *Milk and Peace Drought and War: Somali Culture, Society and Politics,* edited by Markus Hoehne and Virginia Luling, 53–66. New York: Columbia University Press.

Cerulli, Enrico. 1957—64. *Somalia: Scritti Vari Editi ed Inediti*. 3 vols. Rome: Istituto Poligrafico dello Stato.

Christensen, Miyase. 2012. "Online Mediations in Transnational Spaces: Cosmopolitan (Re)Formations of Belonging and Identity in the Turkish Diaspora." *Ethnic and Racial Studies* 35 (2): 888–905.

Colucci, Massimo. 1924. *Principi di Diritto Consuetudinario della Somalia Italiana Meridionale*. Florence: Società Editrice La Voce.

D'Alisera, JoAnn. 2004. *An Imagined Geography: Sierra Leonean Muslims in America*. Philadelphia: University of Pennsylvania Press.

Decimo, Francesca. 2007. "Globalizing Diasporic Networks: Somali Female Workers in Italy." In *From Mogadishu to Dixon: The Somali Diaspora in a Global Context*, edited by Abdi M. Kusow and Stephanie R. Bjork, 97–117. Trenton, NJ: Red Sea Press.

Declich, Francesca. 1992. "Il Processo di Formazione della Identità Culturale dei Bantu della Somalia Meridionale." PhD diss., Istituto Universitario Orientale, Naples, Italy.

Directorate of Immigration (Ulkomaalaisvirasto). 2006. Alien's passport and refugee's travel document (Muukalaispassi ja pakolaisen matkustusasiakirja). Electronic document, http://www.migri.fi/matkustusasiakirjat, accessed April 2007.

El-Solh, Camillia Fawzi. 1991. "Somalis in London's East End: A Community Striving for Recognition." *Journal of Ethnic and Migration Studies* 17 (4): 539–52.

Eno, Mohamed A. 2008. *The Bantu-Jareer Somalis: Unearthing Apartheid in the Horn of Africa*. London: Adonis and Abbey.

Eno, Mohamed A., Omar A. Eno, and Abderrazak Dammak. 2016. "From Linguistic Imperialism to Language Domination: 'Linguicism' and Ethno-Linguistic Politics in Somalia." *Journal of Somali Studies* 3 (1–2): 9–52.

Eno, Omar A. 1997. "The Untold Apartheid Imposed on the Bantu/Jarer People in Somalia." In *Mending Rips in the Sky: Options for Somali Communities in the 21st Century*, edited by Hussein M. Adam and Richard Ford, 209–20. Lawrenceville, NJ: Red Sea Press.

———. 2004. "Landless Landlords, and Landed Tenants: Plantation Slavery in Southern Somalia (1840–1940)." In *Putting the Cart before the Horse: Contested Nationalism and the Crisis of the Nation-State in Somalia*, edited by Abdi M. Kusow, 135–54. Trenton, NJ: Red Sea Press.

Eno, Omar A., and Mohamed A. Eno. 2007. "The Journey Back to the Ancestral Homeland: The Return of the Somali Bantu (Wazigwa) to Modern Tanzania." In *From Mogadishu to Dixon: The Somali Diaspora in a Global Context*, edited by Abdi M. Kusow and Stephanie R. Bjork, 13–43. Trenton, NJ: Red Sea Press.

Evans-Pritchard, E. E. 1940. *The Nuer: A Description of the Modes of Livelihood and Political Institutions of a Nilotic People*. Oxford, UK: Clarendon Press.

Evans-Pritchard, E. E., and Meyer Fortes, eds. 1940. *African Political Systems*. Oxford, UK: Oxford University Press.

Faist, Thomas. 2000. *The Volume and Dynamics of International Migration and Transnational Social Spaces*. Oxford, UK: Clarendon Press.

Falzon, Mark-Anthony. 2004. *Cosmopolitan Connections: The Sindhi Diaspora, 1860–2000.* Leiden, Netherlands: Brill.

Fangen, Katrine. 2007. "The Need to Belong and the Need to Distance Oneself: Contra-identification among Somali Refugees in Norway." In *Somalia: Diaspora and State Reconstruction in the Horn of Africa,* edited by A. Osman Farah, Mammo Muchie, and Joakim Gundel, 78–88. London: Adonis and Abbey.

Farah, Abdulkadir Osman. 2013. "Transnationalism and Civic Engagement: The Role of Somali Civil Society in Development and Security." In *Peace and Security: Keys to Stability and Sustainable Development in the Horn of Africa,* edited by Ulf Johansson Dahre, 147–61. Lund, Sweden: Meida-Tryck Lund University.

———. 2015. *Somalis: In Search of Nationhood, Statehood, and Transnational Connections.* London: Adonis and Abbey.

———. 2016. "Transnational Efforts for Justice and Social Empowerment: The Role of NGOs and Transnational Communities." *Northeast African Studies* 13 (2).

Farah, Abdulkadir Osman, and Helle Stenum. 2014. *Somalis in Copenhagen.* New York: Open Society Foundations. https://www.opensocietyfoundations.org/sites/default/files/somalis-copenhagen-20141031.pdf.

Farah, Nuruddin. 2000. *Yesterday, Tomorrow: Voices from the Somali Diaspora.* London: Cassell.

Ford, Richard, Hussein M. Adam, and Edna Adan Ismail, eds. 2003. *War Destroys, Peace Nurtures: Reconciliation and Development in Somalia.* Lawrenceville, NJ: Red Sea Press.

Gifford, Lindsay, and Rachel Hall-Clifford. 2008. "From Catcalls to Kidnapping: Towards an Open Dialogue on the Fieldwork Experiences of Graduate Women." *Anthropology News* 49 (6): 26–27.

Gewertz, Deborah B., and Frederick K. Errington. 1999. *Emerging Class in Papua New Guinea: The Telling of Difference.* Cambridge, UK: Cambridge University Press.

Gough, Kathleen. 1971. "Nuer Kinship: A Re-examination." In *The Translation of Culture: Essays to E. E. Evans-Pritchard,* edited by T. O. Beidelman, 79–121. London: Tavistock.

Hage, Ghassan. 2005. "A Not So Multi-Sited Ethnography of a Not So Imagined Community." *Anthropological Theory* 5 (4): 463–76.

Hall, Stuart. 2003 [1990]. "Culture, Identity and Diaspora." In *Theorizing Diaspora,* edited by Jana Evans Braziel and Anita Mannur, 233–46. Malden, MA: Blackwell.

Hannerz, Ulf. 1990. "Cosmopolitans and Locals in World Culture." *Theory, Culture and Society* 7: 237–51.

———. 2003. "Being There . . . and There . . . and There! Reflections on Multi-Site Ethnography." *Ethnography* 4 (2): 201–16.

Hansen, Stig Jarle. 2014, February 24. "An In-Depth Look at Al-Shabab's Internal Divisions." CTC Sentinel Special Issue 7 (2): 9–12. West Point, NY: Combating Terrorism Center at West Point. https://www.ctc.usma.edu/posts/an-in-depth-look-at-al-shababs-internal-divisions. Accessed February 17, 2016.

Hautaniemi, Petri. 2007. "Diasporic Authenticity: Connecting Genes and Building Families through DNA-Testing in Somali Family Reunification in Finland." In

*From Mogadishu to Dixon: The Somali Diaspora in a Global Context,* edited by Abdi M. Kusow and Stephanie R. Bjork, 119–33. Trenton, NJ: Red Sea Press.

Helander, Bernhard. 1991. "The Somali Family." In *Somalia: A Historical, Cultural and Political Analysis* (Conference Report 1), edited by Kim Barcik and Sture Normark, 17–28. Uppsala, Sweden: Life and Peace Institute.

———. 1996. "Rahanweyn Sociability: A Model for Other Somalis?" In *Voice and Power: The Culture of Language in North-East Africa,* edited by R. J. Hayward and I. M. Lewis, 195–204. London: SOAS/Oxford University Press.

———. 1998. "The Emperor's New Clothes Removed: A Critique of Besteman's 'Violent Politics and the Politics of Violence.'" *American Ethnologist* 25 (3): 489–501.

———. 2003. *The Slaughtered Camel: Coping with Fictitious Descent among the Hubeer of Southern Somalia.* Uppsala Studies in Cultural Anthropology 34. Uppsala, Sweden: Acta Universitatis Upsaliensis.

Herzfeld, Michael. 1997. *Cultural Intimacy: Social Poetics in the Nation-State.* New York: Routledge.

Hoehne, Markus V. 2006. "Political Identity, Emerging State Structures, and Conflict in Northern Somalia." *Journal of Modern African Studies* 44 (3): 1–18.

———. 2007, November 7. "Puntland and Somaliland Clashing in Northern Somalia: Who Cuts the Gordian Knot?" *Crisis in the Horn of Africa, Online Essays.* Brooklyn, NY: Social Science Research Council. http://hornofafrica.ssrc.org/Hoehne/. Accessed March 16, 2015.

———. 2009. "Mimesis and Mimicry in Dynamics of State and Identity Formation in Northern Somalia." *Africa* 79 (2): 252–81.

———. 2010. "Political Representation in Somalia: Citizenship, Clanism, and Territoriality." In *Accord 21: Whose Peace Is It Anyway? Connecting Somali and International Peacemaking,* edited by Mark Bradbury and Sally Healy, 34–37.

———. 2014. "Continuities and Changes Regarding Minorities in Somalia." *Ethnic and Racial Studies* 38 (5): 1–15.

———. Forthcoming. "Territoriality and Belonging in Rupture: The Emergence of 'Mini-States' and Regional Administration and the Diminishing Relevance of Cross-cutting Ties in Somalia after 1990." In "Rupture and Rule: State Formation as the Production of Property and Citizenship," edited by Christian Lund and Michael Eilenberg. Special issue, *Development and Change.*

Holy, Ladislav. 1996. *Anthropological Perspectives on Kinship.* London: Pluto Press.

Horst, Cindy. 2006. *Transnational Nomads: How Somalis Cope with Refugee Life in the Dadaab Camps of Kenya.* Vol. 19 of *Studies in Forced Migration,* edited by Dawn Chatty. New York: Berghahn.

———. 2007a. "Connected Lives: Somalis in Minneapolis Dealing with Family Responsibilities and Migration Dreams of Relatives." In *Somalia: Diaspora and State Reconstitution in the Horn of Africa,* edited by A. Osman Farah, Mammo Muchie, and Joakim Gundel, 89–101. London: Adonis and Abbey.

———. 2007b. "The Somali Diaspora in Minneapolis: Expectations and Realities." In *From Mogadishu to Dixon: The Somali Diaspora in a Global Context,* edited by Abdi M. Kusow and Stephanie R. Bjork, 275–94. Trenton, NJ: Red Sea Press.

Horst, Cindy, and Nicholas Van Hear. 2002. "Counting the Cost: Refugees, Remittances, and the 'War against Terrorism.'" *Forced Migration Review* 14: 32–34.

Huisman, Kimberly A., Mazie Hough, Kristin M. Langellier, and Carol Nordstrom Toner, eds. 2011. *Somalis in Maine: Crossing Cultural Currents.* Berkeley, CA: North Atlantic.

Hutchinson, Sharon E. 1996. *Nuer Dilemmas: Coping with Money, War, and the State.* Berkeley: University of California Press.

Immonen, Olli. 2015, 24 July. Facebook post. https://www.facebook.com/olli.immonen .3/posts/10153483050174847. Accessed August 22, 2015.

Infopannki.fi [Infobank]. 2015. *Children's Health [Lapsen Terveys;* webpage]. City of Helsinki. http://www.infopankki.fi/en/living-in-finland/health/children-s-health. Accessed March 16, 2015.

Isotalo, Anu. 2007. "Did You See Her Standing at the Marketplace?" Gender, Gossip, and Socio-Spatial Behavior of Somali Girls in Turku, Finland." In *From Mogadishu to Dixon: The Somali Diaspora in a Global Context,* edited by Abdi M. Kusow and Stephanie R. Bjork, 181–206. Trenton, NJ: Red Sea Press.

Jaakkola, Magdalena. 2000. "Finnish Attitudes towards Immigrants in 1987–1999." *Yearbook of Population Research in Finland* 36: 129–61. Helsinki: Population Research Institute.

Jinnah, Zaheera. 2010. "Making Home in a Hostile Land: Understanding Somali Identity, Integration, Livelihood, and Risks in Johannesburg." *Journal of Sociology and Social Anthropology* 1 (1–2): 91–99.

Johansen, R. Elise B. 2006. "Care for Infibulated Women Giving Birth in Norway: An Anthropological Analysis of Health Workers' Management of a Medically and Culturally Unfamiliar Issue." *Medical Anthropology Quarterly* 20: 516–44.

Kapchits, Georgi. 2010. "Lamberti's Maps of Somali Dialects and the Current Sociolinguistic Situation in South Somalia." Paper presented at 5000 Years Semitohamitic Languages in Asia and Africa [5000 Jahre Semitohamitische Sprachen in Asien und Afrika—Akten des internationalen Semitohamitistenkongresses], Berlin, July 22–24.

Kapteijns, Lidwien. 2013. *Clan Cleansing in Somalia: The Ruinous Legacy of 1991.* Philadelphia: University of Pennsylvania Press.

Kapteijns, Lidwien, with Maryan Omar Ali. 1999. *Women's Voices in a Man's World: Women and the Pastoral Tradition in Northern Somali Orature, c. 1899–1980.* Portsmouth, NH: Heinemann.

KELA (The Social Insurance Institution of Finland). 2013. *Moving to or from Finland* [brochure]. http://www.kela.fi/documents/10180/578772/Moving_to_or_away_from _Finland_brochure.pdf/1227c8f2-a10e-4d11-a546-c7e4f4f7da4c. Accessed March 19, 2015.

Kroner, Gudrun-Katharina. 2007. "Transit or Dead End? The Somali Diaspora in Egypt." In *From Mogadishu to Dixon: The Somali Diaspora in a Global Context,* edited by Abdi M. Kusow and Stephanie R. Bjork, 45–70. Trenton, NJ: Red Sea Press.

Kulsoom, Ally. 2002. "Analytical Study of Racism, Discrimination, and Xenophobia in the Education Sector in Finland." EUMC/RAXEN 3. Helsinki: Finnish League for Human Rights.

Kusow, Abdi M. 1995. "The Somali Origin: Myth or Reality." In *The Invention of Somalia,* edited by Ali Jimale Ahmed, 81–106. Lawrenceville, NJ: Red Sea Press.

———. 1998. "Migration and Identity Processes among Somali Immigrants in Canada." PhD diss., Wayne State University, Detroit, MI.

———. 2003. "Beyond Indigenous Authenticity: Reflections on the Insider/Outsider Debate in Immigration Research." *Symbolic Interaction* 26 (4): 591–99.

———. 2004. "Contested Narratives and the Crisis of the Nation-State in Somalia: A Prolegomenon." In *Putting the Cart before the Horse: Contested Nationalism and the Crisis of the Nation-State in Somalia,* edited by Abdi M. Kusow, 1–14. Trenton, NJ: Red Sea Press.

———. 2014. "The Somali Question." *Journal of Somali Studies* 1 (1): 91–101.

Kusow, Abdi M., and Mohamed A. Eno. 2015. "Formula Narratives and the Making of Social Stratification and Inequality." *Sociology of Race and Ethnicity* 1 (3): 1–15.

Laitin, David D., and Said S. Samatar. 1987. *Somalia: Nation in Search of a State.* Boulder, CO: Westview Press.

Lamberti, Marcello. 1984. "The Linguistic Situation in the Somali Democratic Republic." In *Proceedings of the Second International Congress of Somali Studies.* Vol. 1, *Linguistics and Literature,* edited by Thomas Labahn, 155–200. Hamburg: Helmut Buske.

———. 1986. *Maps of Somali Dialects in the Somali Democratic Republic.* Hamburg: Helmut Buske.

Lewis, I. M. 1957. *The Somali Lineage System and the Total Genealogy* [mimeo]. London: Crown Agents.

———. 1961. *A Pastoral Democracy: A Study of Pastoralism and Politics among the Northern Somali of the Horn of Africa.* London: Oxford University Press.

———. 1962. *Marriage and the Family in Northern Somaliland.* Kampala, Uganda: East African Institute of Social Research.

———. 1969. "From Nomadism to Cultivation: The Expansion of Political Solidarity in Southern Somalia." In *Man in Africa,* edited by Mary Douglas and Phyllis M. Kaberry, 59–77. London: Tavistock.

———. 1986. "Islam in Somalia." In *Somalia in Word and Image,* edited by Katheryne S. Loughran, John Loughran, John William Johnson, and Said Sheikh Samatar, 139–67. Washington DC: Foundation for Cross Cultural Understanding, in cooperation with the University of Indiana.

———. 1994. *Blood and Bone: The Call of Kinship in Somali Society.* Lawrenceville, NJ: Red Sea Press.

———. 1998a [1955]. *Peoples of the Horn of Africa: Somali, Afar and Saho,* 4th ed. Lawrenceville, NJ: Red Sea Press.

———. 1998b. "Doing Violence to Ethnography: A Response to Catherine Besteman's Representing Violence and 'Othering' Somalia." *Cultural Anthropology* 13 (1): 100–108.

———. 2002 [1965]. *A Modern History of the Somali: Nation and State in the Horn of Africa,* 4th ed. Athens: Ohio University Press.

——. 2008. *Understanding Somalia and Somaliland: Culture, History, Society*. New York: Columbia University Press.

Lilius, Suzanne Muddle, ed. 2001. *Proceedings of the EASS/SSIA International Congress of Somali Studies: Variations on the Theme of Somaliness*. Turku, Finland: Centre for Continuing Education, Åbo Akademi University.

Lindley, Anna. 2009. "The North–South Divide in Everyday Life: Londoners Sending Money 'Home.'" *Bildhaan* 9: 39–62.

——. 2010. *The Early Morning Phone Call: Somali Refugees' Remittances*. Vol. 28 of *Studies in Forced Migration*, edited by Dawn Chatty. New York: Berghahn.

Loughran, Katheryne S., John L. Loughran, John William Johnson, and Said Sheikh Samatar, eds. 1986. *Somalia in Word and Image*. Washington, DC: Foundation for Cross Cultural Understanding, in cooperation with the University of Indiana.

Luling, Virginia. 1971. "The Social Structure of Southern Somali Tribes." PhD diss., University of London.

——. 1984. "The Other Somalis: Minority Groups in Traditional Somali Society." In *Proceedings of the Second International Congress of Somali Studies*, edited by Thomas Labahn, 39–55. Hamburg: Helmut Buske.

——. 2002. *Somali Sultanate: The Geledi City-State over 150 Years*. London: HAAN; Piscataway, NJ: Transaction.

——. 2006. "Genealogy as Theory, Genealogy as Tool: Aspects of Somali 'Clanship.'" *Social Identities* 12 (4): 471–85.

——. 2007. "A Game of Chance: Somali Asylum Applicants in the UK." In *Somalia: Diaspora and State Reconstitution in the Horn of Africa*, edited by A. Osman Farah, Mammo Muchie, and Joakim Gundel, 43–58. London: Adonis and Abbey.

Mainsah, Henry. 2014. "Young African Norwegian Women and Diaspora: Negotiating Identity and Community through Digital Social Networks." *Crossings* 5 (1): 105–19.

Malkki, Liisa H. 1995. *Purity and Exile: Violence, Memory, and National Cosmology among Hutu Refugees in Tanzania*. Chicago: University of Chicago Press.

Mannila, Simo. 2010. "Nordic Immigration Policy and the New Emphasis on Labour Immigration: The Case of Finland as Compared to Sweden and Norway." In *Immigrants and Ethnic Minorities: European Country Cases and Debates* (Report 41/2010), edited by Simo Mannila, Vera Messing, Hans-Peter van den Broek, and Zsuzsanna Vidra, 18–38. Helsinki: National Institute for Health and Welfare.

Mansur, Abdalla Omar. 1995. "Contrary to a Nation: The Cancer of the Somali State." In *The Invention of Somalia*, edited by Ali Jimale Ahmed, 107–16. Lawrenceville, NJ: Red Sea Press.

——. 1997. "Aspects of the Somali Tribal System." In *Mending Rips in the Sky: Options for Somali Communities in the 21st Century*, edited by Hussein M. Adam and Richard Ford, 123–29. Lawrenceville, NJ: Red Sea Press.

Marcus, George E. 1995. "Ethnography in/of the World System: The Emergence of Multi-Sited Ethnography." *Annual Review of Anthropology* 24: 95–117.

Marlowe, David. 1963. "The Galjaal Barsana of Central Somalia: A Lineage Political System in a Changing World." PhD diss., Harvard University.

McMichael, Celia, and Lenore Manderson. 2004. "Somali Women and Well-Being: Social Networks and Social Capital among Immigrant Women in Australia." *Human Organization* 63 (1): 88–99.

Menkhaus, Ken. 1989. "Rural Transformation and the Roots of Underdevelopment in Somalia's Lower Jubba Valley." PhD diss., University of South Carolina.

———. 2010. "The Question of Ethnicity in Somali Studies: The Case of Somali Bantu Identity." In *Milk and Peace Drought and War: Somali Culture, Society and Politics,* edited by Markus Hoehne and Virginia Luling, 87–104. New York: Columbia University Press.

Miller, Daniel, and Don Slater. 2000. *The Internet: An Ethnographic Approach.* Oxford, UK: Berg.

Mohamed, Jama. 2007. "Kinship and Contract in Somali Politics." *Africa* 77 (2): 226–49.

Mohamed, Mohamed-Abdi. 1997. "Somalia: Kinship and Relationships Derived from It." In *Mending Rips in the Sky: Options for Somali Communities in the 21st Century,* edited by Hussein M. Adam and Richard Ford, 145–59. Lawrenceville, NJ: Red Sea Press.

Moore, Sally Falk. 1987. "Explaining the Present: Theoretical Dilemmas in Processual Ethnography." *American Ethnologist* 14 (4): 727–36.

Mukhtar, Mohamed Haji. 1995. "Islam in Somali History: Fact and Fiction." In *The Invention of Somalia,* edited by Ali Jimale Ahmed, 1–27. Lawrenceville, NJ: Red Sea Press.

———. 1997. "Somalia: Between Self-Determination and Chaos." In *Mending Rips in the Sky: Options for Somali Communities in the 21st Century,* edited by Hussein M. Adam and Richard Ford, 49–64. Lawrenceville, NJ: Red Sea Press.

———. 2010. "Language Marginalisation, Ethnic Nationalism, and Cultural Crisis in Somalia." In *Milk and Peace Drought and War: Somali Culture, Society and Politics,* edited by Markus Hoehne and Virginia Luling, 281–300. New York: Columbia University Press.

Official Statistics of Finland. 2004. *Population Database* [electronic database.] Origin, Background Country and Language by Age and Sex 1990–2014, Whole Country. Helsinki: Statistics Finland. http://pxnet2.stat.fi/PXWeb/pxweb/en/StatFin/StatFin__vrm__vaerak/047_vaerak_tau_202_en.px/?rxid=54bc8beb-4d4d-4f62-acd1-fbd28139ace9. Accessed June 23, 2006.

———. 2013. *Population Structure. Appendix Figure 2: Largest Background Groups of Those with Foreign Background in 2013 [webpage].* Helsinki: Statistics Finland. http://www.stat.fi/til/vaerak/2013/02/vaerak_2013_02_2014-12-10_kuv_002_en .html. Accessed March 5, 2015.

———. 2015. *Population Structure. Appendix Table 2. Population According to Language 1980–2015.* Helsinki: Statistics Finland. http://www.stat.fi/til/vaerak/2015/vaerak_2015_2016-04-01_tau_002_en.html. Accessed May 13, 2016.

Pirkkalainen, Päivi. 2009. "The Finland-based Somali Diaspora Associations and Their Involvement in Co-development." In *Migration for Development in the Horn of Africa: Health Expertise from the Somali Diaspora in Finland,* edited by Thomas Lothar Weiss, 74–90. Helsinki: International Organisation for Migration. publications.iom.int/bookstore/free/MIDA_Health_book.pdf#page=74. Accessed November 1, 2015.

Pred, Allan. 1997. "Somebody Else, Somewhere Else: Racisms, Racialized Spaces, and the Popular Geographical Imagination in Sweden." *Antipode* 29 (4): 383–416.

Sahlins, Marshall David. 1972. *Stone Age Economics.* Chicago: Aldine-Atherton.

Samatar, Ahmed I. 1988. *Socialist Somalia: Rhetoric and Reality.* London: Zed.

———. 2001. "The Somali Catastrophe: Explanations and Implications." In *Proceedings of the EASS/SSIA International Congress of Somali Studies: Variations on the Theme of Somaliness* edited by Muddle Suzanne Lilius, 7–30. Turku, Finland: Centre for Continuing Education, Åbo Akademi University.

Shandy, Dianna J. 2001. "Routes and Destinations: Nuer Secondary Migration in the United States." In *Negotiating Transnationalism,* edited by MaryCarol Hopkins and Nancy Wellmeier, 9–31. Arlington, VA: American Anthropological Association.

———. 2007. *Nuer-American Passages: Globalizing Sudanese Migration.* Gainesville: University Press of Florida.

Simons, Anna. 1994. "Somalia and the Dissolution of the Nation-State." *American Anthropologist* 96 (4): 818–24.

———. 1995. *Networks of Dissolution: Somalia Undone.* Boulder, CO: Westview Press.

Sorainen, Olli. 2003. *Finland: Trends in International Migration.* Helsinki: Ministry of Labour.

Southall, Aidan. 1970. "The Illusion of Tribe." *Journal of Asian and African Studies* 5 (1): 28–50.

———. 1986. "The Illusion of Nath Agnation." *Ethnology* 25: 1–20.

Stanford University. 2016, March 30. *Mapping Militant Organizations: Islamic Courts Union* [webpage]. http://web.stanford.edu/group/mappingmilitants/cgi-bin/groups/view/107. Accessed May 12, 2016.

Tapaninen, Anna-Maria, and Miia Halme-Tuomisaari. 2015. "Why Is DNA Not Enough? The Quest for Truth in Decision-Making on Family Reunification in Finland." Paper presented at the Twelfth Somali Studies International Association Congress, Helsinki, August 22.

Tiilikainen, Marja. 2003. *Arjen Islam: Somalinaisten Elämää Suomessa* [Everyday Islam: The Life of Somali Women in Finland]. PhD diss., Tampere, Finland: Vastapaino.

———. 2007. "Continuity and Change: Somali Women and Everyday Islam in the Diaspora." In *From Mogadishu to Dixon: The Somali Diaspora in a Global Context,* edited by Abdi M. Kusow and Stephanie R. Bjork, 207–30. Trenton, NJ: Red Sea Press.

Tiilikainen, Marja, Abdirashid Ismail, Elina Tuusa, Maryan Abdulkarim, and Abdurasak Adam. 2013. *Somalis in Helsinki*. New York: Open Society Foundations. https://www.opensocietyfoundations.org/sites/default/files/somalis-helsinki-20131121.pdf. Accessed July 1, 2015.

Tiilikainen, Marja, and Salada M. Robleh. 1999. "Cultural Change and Problems Faced by Somali Families in Two Nordic Countries." Paper presented at the Seventh International Congress of Somali Studies, Toronto, Canada, July 8–11.

Trandafoiu, Ruxandra. 2013. *Diaspora Online: Identity Politics and Romanian Migrants*. Oxford, UK: Berghahn.

Turner, Victor. 1969. *The Ritual Process: Structure and Anti-structure*. Chicago: Aldine.

———. 1974. *Dramas, Fields, and Metaphors: Symbolic Action in Human Society*. Ithaca, NY: Cornell University Press.

United Nations High Commissioner on Refugees [UNHCR]. 2015, June 18. *Worldwide Displacement Hits All-Time High as War and Persecution Increase* [webpage]. http://www.unhcr.org/print/558193896.html. Accessed February 17, 2016.

———. 2016. *Resettlement: A New Beginning in a Third Country* [webpage]. http://www.unhcr.org/pages/4a16b1676.html. Accessed February 17, 2016.

Vaattovaara, Mari, and Matti Kortteinen. 2003. "Beyond Polarisation versus Professionalisation? A Case Study of the Development of the Helsinki Region, Finland." *Urban Studies* 40 (11): 2127–45.

van Gennep, Arnold. 1960 [1908]. *The Rites of Passage*. Translated by Monika B. Vizedom and Gabrielle L. Caffee. Chicago: University of Chicago Press.

Verdon, Michel. 1982. "Where Have All Their Lineages Gone? Cattle and Descent among the Nuer." *American Anthropologist* 84: 566–79.

Vilkama, Katja. 2011. Yhteinen Kaupunki, Eriytyvät Kaupunginosat? Kantaväestön ja Maahanmuuttajataustaisten Asukkaiden Alueellinen Eriytyminen ja Muuttoliike Pääkaupunkiseudulla [Shared city or divided neighborhoods? Residential segregation and selective migration of the native and immigrant populations in the Helsinki metropolitan area]. Helsinki: Helsingin Kaupungin Tietokeskus [City of Helsinki urban facts].

Warfa, Nasir, Sarah Curtis, Charles Watters, Ken Carswell, Davic Ingleby, and Kamaldeep Bhui. 2012. "Migration Experiences, Employment Status and Psychological Distress among Somali Immigrants: A Mixed-Method International Study." *BMC Public Health* 12: 749. http://bmcpublichealth.biomedcentral.com/articles/10.1186/1471-2458-12-749. Accessed January 2, 2016. doi: 10.1186/1471-2458-12-749

Willis, Paul. 1977. *Learning to Labour: How Working Class Kids Get Working Class Jobs*. Farnborough, UK: Saxon House.

# INDEX

Page numbers in *italics* refer to illustrations.

Abdi, Cawo M., 18, 45–46, 119
Abdullahi, Mohamed Diriye, 124
Aeroflot, 25, 140
Af-Maay (also Maay Maay), 53, 60, 62, 62, 67, 168n8
Af-Maxaa, 53, 62, 62, 168n8
Af-Yaal ("the language keepers"), 168n8
agriculture, 124, 163
agropastoralism, 14–15, 15
Ahmed, Ali Jimale, 17
Ahmed, Christine Choi, 125, 151
alcohol consumption, 29, 39–40, 65, 76, 78–82, 107, 118, 146, 147, 169n6
Alitolppa-Niitamo, 168n6
All Things Somali Facebook page, 31
Al-Sharmani, Mulki, 21, 31, 84–85, 87, 91, 117–18
AMISON (African Union Mission in Somalia), 154
ancestral clan territories, 22, 41, 43, 57, 67, 71, 154, 161, 163
anti-immigrant sentiment, 27–28, 30–32
Arabic language, 67, 92
arranged marriages, 94–95
Asheraaf Sarman minority group, 65
asylum seekers: clan affiliations with, 55, 58; clan as decision factor, 8, 10; reception centers, 50–51; research on, 17; reunification and, 166n16; social capital and, 95–96; Somalis in Finland, 24–25, 27, 166n15

Australia, 55, 111
autonomy: clan as barrier to, 100; clan obligations and, 137; Finnish ideology of, 21, 40, 84, 102, 170n20; internet and social media influence on, 92–93; self-reliance and, 99, 135, 137, 150, 155–56; young Somalis desire for, 40, 75–89, 92–93, 97–99, 143, 146, 150–51

balanced reciprocity, 118–19, 142
Barnes, Cedric, 18–19, 22–23
Barre military regime: campaign against tribalism, 10, 31, 58, 138–39; clan affiliations and, 10–11, 17, 155; clan hierarchy in, 22; cultural trauma inflicted by, 109; divide and rule policy, 165n3; National Security Service (NSS) initiatives, 10–11, 17, 138–39; scientific socialism, 10; Western aid and, 11
Baydhabo, 3–4, 62, 89–90
Benaadiri (Reer Xamar) minority group, 34, 60, 69, 161
Besteman, Catherine, 11, 18–19, 162–63, 166n12
Bjork, Stephanie, 7, 32–34
Black Hawk Down, 11, 165n2
Bosaaso, 91, 153
Bourdieu, Pierre: clan feeling and, 20; construction of difference in, 59; on cultural capital, 69; on cultural competence, 51–52; on distinction, 123, 125, 126; on family accumulation of capital, 83; on family feeling, 20, 48–49;

Bourdieu, Pierre (*continued*): on forms of
    capital, 49; on habitus, 49, 59; on official
    kin, 113; on practical relationships,
    119–20; on social capital, 21, 48–49, 83;
    on symbolic capital, 168n8
*buraanbur* (women's oral poetry), 105–11,
    114, 127, 132
Burton, Frank, 47

Caldwell, Melissa L., 40
Canada, 23, 94, 111, 114
capital: asylum seekers and, 95–96; clan af-
    filiation/identity and, 40, 48–49, 90; clan
    obligations and, 120–21; dispersal of
    social capital, 96–97; exchange of capital
    in weddings, 87, 118–26; social capital in
    clans, 21, 48–49, 83–88, 120–21, 134–
    38; social capital in integrated networks,
    99–102. *See also* cultural capital
caste (Madhibaan caste group), 52–53
Caydiid, Muhammad Faarax, 165n2
celebration: *Ciid* religious holiday, 32, 83,
    169n9; Finnish intercultural events, 28,
    98, 121–22; graduation ceremonies, 50;
    Restaurant Day as multicultural event,
    38; *Soomaalinimo* in independence day
    celebrations, 31. *See also* weddings
cell phones: *aroos* video distribution,
    128–29; clan obligation and, 131–32,
    148; dispersed social capital and, 96,
    119; fieldwork and, 88; nicknames and,
    66; public internet and, 67, 93; remit-
    tances and, 86; social autonomy of young
    Somalis and, 75–76. *See also* internet and
    social media
Central Rangelands Development Project
    (CRDP), 16–17, 135–36
children: child benefits and subsidies,
    84–85; *Ciid* holiday and, 33; clan lineage
    and, 119–20; dating practices, 29;
    exposure to clan, 47, 73–74; exposure to
    Finnish culture, 28–29, 39; family size,
    27, 29–30, 81, 85, 132, 158–59; field-
    work and, 36–37; Finnish schools and,
    28, 30, 62; in Helsinki Somali house-
    holds, 44; international travel, 73–74, 96,
    153; language learning and, 33, 62, 69;
    nicknames and, 89; of Somali minorities,
    53–54, 114–15; wedding videos and, 127
Cigaal, Maxamed Xaaji Ibraahim, 134

*Ciid* religious holiday, 32, 83, 169n9
circumcision, 17, 96, 153, 171n5
clan affiliation/identity: clan feeling, 20–21,
    48–49, 90, 125, 138–40, 157–58; colo-
    nialism and, 10; cultural intimacy and,
    12–13, 37–38, 55–57, 157; food as clan
    identifier, 70, 124–25; *Jaalle* alternative
    for, 10–11; Sab-Samaale distinction and,
    14–15, 15, 60; sensitivity of clan identity,
    7–9; sites of kinship, 158–59; *Soomaa-
    linimo* compared with, 31, 111; transna-
    tional cultural capital and, 40, 48–49, 90.
    *See also* telling clan
clan and social networks: clan-based associa-
    tions, 54–57, 63–64, 168n6; clan obliga-
    tions and, 120–21, 133–34, 145, 150;
    cosmopolitanism and, 47, 137–38; culti-
    vating clan networks, 20–22, 41, 48–50,
    85, 120–21, 125, 139–40, 145; dispersed
    networks, 85, 120–21, 125, 139–40, 145;
    horizontal links between clans, 41, 67,
    110, 126, 141, 159; integrated networks,
    99–102; mixed networks, 140–42; modes
    of contact, 170n21; movement in social
    networks and, 20–21, 97, 100–102,
    119–21; nonrelative Somali networks,
    49, 100, 119–20, 121, 123, 133, 140–43,
    146–47, 151–52, 156; rites of integration,
    41, 110–14; Somali modernity and, 158;
    Somali Somali association, 162; video
    viewing and, 127–29, 128, 159, 171n12;
    *xeer* social contract and, 10, 14–15
clan competence, 21, 51–52
clan conflicts, 105–10
clan cultivation, 20–21
clan hegemony, 41, 107–10
clan hierarchy, 22–23, 108–10, 123, 127
clan identity. *See* clan affiliation/identity
clan legitimacy: crises of legitimacy, 41,
    152; injustice/oppression-based narra-
    tives, 162–63; of kin ties, 106, 108, 127,
    132; lineage-based narrative, 22–23, 52,
    73, 109, 114–15, 163; telling clan and,
    40, 47–48, 154, 157, 161; territorial-
    based narrative, 22–23; total genealogy
    and, 14
clan networks. *See* clan and social networks
clannism (clannishness): blaming clan-
    nishness, 10–12, 54–56, 102, 135–36,
    149–50, 157; discord among clans and,

77, 139; political violence and, 160; terms for, 52; weddings and, 111

clan obligations: autonomy/equality balance with, 40, 89, 99–102; balanced reciprocity and, 118–19, 142; clan associations and, 57; clan feeling and, 20–21, 48–49, 90, 125, 138–40, 157–58; clan network as social capital and, 120–21; crisis help and, 41; death/funeral obligations, 133–35, 152–53; donations of money, 87, 121, 146; Finnish welfare state and, 152; loans, 48, 99, 121, 131–32, 142–44; protection and safety, 51, 146, 153–55; qaaraan (clan assistance), 87, 152; remittances, 17–18, 40–41, 48, 85–87, 95–96, 158, 169n11, 170n13

clan practicality (practical relationships), 20, 65, 119, 126, 137

clanship, 41, 48, 60, 72, 138, 155–56

clan territory, 22, 45, 57, 63, 67, 71, 117, 141, 154

cohabiting, 29, 40, 99

colonial ethnography, 13–18

colonialism: clan affiliation and, 10; influence on telling, 67, 70; kinship study and, 16; migration pathways and, 94; postcolonial Somali scholarship, 17–18; Somali colonial partitions, 68

cosmopolitanism, 47, 91, 137–39

crisis: asking for help, 136–42; being asked for help, 143–50; civil war clan network, 52, 135–36; clan legitimacy and, 41, 47, 152; clan obligations and, 41, 136, 150; everyday crises, 150–51; liminality and, 155–56; loans and remittances, 48, 87, 99, 121, 131–32, 143–44; mixed networks and, 140–42; nonrelative support, 100, 121, 151–52, 156; self-reliance and, 135, 137, 155–56

cultural capital: clan competence/effort and, 21, 108, 158; conversion of social capital and, 49; Finnish cultural capital, 41, 102, 121; forms of cultural capital, 49, 51–52, 90; political asylum as, 96; socialization and, 69; telling clan and, 92; transnational cultural capital and, 40, 48–49, 90; in weddings, 122–24. See also economic capital; social capital

cultural competence: clan competence, 21, 40, 41, 51–52, 59, 73, 90, 92–93, 106,

108, 140, 158; cosmopolitanism as, 137; Finnish cultural competence, 84, 97, 137, 145; language and dialect, 49; personality as, 123; transmission of, 127

cultural identity, 164

cultural intimacy: blaming clannishness, 10–12, 54–56, 102, 135–36, 149–50, 157; buraanbur and, 110; clan scholarship and, 18, 34, 37–38, 72, 145; defined, 12–13; hiding clan and, 55–57, 157; self-reliance and, 135, 137, 155–56

D'Alisera, JoAnn, 29, 38

dialects. See language

distinction: amplified efforts at distinction, 93, 124, 161; aroosyo performance of, 122–27; habitus and, 49, 59, 149–50; lifestyle choices and, 97; new forms of, 160; Somali Bantu performance of, 163–64; status claims, 22; telling clan and, 48–49, 59, 90, 92; women's clan performance and, 41

Djibouti (French Somaliland): "Djibouti-style" as telling sign, 41, 123–24, 126; horizontal associations and, 159; online communities, 92–94

DNA testing, 27, 58, 166n16

dress and adornment: dahab (gold jewelry), 94, 104–5, 104, 112, 121–22, 125–26, 151, 159; displays of clan competence and, 41; family honor and, 30, 103; henna (cillaan), 101, 105, 122, 123–24; men's clothing, 81–82, 148; Somali Bantu T-shirts, 163–64; women's wedding costume, 105, 170n1; xijaab/hijab traditions, 44, 81, 83, 88, 99

Dubai, 125

East Helsinki, 38

economic capital, 11, 41, 87, 95–96, 108, 122, 142. See also cultural capital; social capital

economy: avoidance of crisis and, 41; carriers and, 95–96; conversion of social capital and, 49; donations of money, 87, 121, 146, 152; economic aid to Somalia, 11; employment of Somali residents, 25–27, 30, 34, 41, 83–85, 100–102, 137; Finnish economic environment, 25, 27; Helsinki Somali social inequality, 76;

economy (*continued*): informal economy,
48–49, 63, 95, 97, 101, 112–13, 122–25,
128, 153; loans, 48, 99, 121, 131–32,
142–44; management of transnational
capital, 40, 96–97; *meher* (divorce payment), 113, 171n7; progressive state
social policies and, 27, 40, 83–87, 96,
170n20; remittances, 17–18, 40–41, 48,
85–87, 95–96, 158, 169n11, 170n13;
self-reliance and, 99, 135, 137, 150,
155–56; social capital in clans, 21, 48–49,
83–88, 120–21, 134–38; social capital in
integrated networks, 99–102; symbolic
capital, 21–22, 49–50, 108, 121, 126,
168n7. *See also* cultural capital; economic
capital; social capital; symbolic capital
education: cosmopolitanism and, 137;
distinction and, 123; ethos of integration
and, 101; Finnish ideology and, 84, 95;
language instruction in Finnish schools,
43–44, 62, 83, 96, 98; ranking of Finnish
education system, 29, 95; remittances
and, 86–87; Somali childhood in Finland,
28, 30, 39; Somali diaspora education
sites, 94; Somali educational achieve-
ment, 50, 167n3; Somalis in higher
education, 50, 90–91, 98, 136
Egypt, 31
employment/unemployment, 25–27, 30, 34,
41, 83–85, 100–102, 137, 144
endogamy, 117
Eno, Mohamed A., 45, 158, 163, 167–68n5
Eno, Omar A., 52
Errington, Frederick K., 148
Espoo (Finland), 19
Estonia, 25, 26, 27, 62, 85
Ethiopia: Ogaadeen disputed territory, 11;
Somali diaspora and, 43–44, 90, 94, 154;
telling time in, 70
ethnographic approach: collaborative anthropology, 9, 20; communication technology in, 9, 35; diagnostic events, 105;
Finland as fieldwork site, 23–25; gender
and, 36; globalization and, 8–9; informed
consent, 36, 74, 89–90; insider vs. outsider status, 10, 12, 20, 46, 47, 72, 157;
language and, 36, 167n20, 167nn19–20;
methodology, 20, 37, 136; multisited
ethnography, 37, 46–47; multivocality,
8; participant observation, 34, 37, 143,
146–47, 150; photography and record-

ings, 37; practice theory and, 20, 157;
privacy/anonymity of consultants, 37;
researcher community role, 80, 167n19;
social network approach, 33–34, 71–72;
Somali kinship studies, 9–11, 13–16, 18,
160; Somali views of researchers, 33, 37,
39, 73, 88; survey participants overview,
36–37; surveys, interviews and, 33–37,
55, 72–74, 136, 170n15; telling clan and,
56, 66, 71–72
Evans-Pritchard, E. E., 13–14, 16

family: clan/family honor, 30, 80, 83, 97,
99, 103; family reunification, 27, 58,
95–98, 132, 166n16; family size, 27,
29–30, 81, 85, 132, 158–59; family
structure, 27, 29–30; home decor and
lifestyle, 44, 81, 123; household internet
access, 91–93; households as interview
sites, 35–37; incense household use, 44,
49, 103; language in Somali households,
49; official kin, 113, 125; patrilineal descent, 10–11, 13–16, 106, 113–15, 117,
125, 165n4; visiting households, 32, 48,
63–64, 106, 127, 147, 156, 170n3; young
Somalis separation from, 40, 75–89,
92–93, 97–99, 143, 150–51
Farah, Abdulkadir Osman, 11–12
Farah, Mo, 31
Finland—national culture: ethos of integration, 30–31, 76, 99–102, 168n2;
Finnish welfare state, 83, 86–87, 95–97,
143, 152; gender equality, 21, 84, 102,
169n7, 169n10, 170n4; Green Party, 38;
Helsinki Finnish social spaces, 32; housing benefits, 7, 84; military conscription,
39; mobile phones importance in, 35;
official languages, 62; progressive social
policy, 27, 40, 83–87, 96, 170n20; sauna
tradition and, 23, 29, 32; SDP (Social
Democratic Party), 38; secular society,
29–30; True Finn Party (*now* Finns Party;
*Perussuomalaiset*), 31, 38, 166n18. *See
also* integration
Finland—Somali diaspora: clan-based
associations, 54–57, 63–64, 168n6; diasporic moments, 40–41; emigration from
Finland, 35, 132, 140; Finnish anti-immigrant sentiment, 27–28, 30–32; Finnish
citizenship, 39, 96; Finnish lifestyle, 34,
40–41, 97–100, 135–37, 143; genera-

tional differences, 38–39; Helsinki Somali social spaces, 32, 37–38, 66–67, 170nn3–4, 171n5; housing type and locations, 76, 168n1; integration experiences, 34, 39–41, 98–102; migration routes, 25–27, 26, 66; municipal apartment housing, 40, 44, 58, 75–85, 86, 88–89, 91–93, *104*, 162–64; other Finnish minorities, 25, 27; places of integration, 98–99, 148; recent arrival stigma, 66, 96; Somali civil war refugees, 50–51; Somali immigration, 21, 25–26, 26, 166n14, 166n17; "Somali Shock" reception, 24; SSIA conference reception, 7–9; terms for Somalis in Finland, 39; views of Americans, 33. *See also* Finland—national culture; Somali diaspora; young Somalis in Finland
Finland-Swedes. *See* Swedish-Finns
Finnish welfare state, 27, 83, 86–87, 95–97, 143
France, 70, 90, 94
Fresh off the Boat (FOB), 66, 96

gender: as fieldwork issue, 36; gender equality in Finland, 21, 84, 102, 169n7, 169n10, 170n4; gender segregation, 63, 67, 111–14; gender studies, 16–17; jewelry as gendered property, 112, 151; performance of clan and, 41; Somali gender norms, 29–30, 40, 82–83. *See also* women
Gewertz, Deborah B., 148
globalization, 8–9, 48
Gosha minority group. *See* Somali Bantu minority group
Gough, Kathleen, 16
Gulf States, 86, 94, 102

Hage, Ghassan, 37
Hakunila (Vantaa suburb, Finland), 27–28
Hall, Stuart, 164
Halonen, Tarja, 28, 84
Hargeysa, 2, 18, 70, 154
Hautaniemi, Petri, 27, 97–98, 166n16
Helander, Bernhard, 14–15, 117, 166n12
Helsinki (Finland): Café Vanha, 148; clan associations in, 63–64; *Esplanadin Puisto* (Esplanadi Park), 38; ethnic minority neighborhoods, 76–77, 77; ethnography in, 19–20; Finnish and Somali social spaces, 32, 38, 63, 66–67,

79, 170nn3–4, 171n5; Itäkeskus (*Itis*) Shopping Center, 32, 38, 131; Kandahar apartment complex, 77–82, 86, 88–89, 92, 96, 146, 160; Mogadishu Avenue, 76; proposed mosque construction, 31; public transportation, 35, 57–58, 71, 84; Rastila neighborhood, 7, 76, 115; residential economic disparity, 76; residential segregation, 76–77, 168n2; SSIA 2015 conference site, 8–9; *Teatteri* restaurant/nightclub, 38; Tiger (*Tiikeri*) night club, 32, 79–80
henna (*cillaan*), 101, 105, 122, 123–24
Herzfeld, Michael, 12, 55–56
Hoehne, Markus V., *15*, 19, 114, 117, 134, 159–60
Horn of Africa Somali diaspora, 21, 24
Horst, Cindy, 17–18

Immonen, Olli, 31, 166–67n18
India, 53
integration (into Finnish culture): avoidance of Somalis, 41, 65, 100–102, 146–49; civil war atrocities and, 99; clan status claims and, 102; clan support and, 143–50, 156; cosmopolitanism and, 137; employment and, 30, 34, 56, 101, 137, 150; Finnish cultural competence, 84, 97, 137, 145, 147; Finnish ethos of integration, 30–31, 76, 99–102, 168n2; Finnish language acquisition, 43, 58, 83, 98, 101; Finnish social networks, 20, 30, 99–102, 137, 148–50; integration experiences, 34, 39–41, 98–102; places of integration, 98–99, 148. *See also* young Somalis in Finland
internet and social media, 19, 31–32, 63, 66–70, 88–90, 91–94, 129. *See also* cell phones
Iraq, 54
Islam: *Ciid* religious holiday, 32, 83, 169n9, 170n14; Finnish anti-Islam sentiment, 31; Finnish marriage law and, 171n8; Helsinki mosques, 31–33, 58, 81, 149, 169n9; men's clothing, 81–82; Qurayshitic lineage, 14; Ramadan, 169n9, 170n14; *sako* as remittances, 87, 170n14; views of Americans, 33; Western secular society and, 29, 82; *xijaab/hijab* traditions, 44, 81, 83, 88, 99; young urban Somali practices, 81–83

Isotalo, Anu, 169n7
Italian Somaliland, 67, 68
Italy, 94

jareer racial group. See Somali Bantu minority group
Joensuu (Finland), 27, 28, 50–51
Jubbaland, 159

Kahin, Dahir Rayale, 134
Kapchits, Georgi, 45, 59–60, 62, 167n4
Kapteijn, Lidwien, 19, 105–6, 110
Kaunaiinen (Finland), 19
Kenya: Dadaab refugee camp, 17–18, 86–87; declining relevance of Somali clans, 18; Nairobi Somalis, 18; Somali diaspora and, 94
kinship: kinship as usual, 160; overview of Somali kinship, 15; patrilineal descent, 10–11, 13–16, 106, 113–15, 117, 125, 165n4; segmentary lineage system, 13–19, 22–23, 46, 67, 158–59, 165n4; Somali kinship studies, 9–11, 13–16; tol kinship alliances, 14, 20; total genealogy principle, 14, 22–23
Koonfur (South), 67–68, 70–71, 159–60
Kortteinen, Matti, 168n2
Kroner, Gudrun-Katharina, 31
Kusow, Abdi M., 10, 22, 89–90, 111, 161, 163

Lamberti, Marcello, 60, 60, 67
language: Af-Maay language, 53, 60, 60, 62, 67, 168n8; Af-Maxaa (standard Somali language), 53, 61–62, 62, 168n8; code switching, 33, 92; cross-clan linking and, 67; dialect as telling sign, 59–62, 60–62, 66, 67, 69, 88–90, 108; English-language clan references, 165n4; exaggeration in telling clan, 59, 67; fieldwork and, 36, 167n20, 167nn19–20; generational differences in, 69; gossip in clan networks, 80, 99–100, 107, 146–48, 150–51; greeting practices, 66; language instruction in Finnish schools, 43–44, 62, 83, 98; migrant generational differences, 38–39; names as telling signs, 59, 65–66, 89; North-South clan references, 67–71; online telling and, 92–94; Somali Bantu

ancestral languages, 53; Somali language, 24, 36, 62, 92, 101; Somali names, 37, 58–59, 65–66; spoken languages in Finland, 24, 62, 67; surveys, interviews and, 36–37; translators and interpreters, 36, 69, 101, 144–45
Lewis, Ioan M., 13–14, 16, 18–19, 21, 22–23, 158, 166n9
Lindley, Anna, 17–18, 86, 169n11
London (England), 18, 23
Luling, Virginia, 14, 52, 64, 81, 138, 160, 167–68n5, 171nn8–9

Madhibaan (Midgaan) minority group, 51–54, 65, 163
Mainsah, Henry, 160
Manderson, Lenore, 55, 111
marriage: arranged marriages, 94–95; divorce, 30, 78, 81, 113, 150–51, 168–69n3; endogamy, 117; exogamy, 117; Finnish marriage law, 171n8; Finnish-Somali marriages, 112–13, 116, 121–22, 171n6; marriage taboos, 48, 53–54, 114–18, 158; meher (divorce payment), 113, 171n7; nikaax (wedding contract) and, 107, 111–13, 114, 127, 131–33; polygynous marriages, 27, 97–98, 170n22; spouse preference, 53, 114–18, 152, 161. See also weddings
Marxism, 16
McMichael, Celia, 55, 111
Menkhaus, Ken, 16
Minneapolis (Minnesota), 23, 87, 165n2
minority groups: Asheraaf Sarman minority group, 65; Benaadiri (Reer Xamar) minority group, 34, 60, 69, 161; clan competence and, 51–53, 73, 123; clan status claims of, 23, 74, 163; current/future arrivals, 161–62; Helsinki Benaadiri population, 34; Madhibaan (Midgaan) minority group, 51–54, 65, 163; marriage taboos, 48, 53–54, 114–18, 158; Soomaalinimo and, 115, 163; Swedish-Finns (Finland-Swedes), 148–49, 171n2. See also Somali Bantu minority group
Mogadishu: Battle of Mogadishu, 165n2; clan areas in, 44–45; clan cleansing in, 18; "Mogadishu feeling" of cosmopolitanism, 138–39; neighborhoods and clan

areas, 43–46, 55, 139–40; Simons CRDP project in, 16–17, 135–36; as travel destination, 153; *Xamar* as name of, 68–69
*Mogadishu Avenue* Finnish sitcom, 76
Mohamed, Jama, 10
Moore, Sally Falk, 105
morality, 28–31, 40, 163, 169n7
Moscow, 25, 26
movement: accidental movement, 25; automobiles and, 103–4; carriers, 95–96; dispersal of social capital, 96–97; forms of Somali movement, 40; Helsinki as site for youth autonomy, 75–83, 87–89, 169n7; Helsinki Finnish and Somali social spaces, 32, 38, 66–67, 79; Helsinki Somali frequent movement, 35–36; household size flexibility, 81; international travel, 78, 96–98, 118, 160; internet access and, 32, 67, 91; liminal spaces and, 40, 89, 93; migration patterns and strategies, 94–95; migration routes, 25–27, 26, 66; places of integration, 98–99, 148; reunification and, 27, 58, 95–98, 132; social networks importance for, 20–21, 97, 100–102, 119–21; Somali diaspora youth movement, 40–41; structural functionalist analysis and, 20, 166n6; visits to Somalia and the Horn, 35, 47, 73–74, 96, 97–98, 109, 123, 135, 152–53, 161, 171n4

names: nicknames, 66, 89; screen names, 93; Somali names, 37, 58–59, 65–66; as telling signs, 59, 65–66, 89, 93
national identity (*Soomaalinimo*), 31, 111
National Security Service (NSS), 10–11, 17, 138–39
*nikaax* (wedding contract ceremony), 107, 111–13, 114, 127, 131–33
Nordic welfare state, 40, 83, 95, 161
Norway, 76
nudity, 29
Nuer, 13–14, 16

Ogaadeen War, 11

Paltalk, 88–93
pastoral nomadism, 14–15, 15, 53–54, 124, 163
Pirkkalainen, Päivi, 56

poetry, 18
practice theory, 20, 157
Puntland State of Somalia, 44, 67–68, 91, 134, 139, 141, 159–60, 171n1

*qaad*, 79, 81, 101, 128, 169n5, 169n11

R&B music, 32, 79, 106
race/racism: anti-immigrant sentiment, 27–28, 30–32, 89; ascribed physical features and, 53, 64, 66, 72, 162; attacks against young Somalis, 28, 78; blaming racism, 30–31, 150; *jareer* as racial term, 53–54, 114, 162; Somali minorities and, 53–54, 64, 114–15; suspension of clanship as response to, 41, 156; transnational Somali unity and, 156; xenophobia and, 28, 96, 101–2
refugees: Dadaab refugee camp, 17–18, 86–87; modern refugees, 94, 161–62; reception centers, 32, 50–51, 140; resettlement initiatives, 166n13; Somali Bantus as "modern refugees," 161–62; Somali civil war refugees, 50–51; telling clan and, 10, 50–52, 54–55, 58, 73, 98; "Titanic" recent arrival term, 66
regional identity: clan territory, 22, 45, 57, 63, 67, 71, 117, 141, 154; geographical discontinuity and, 37; Helsinki neighborhoods and, 76–77; Mogadishu neighborhoods and, 43–46, 55, 139–40, 159; North-South clan references, 67–71, 139, 146, 159–60; place as clan reference, 43–47, 54–55, 66–69, 91, 139; regional foods and, 70, 124–25; *Soomaali qaldan* and, 68; telling time and, 69–70; territorial-based narrative, 22–23
Russia. *See* Soviet Union and Russia

Sab, 14, 15, 60
Samaale, 14, 15, 60
satellite television, 66
Saudi Arabia, 54, 94
sauna tradition, 23, 29, 32
screen names, 93
Shandy, Dianna J., 80, 166n13
Sierra Leone, 29
Simons, Anna, 11, 16–17, 135–36, 142, 155–56

social capital: asylum seekers and, 95–96; clan network as social capital, 120–21, 157–58; conversion into economic/cultural capital, 49; dispersal of social capital, 96–97; social capital in clans, 21, 48–49, 83–88, 120–21, 134–38; social capital in integrated networks, 99–102. *See also* cultural capital; economic capital

social media. *See* internet and social media

Somali Bantu minority group: *Af-Maay* language, 53, 60, 60, 62, 67, 168n8; clan identity and, 52–53, 65, 74; cultural identity and, 163–64; history of, 53–54; *jareer* racial designation, 53–54, 64; Somali Bantu association, 162; Somali minority status, 114–15, 162; U.S. resettlement initiative, 23, 41, 63–64, 161–62

Somali civil war: Battle of Mogadishu, 165n2; clan cleansing, 18; clan identity and, 52, 135–36, 146; failed state studies and, 18–19; Finnish lifestyle integration and, 99; liminality in, 155–56; Somali mass emigration and, 25, 94

Somali diaspora: clan identity and, 11–12; cultural identity and, 163–64; declining relevance of clans, 17–18, 21–22; diasporic moments, 40; internet and social media use, 19, 31–32, 63, 66–70, 88–90, 91–94, 129; refugee status, 10; research on, 17–18, 157; Somalia as homeland, 171n3; Somali modernity, 158; Somalis in higher education, 50, 90–91, 98, 136. *See also* Finland—Somali diaspora; transnational identity; young Somalis in Finland

Somaliland Republic (British Somaliland region): diaspora allegiance to, 44, 109, 119, 132–34, 171n1; horizontal associations and, 159–60; Lewis kinship study in, 13–14, 166n9; map of, 141; "North" as reference to, 67–68; remittance practices in, 86; as travel destination, 153

Somali Shock, 24

Somali Somalis, 162–64

Somali Studies International Association (SSIA), 7–9, 12, 37, 90, 154, 163, 165n1

*Soomaalinimo* (Somali national identity): *aroosyo* and, 111; boundary of Somaliness, 14, 40, 48–49, 115, 152, 157, 163;

diaspora environment and, 31; minority groups and, 115, 163; telling clan and, 47–50, 161; *xeer* (social contract), 10, 14

*Soomaali qaldan*, 68

South Africa, 18

Soviet Union and Russia: Ethiopian alignment with, 11; Moscow diasporic moments, 40; Russian emigration to Finland, 25, 26, 27; Somali civil war and, 166n14; Somali diaspora and, 54, 94; as Somali emigration outpost, 25, 26; as Somali national security model, 10–11

status claims: clan associations and, 22–23, 89; clan conflicts and, 107–10; context of asking and, 46, 158; dialect and, 49; integration and, 102; minority groups and, 23, 74, 163; regional identity and, 125; Sab-Samaale distinction and, 14, 56–57; telling clan and, 40, 48. *See also* telling clan

structural functionalist analysis and, 20, 166n6

Suomen-Somalia Verkosto (Finnish-Somalia Network), 56–57

Sweden, 24, 25, 27, 34, 62, 76, 140, 148–49, 171n2

Swedish-Finns, 148–49, 171n2

symbolic capital, 21–22, 49–50, 108, 121, 126, 168n7

telling clan: acceptance of clan tellings, 65; Barre proscription of, 58; clan-based associations, 54–57, 63–64; clan competence and, 21, 51–53; clan neutrality, 56; context of asking and, 45–46; cross-clan interactions and, 64, 67; cultural intimacy and, 37–38, 135; by current/future arrivals, 161; DNA testing and, 27, 58, 166n16; in everyday encounters, 43–47, 57–58, 66; exaggeration and, 59, 67; exchange of capital and, 20, 40, 48–49; in fieldwork moments, 56, 66, 71–74, 89–91, 143–45; in graduation ceremonies, 50; hiding clan, 51–53, 65; internet practices for, 92–94; Irish Catholic and Protestant telling compared with, 47; kinship structure maintenance, 48–49; place as clan reference, 43–47, 54–55, 66–69, 91, 139; in refugee encounters, 50–51,

54–55, 58, 73, 98; refugee forced telling, 10, 51–52; resettlement and, 41; screen names and, 93; security culture and, 17; *sheegato* (newcomer who identifies with natives), 52, 167–68n5; status claims and, 40, 47–48; telling signs as alternatives, 58–67, 71–72, 89; in weddings, 41, 49–50, 63, 64. *See also* status claims
Tiilikainen, Marja, 167n1
"Titanic" recent arrival term, 66
Toronto (Canada), 23
transnational identity: research on, 17; Somali transnational experience in Finland, 39; transnational capital, 31, 40, 48–49; transnational clan networks, 48, 127; transnational families, 21, 27, 84–85. *See also* movement; Somali diaspora
tribe: attitudes toward, 52; avoidance of tribalism, 136–38; Barre anti-tribalism campaign, 10–11, 58; blaming tribe, 11–13; "clan" vs. "tribe" term, 165n4; diaspora tribalism, 52–53, 55–56; interdependency of members, 155–56; Lewis research and, 18; in refugee camps, 55–56; scholarship on, 18, 156. *See also* clannism
Turkish Airlines, 97
Turku (Finland), 24, 75, 78–79, 80, 169n7
Turner, Victor, 155–56

United Arab Emirates, 18
United Kingdom: *aroosyo* celebrations in, 114; Cardiff Somaliland population, 132; *qaad* in, 169n5; Somalia colonial linkage with, 94; Somali population in, 18, 23, 34, 87, 132
United States: "Black Hawk Down" battle, 11, 165n2; declining relevance of Somali clans, 18; economic aid to Somalia, 11; ethnic associations in, 162–64; jewelry as gendered property in, 112; post-9/11 international reputation, 33; secular society as immigrant deterrent, 29; Somali Bantu resettlement in, 161–62; Somali population in, 23, 25, 87, 94; War on Terror, 33

Vaattovaara, Mari, 168n2
Vantaa (Finland), 19, 28, 35, 38, 63, 66, 120

WaGosha minority group. *See* Somali Bantu minority group
*Waqooyi* (North), 67–68, 159–60
weddings (*aroosyo*): *buraanbur* as clan status claim, 105–11, 114, 127, 132, 150; clan affirmation in, 41, 49–50, 63, 64, 105–11; clan and lineage issues, 114–18, 128, 132; description of, 103–10, *104*; exchange of capital and, 87, 118–26; as fieldwork site, 37, 72, 75; Finn-Somali marriages, 112–13, 116, 121–22; horizontal associations and, 159; *nikaax* (wedding contract) and, 107, 111–13, 114, 127, 131–33; performance of clan and, 41, 105–9, 126; preparation for, 64, 103–4, 118–19, 122, 122–23, 144; as Somali diaspora social space, 32, 110–11, 170n3, 171n5, 171n10; *Soomaalinimo* performance in, 111; *sooryo* (bride wealth), 113; video viewing, 83, 126–29, 128, 159; *xeedho* tradition, 124–25. *See also* marriage
Willis, Paul, 89
women: *aroosyo* importance for, 110–12, 114; arranged marriages and, 94–95; body/dress as performance of clan, 64, 122, 122–26; *buraanbur* role of, 105–11, 114, 127, 132; clan/family honor and, 30, 80, 83, 97, 99, 103; contributions to remittances, 169n11; *dahab* (gold jewelry), 94, *104*, 104–5, 112, 121–22, 125–26, 151, 159; female genital cutting, 17; feminist kinship study, 16; gender equality in Finland, 84; gossip in clan networks, 80, 99–100, 107, 146–48, 150–51; internet anonymity and, 92–94; polygynous marriages and, 27, 97–98, 170n22; social autonomy of young women, 30, 81–86, 98–99; Somali women social spaces, 28, 170n4; unmarried women, 36, 81–84, 87–88, 118, 146–47, 170n2; women as fieldwork consultants, 36; *xeedho* tradition and, 124–25; *xijaab/hijab* traditions, 44, 81, 83, 88, 99. *See also* gender
World Bank, 17

*Xamaraawi*, 68–69, 71
*xawilaad*, 86
*xeer* (social contract), 10, 14

xenophobia, 28, 96, 101–2

Yemen, 94
young Somalis in Finland: clan identification
  of, 40–41, 72–74; clothing as personal
  expression, 81–82, 146; dating practices,
  29, 40, 82, 84, 146; desire for autonomy,
  40, 75–89, 92–93, 97–99, 143, 146–47,
150–51; internet anonymity and, 92–94;
Kandahar apartment complex, 77–82, 86,
88–89, 92, 96, 146, 160; musical tastes,
105–6; parental expectations for, 29,
82–86; premarital sex, 29; racial attacks
against, 28; Somali nightlife in Helsinki,
32, 79–80, 169n4, 169nn6–7; "too Finnish" youth experiences, 40, 79–80, 169n7

STEPHANIE R. BJORK is Professor of Anthropology at Paradise Valley Community College. She is coeditor of *From Mogadishu to Dixon: The Somali Diaspora in a Global Context*.

INTERPRETATIONS OF CULTURE IN THE NEW MILLENNIUM

Peruvian Street Lives: Culture, Power, and Economy among Market
   Women of Cuzco   *Linda J. Seligmann*
The Napo Runa of Amazonian Ecuador   *Michael Uzendoski*
Made-from-Bone: Trickster Myths, Music, and History from the
   Amazon   *Jonathan D. Hill*
Ritual Encounters: Otavalan Modern and Mythic Community
   *Michelle Wibbelsman*
Finding Cholita   *Billie Jean Isbell*
East African Hip Hop: Youth Culture and Globalization
   *Mwenda Ntarangwi*
Sarajevo: A Bosnian Kaleidoscope   *Fran Markowitz*
Becoming Mapuche: Person and Ritual in Indigenous Chile
   *Magnus Course*
Kings for Three Days: The Play of Race and Gender in an Afro-Ecuadorian
   Festival   *Jean Muteba Rahier*
Maya Market Women: Power and Tradition in San Juan Chamelco,
   Guatemala   *S. Ashley Kistler*
Victims and Warriors: Violence, History, and Memory in Amazonia
   *Casey High*
Embodied Protests: Emotions and Women's Health in Bolivia
   *Maria Tapias*
Street Life under a Roof: Youth Homelessness in South Africa
   *Emily Margaretten*
Reinventing Chinese Tradition: The Cultural Politics of
   Late Socialism   *Ka-ming Wu*
Cape Verde, Let's Go: Creole Rappers and Citizenship in Portugal
   *Derek Pardue*
The Street Is My Pulpit: Hip Hop and Christianity in Kenya
   *Mwenda Ntarangwi*
Cultural Heritage in Mali in the Neoliberal Era   *Rosa De Jorio*
Somalis Abroad: Clan and Everyday Life in Finland   *Stephanie R. Bjork*

The University of Illinois Press
is a founding member of the
Association of American University Presses.

---

Cover designed by Jennifer S. Holzner
Cover image by Mikko Paananen.

University of Illinois Press
1325 South Oak Street
Champaign, IL 61820-6903
www.press.uillinois.edu